What We Learned

What We Learned

Two Generations Reflect on Tsimshian Education and the Day Schools

HELEN RAPTIS

WITH MEMBERS OF THE TSIMSHIAN NATION

The members of the Tsimshian Nation are
Mildred Roberts, Wally Miller, Sam Lockerby, Verna Inkster,
Clifford Bolton, Harvey Wing, Charlotte Guno,
Don Roberts Junior, Steve Roberts, Richard Roberts,
Carol Sam, and Jim Roberts

UBC Press • Vancouver • Toronto

25 24 23 22 21 20 19 18 17 16   5 4 3 2 1

Printed in Canada on FSC-certified ancient-forest-free paper
(100% post-consumer recycled) that is processed chlorine- and acid-free.

_____

Library and Archives Canada Cataloguing in Publication

Raptis, Helen, 1962-, author
   What we learned : two generations reflect on Tsimshian education and the day schools / Helen Raptis with members of the Tsimshian Nation ; the members of the Tsimshian Nation are Mildred Roberts, Wally Miller, Sam Lockerby, Verna Inkster, Clifford Bolton, Harvey Wing, Charlotte Guno, Don Roberts Junior, Steve Roberts, Richard Roberts, Carol Sam, and Jim Roberts.

Includes bibliographical references and index.
Issued in print and electronic formats.
ISBN 978-0-7748-3019-5 (bound). – ISBN 978-0-7748-3020-1 (pbk.). –
ISBN 978-0-7748-3021-8 (pdf). – ISBN 978-0-7748-3022-5 (epub). –
ISBN 978-0-7748-3023-2 (mobi)

   1. Tsimshian Indians – Education – British Columbia. 2. Indians of North America – British Columbia – Residential schools. I. Title.

E96.65.B7R36 2016   371.829'974128071185   C2015-906800-2
                                                      C2015-906801-0

_____

Canada

UBC Press gratefully acknowledges the financial support for our publishing program of the Government of Canada (through the Canada Book Fund), the Canada Council for the Arts, and the British Columbia Arts Council.

This book has been published with the help of a grant from the Canadian Federation for the Humanities and Social Sciences, through the Awards to Scholarly Publications Program, using funds provided by the Social Sciences and Humanities Research Council of Canada.

UBC Press
The University of British Columbia
2029 West Mall
Vancouver, BC V6T 1Z2
www.ubcpress.ca

For the students of
Spaksuut (Port Essington) – past and future –
that these stories
may help you *suwilaawks* (to learn)

Contents

Illustrations / ix

Foreword / xi
James McDonald

Acknowledgments / xiii

1 A Class List and a Puzzle: Researching Indigenous Education / 3

2 Indigenous Schooling as Assimilation: From Segregation to Integration / 27

3 Tsimshian Education versus Western-Style Schooling / 35

4 Walking on Two Paths: Education and Schooling at Port Essington among the Pre-1950s Generation / 56

5 Buried Seeds Taking Root: Dispossession and Resurgence at Terrace among the Post-1950s Generation / 103

6 Stability and Change: Education and Schooling across Time and Place / 129

Epilogue / 151

Notes / 156

Bibliography / 182

Index / 195

Illustrations

Map of British Columbia situating Port Essington / 8

Port Essington Indian Reserve facing the Skeena River, 1888 / 9

Streets and buildings, Port Essington, 1915 / 10

Skeena Commercial Cannery, Port Essington, circa 1910 / 11

Port Essington Indian Day School, 1890s / 41

Dennis Jennings, Fanny Noble, and the students of Port Essington Indian Day School, December 1916 / 44

Prince Rupert Exhibition Entry A / 46

Prince Rupert Exhibition Entry B / 47

Fish drying in the sun / 59

Tsimshian women, 1930s / 61

Mildred Roberts, Kitsumkalum, February 18, 2012 / 68

The Happy Gang, February 1946 / 71

Wally Miller at home, Kitsumkalum, August 2010 / 72

Remains of water flume, Port Essington / 76

Sam Lockerby, Kitsumkalum, August 2010 / 77

Verna Inkster at home, Kitsumkalum, 2010 / 79

Richard and Verna Inkster with wedding party, 1957 / 81

Four generations, Kitsumkalum, July 2011 / 82

Port Essington Elementary School, 1947–48 / 85

Clifford Bolton's National Rifle Association medals and badges / 87

Clifford Bolton's graduating class, Lytton / 89

Clifford Bolton with the canoe he carved for the village of Kitselas / 90

Pole-raising ceremony, 1981 / 90

Fishing, Port Essington / 94

Faith and Harvey Wing, Kitsumkalum, August 2010 / 96

Principal Charlotte Guno and 'Na Aksa Gila Kyew Learning Centre's 2009 graduating class / 100

Christmas play, Port Essington Elementary School, 1950s / 105

Don Roberts Junior, Port Essington, 2010 / 107

Mrs. McDougall's class, Port Essington Elementary School students, 1950s / 110

Steve Roberts, Kitsumkalum, August 18, 2010 / 112

The Roberts family, 1960 / 114

Richard Roberts, Kitsumkalum, August 17, 2010 / 117

Carol Sam with older sister Stella, Port Essington, circa 1961 / 119

Carol Sam with younger brother Jim, Kitsumkalum, August 2010 / 122

Port Essington shoreline today / 154

Foreword

HELEN RAPTIS PROVIDES us with an important case study of "Indian education" and the interface between Indigenous education and Canadian Indian policy. Unlike the current emphasis on the residential school system, her focus is on day schools, particularly the day schools at the west coast cannery town of Port Essington. For nearly a century, from 1871 until the destructive fires of the 1960s, Port Essington was an outpost of direct and indirect assimilation of Aboriginal populations in the northwest of British Columbia. For Aboriginal residents, the centre was the Port Essington Indian Reserve, which, despite its sorry history as a colonial administrative tool, recognized an ancient Tsimshian presence and the way of life that contextualizes the narrative of the case study.

The Port Essington Indian Reserve was deeded to the Kitsumkalum and Kitselas Indian Bands. These names represent the government's reorganization of the Indigenous Gitsmgeelm and Gits'ilaasú communities into distinct Indian bands with registered membership controlled by Canadian Indian policies, especially the Indian Act. Raptis's study offers insight not only on how this control changed the communities in a more profound way than simply renaming them but also on how the ancient social and economic patterns that brought the communities to Port Essington and the coast responded. Governmental education was the key to the changes, just as traditional education was central to the persistence of the cultural patterns and processes. Raptis's interweaving of documentary evidence with oral history and her examination of two distinct generations reveal the challenges that the communities faced over time as the traditional residential communities of Gitsmgeelm and Gits'ilaasű were transformed into the very different colonial administrative Indian bands of Kitsumkalum and Kitselas.

These challenges underlie the theme of stability and change. This book preserves significant memories for the communities, giving texture to the fabric of what was lost with the fires. Although Port Essington no longer functions as their home port, the two Tsimshian communities have never lost their connection to the coast. Port Essington remains a high symbol of that linkage, particularly through the special coastal Indian reserve. Community members still occupy the coast, living in the cities and reserve villages, just as those who make their residence inland still return to the coast for cultural and subsistence reasons. This book is an important contribution to the communities, preserving their past not just as a memory but also as a way of life that will continue into tomorrow.

James McDonald
Department of Anthropology
University of Northern British Columbia

Acknowledgments

THE CREATORS OF *What We Learned* wish to acknowledge generous financial support for this research from the Social Sciences and Humanities Research Council of Canada, Grant No. 410–2008–0762. Thanks are also due to many people whose help was immeasurable: Jean Eiers-Paige of the Prince Rupert City and Regional Archives; Blair Galston, archivist at the United Church of Canada, Bob Stewart Archives; staff at Library and Archives Canada as well as at the British Columbia Archives; Kitsumkalum administrative staff Cynthia Bohn, Wayne Bolton, and Sandra Christiansen; Kitsumkalum Treaty negotiator Alex Bolton; and University of Victoria research assistants Sam Bowker and Eve Chapple. Special appreciation goes to Dr. Anne Marshall, Judy (Edosdi) Thompson, and Dr. James McDonald for all their help; to Frank Freiburg for offering his photographs; and to the Kitsumkalum Band Council for approving the project. This book would never have come to fruition without the careful guidance of Darcy Cullen and Lesley Erickson of UBC Press and the helpful suggestions of two anonymous reviewers. Finally, my sincere thanks to Moira Cairns, whose impeccable editing helped me to see the forest among the trees.

What We Learned

I

A Class List and a Puzzle:
Researching Indigenous Education

WHEN TSIMSHIAN ELDER Verna Inkster (née Spalding) was growing up in Port Essington on the northwest coast of British Columbia during the first half of the twentieth century, her parents stressed the importance of self-reliance. Like many Tsimshian couples, Verna's parents regularly took their children out to camp in their traditional territories in order to teach them survival skills, such as preserving seafood and wildlife procured by fathers and uncles. Verna also learned to harvest berries and seaweed, which were dried in the sun and preserved in large oil cans. Verna's education, much like that of her Tsimshian ancestors, consisted of watching elders and learning the traditional skills and knowledge – passed down over the millennia – that would help her to assume a place in the community's social fabric. When not at camp, families resided at Port Essington, a town developed on a former autumn camping site that the Tsimshian people called Spaksuut (pronounced "Spokeshute"). Children attended the Methodist-run Port Essington Indian Day School. Verna generally enjoyed her four years at the school.

> We did reading and writing. We learned about *Jack and Jill*. I think everyone memorized it. We did a lot of drawing for art ... We did lots of singing, and there were Christmas concerts where we sang songs such as "Silent Night." At recess and after lunch, we'd play outside, mostly baseball. We'd also go around and pick berries and eat them with our lunch.[1]

Verna's recollections offer a rare view into the two educational worlds
in which the Aboriginal children of Port Essington manoeuvred in the
early twentieth century: the traditional hunter-gatherer lifestyle passed down
through the generations and the formal day school, where children were
"Anglicized." The differences between these two forms of education afford
an important opportunity to examine educational developments within
a context of crosscultural contact. As Métis scholar Emma LaRocque has
pointed out, "living cultures do not remain fixed in time; they adapt and
change as required over time."[2] This acknowledgment of inevitable adaptation and change raises several important questions about Indigenous
education. How has Indigenous education evolved over time and place?
What has remained stable and what has changed? What factors have
prompted stability and change? How was education – both traditional
and Western-style – experienced by the children who were being educated?
What impacts have former pupils' educational experiences had on their
adult lives overall?

Historians studying Indigenous education have tended to focus on the
limited notion of formal schooling as opposed to the broader, more
comprehensive concept of education, leading one historian to note that
"residential schooling has become synonymous with the history of Aboriginal education."[3] Yet "more Indian children in Canada passed through
seasonal or regular day schools than through the portals of the more
impressive boarding facilities."[4] This book moves beyond residential
schooling to explore the many, varied dimensions of education experienced by two generations of Tsimshian students between the 1930s and
the 1970s at Port Essington and Terrace, British Columbia. In particular,
it presents the recollections of seven elderly Tsimshian born during the
1930s and 1940s and of five middle-aged adults born during the 1950s
and 1960s. All twelve students lived at Port Essington for part of their
childhood, during which they found themselves transitioning from one
world into another. The group of elders received a traditional Tsimshian
education, provided by their families mainly while out at their traditional
camping grounds. This group also experienced formal schooling at Port
Essington Indian Day School and, after 1947, entered the public system
by attending the integrated Port Essington Elementary School. Two of the
students from this generation also attended residential school after completing elementary school. In contrast, the five participants from the
younger generation were schooled entirely in integrated settings. Their
experiences were more challenging as they made the difficult transition
from the tranquil world of Port Essington, where they were surrounded

by extended family, to the reserve at Kitsumkalum, where the distance from schools in Terrace required them to travel daily by bus with unfamiliar populations.

Members of both generations note that both Western-style schooling and their broader Tsimshian education played important, albeit unequal, roles as they transitioned into their adult lives. Their narratives indicate that the elders were exposed to more of their Tsimshian traditions than were the younger generation. In many ways, members of the generation born after the Second World War have retained little of their Tsimshian language and culture. At the same time, after entering the workforce, they strove to retain their places in the mainstream economy, which shifted and changed around them due to global economic developments.

What We Learned offers readers a historical study of how these twelve former students from two different generations experienced educational change during a particularly dynamic period in Canadian history.[5] Archival documents and the elders' oral histories illustrate that they experienced both the broad, holistic notion of Tsimshian education as well as the more restricted Western concept of formal schooling at Port Essington Indian Day School. The stories of the younger generation, however, focus mainly on formal schooling, indicating that within one generation the broad Tsimshian notion of education gave way to a more limited concept of schooling. Their stories also evoke troubling themes: cultural loss, disconnection, and discrimination. Yet their narratives illustrate resilience and triumph, revealing the character of Tsimshian resistance and adaptation with respect to both formal schooling and entry into the paid labour force.

CLARIFICATION OF TERMS

The words "Aboriginal," "First Nations," "Indian," "Indigenous," and "Native" are used interchangeably throughout this book to reflect their common usage at various points in time. It is also important to explain the distinction between the words "schooling" and "education" in this study. Recently, a growing number of Indigenous scholars have asserted that schooling is a subcomponent of education, despite the fact that the two terms have become synonymous in common parlance. American researchers K. Tsianina Lomawaima and Teresa McCarty illustrate the conflation of schooling and education like this: "Ask ten Americans to *describe* education, and nine times out of the ten you will hear about schooling ... Our everyday ideas about *education* are constrained by a narrow vision of *schooling*, a thin slice out of the panoply of educational theories, strategies, and experiences developed over human history."[6]

Whereas Western conceptions of education tend to focus on formal – mainly cognitive – aspects of schooling, education within Indigenous epistemology implies a broader, lifelong notion of experience "gleaned from interaction with one another, with all of nature (seen and unseen), as well as with all of the cosmos."[7] Indigenous researchers are increasingly inviting scholars and educators to supplant the narrow concept of schooling with a more expansive view of education.[8] This distinction is fitting for this book, as the Tsimshian have no word for formal schooling. Instead, the word that is used for education is *suwilaawks*, meaning "to learn."

A JOURNEY BEGINS: RESEARCH SOURCES AND APPROACHES

The impetus for this book was a 1947 class list from Port Essington Indian Day School that I (Helen), as the principal investigator of the project, found in the national archives while researching the genesis of the Canadian government's 1951 policy shift from segregated to integrated schooling for Indigenous learners. The names on the list constituted the last group of children to attend the day school before it was closed and the students were integrated into Port Essington Elementary School. This list and the teacher's note declaring the school's closure were intriguing. How and why did the Tsimshian children of Port Essington integrate into a public school when there was no existing legislation in 1947 that would have enabled such a move? Were the people of Port Essington simply more enlightened, egalitarian citizens than other Canadians, or were there other factors at work? How did the former students of Port Essington experience the transition from segregated to integrated schooling? I made a copy of the class list and was determined to learn more about this educational change. When I secured funding from Canada's Social Sciences and Humanities Research Council, I began searching for more documents about the life of the day school.

The backbone of historical research has tended to be document analysis due, in part, to the wealth of written sources.[9] This is particularly true of the government sources recording almost every facet of Indigenous peoples' lives in Canada. The search for background information about the closure of Port Essington Indian Day School began with official government files at the British Columbia Archives in Victoria and at Library and Archives Canada in Ottawa. My research assistants and I found Department of

Indian Affairs files contained in Record Group 10, Volume 6407, to be the most useful. Throughout our investigations, I was awed by the Canadian government's meticulous recordkeeping. Indigenous peoples have been subjected to a level of surveillance surpassed only perhaps by incarcerated populations.[10]

Although these provincial and federal repositories were useful sources of statistics and community information about Port Essington, we were not able to learn much about classroom life at the day school. For this, we turned to the Prince Rupert City and Regional Archives, which had a very useful collection of materials documenting the community of Port Essington, as well as developments and events at both the public school and the day school. At the United Church of Canada's Bob Stewart Archives in Vancouver, we were able to retrieve immeasurably helpful information about the Methodist teachers who taught at the day school from the late 1800s to the mid-1940s. The Prince Rupert School District provided the 1947 minutes of board meetings at which the trustees discussed the integration of the Indigenous children into Port Essington's public school. To fill in gaps in the archival record, we relied on published sources, the most useful being Ernest A. Harris's local history titled *Spokeshute: Skeena River Memory*.

From the documents and published sources, we were able to piece together the comings and goings of the town of Port Essington and the Indian Day School over a period of approximately 100 years. We learned that Port Essington once sat on the northwest coast of British Columbia where the Skeena and Ecstall Rivers meet just south of Prince Rupert. It lay within the traditional territory of the Tsimshian peoples who once used the site in the autumn months before returning to their winter villages farther inland at Kitsumkalum and Kitselas near the present-day towns of Terrace and Kitimat.[11] In 1835 the Coast Tsimshian population of 8,500 occupied territory spanning from the coast to just east of what is now Smithers, north to the border of Alaska near Stewart, and south almost to Bella Bella.[12] In the second half of the nineteenth century, the Tsimshian population was seriously threatened by settler expansion and diseases such as smallpox.[13]

In 1871, when the discovery of gold created a rush inland to the Omineca region, Robert Cunningham and his partner Thomas Hankin received a land grant from the provincial government to establish a store at Port Essington that would sell mining supplies.[14] Others followed their lead, and Port Essington soon became a centre of trade and industry servicing the Skeena River region and the inland goldfields. In 1882, after the gold

rush had subsided, Cunningham built a cannery at Port Essington, followed by a sawmill farther south of the town, and encouraged the Tsimshian to settle there permanently. To ensure a steady supply of labour, he
allocated a portion of his pre-empted land to establish a reserve.[15] With
the growth of fish canning and logging industries during the 1870s, increasing numbers of Tsimshian opted to settle in the area. Many Tsimshian
found employment in the fledgling industries and used canoes and their
knowledge of the Skeena to transport supplies and travellers.[16] Settlers
bought up the remainder of Cunningham's subdivided land.[17] By 1890

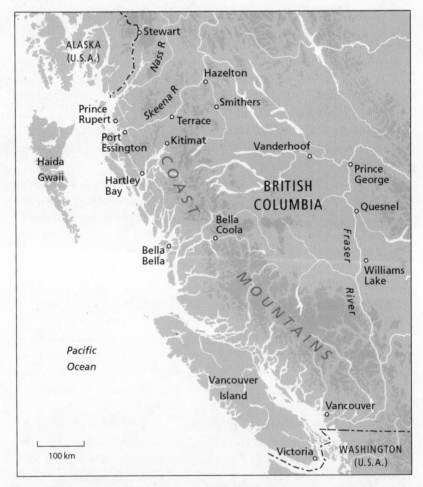

Port Essington, west of Terrace, on the southwest bank of the Skeena River, just
south of Prince Rupert. *Map by Eric Leinberger.*

Port Essington Indian Reserve facing the Skeena River, 1888. *Courtesy of the University of British Columbia, Rare Books and Special Collections, BC, Historical Photos, B124.*

Port Essington had become the area's main docking site, with steamboats replacing canoes as the most common means of shuttling people and goods along the Skeena River and the BC coastline.[18] By 1898 Port Essington included three canneries (Skeena, British-American, and Skeena Commercial), numerous shops, a mill, and several cafés. Its population was ethnically mixed, consisting of "Indians, Whites, Japanese, Chinese, and new immigrants from Europe [particularly Finns]," but the reserve formed the heart of the town.[19] Despite its ethnic diversity, the town was segregated to a certain extent. The reserve occupied the centre front of the town, closest to the Skeena River. Japanese Canadians, who made up half of the town's population, resided northeast of the reserve. Another community, "dubbed Finntown," was close to the Ecstall River, farther east of the Japanese area.[20] Not surprisingly, two school systems operated. Children of Native heritage attended Port Essington Indian Day School, and all the others enrolled in Port Essington Elementary School.[21]

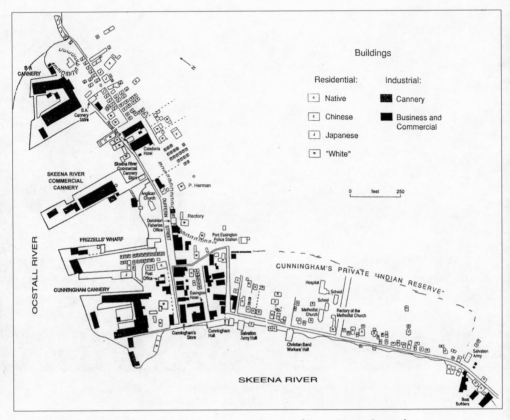

Streets and buildings, Port Essington, 1915. *Courtesy of Prince Rupert City and Regional Archives.*

Like other frontier towns, Port Essington had developed a reputation as being "rough and tumble" by the mid-1920s, when its permanent population of 350 regularly grew to several thousand during the June to July fishing seasons.[22] Due to a rocky, uneven terrain, buildings were connected by boardwalks on "posts, sometimes ten to twenty feet high ... There were several hotels ... a restaurant, a pool room [and] a small hospital."[23] Genteel social activities, such as dances, concerts, and church functions, competed with more lively weekend attractions, such as poker, black jack, and "working ladies."[24] On Saturday evenings, the town's main street allegedly became "a seething mass of humanity, with representatives of every race, and the vast majority of them in some degree of intoxication. The married women of the town very wisely stayed at home ... for the two Provincial constables were totally inadequate to maintain order and brawling frequently halted the stream of people as they eddied around a struggling group."[25]

Port Essington's meteoric rise as an economic hub was followed by a slow but precipitous decline. In 1914 the transcontinental Grand Trunk Pacific Railway, connecting British Columbia to the province of Alberta, was completed, but its terminus was placed north of Port Essington at Prince Rupert. As train travel increasingly replaced sea and river travel, Port Essington began to stagnate. Once-busy passenger boats began to rot on the town's shores, foreshadowing its destiny.[26]

Changes in the fishing industry also played a critical role in Port Essington's decline. In 1929 ten canneries operated around the lower Skeena River – with three at Port Essington.[27] With the advent of refrigeration to transport fish across vast distances, canneries no longer needed to be located close to the fish runs. Fewer, larger canneries concentrated production closer to urban areas in the province's southern region. Coupled with declining fish stocks, these changes squeezed many Skeena-area canneries out of production.[28] Port Essington's last cannery closed its doors in the late 1930s, forcing many residents to leave.[29]

Skeena Commercial Cannery, Port Essington, circa 1910. *Courtesy of Royal BC Museum, Image C-04932 c, British Columbia Archives.*

The federal government's decision to remove Japanese Canadians from coastal areas also contributed to the town's declining vitality. After the bombing of Pearl Harbor in 1941, Canada declared war on Japan, and by January 1942 anti-Japanese hysteria had swept the province. Responding to severe public pressure, the federal government initially relocated one hundred men of Japanese ancestry from coastal areas to work in camps in the province's interior. Soon, however, women and children were also interned. By the end of the war, the government had moved approximately 23,000 people of Japanese descent to interior settlements and had sold their property and belongings below market value.[30] The removal of Japanese families from coastal areas caused enrolment at Port Essington Elementary School to drop from forty-five in 1940 to thirteen in the spring of 1942.[31]

During the 1950s Port Essington witnessed the majority of residents boarding up their businesses and relocating to more central locations. For example, although long-time resident Jimmy Donaldson continued to operate the Ecstall Mill just east of Port Essington, he opened another at Georgetown near Port Simpson, eventually installing his family and business headquarters at Prince Rupert. Of the few families who remained in the area into the 1960s, most were First Nations. More often than not, the menfolk travelled to Prince Rupert or Port Edward for paid employment in fishing and logging industries while the women remained at Port Essington to tend to family, home, and garden.[32]

All but six adults and twenty-four children were away from Port Essington when a strong westerly wind fuelled the flames of a devastating fire that broke out in 1961. With an abundance of vacant buildings, it did not take long for the fire to ravage most of the town. Among the buildings claimed by the fire were a bank, a pool hall, a hotel, a café, a church, a community hall, a large store, and many houses. The Wesley, Brown, Lockerby, Brooks, Bolton, and Starr families were among those left homeless.[33] The following day, the *Vancouver Sun* newspaper reported that a "column of brown smoke lingered ... where only 24 hours before stood the sleepy little fishing village of Port Essington."[34] When a second fire struck on March 25, 1965, Port Essington ceased to exist. Most residents relocated to Prince Rupert or to Kitsumkalum, just outside of Terrace, where a burgeoning logging industry promised steady employment. According to local historian Norma Bennett, Port Essington is "remembered for its boom of prosperity, its winters of liquor, song and laughter, its many-nationed population and its rapid decline into oblivion and neglect."[35]

Archival documents and published historical sources reveal very little about the Indian Day School or the public school at Port Essington. There is no account of how or why the day school closed in 1947, four years in advance of federal legislation that would enable it. Furthermore, despite the thoroughness of the published sources about Port Essington, most give little more than a brief mention of the town's Native occupants. In conducting research for this study, I was troubled by the documents' lack of Indigenous voices. As noted by so many Indigenous researchers, it seems that the Tsimshian were "objects, but not subjects" of their colonizers' narratives.

This observation brings to light that document analysis – like all research approaches – has its limitations. There is a "great gap between administrative record-keeping and people's actual lives" since the documents "chronicle events" but do not explain "how those events came about or how they were experienced by teachers or students."[36] Indeed, traditional historical source documents tend to ignore the views and experiences of regular people while favouring the voices of people in authority. This has been particularly striking in the treatment of Aboriginal peoples, who have tended to be "generalized as a mass ... continuously unidimensional and on the margins."[37] Oral history approaches seek to address such gaps[38] by bringing voices that have previously been marginalized into a central position.[39] Since oral history represents "the recollections of a single individual who participated in or was an observer of the events to which s/he testifies,"[40] it "is where people and history meet."[41] For that reason, this study looks beyond the documents and incorporates oral histories of former students themselves.

Historical scholarship has largely been silent on how to conduct research respectfully in collaboration with Indigenous communities. In preparing to work with former students from Port Essington and Terrace, my research assistants and I turned to the growing body of "indigenist" research contributed by Indigenous scholars such as Shawn Wilson, Cora Weber-Pillwax, and Margaret Kovach – to name but a few. The next section describes our journey as we prepared ourselves to conduct research respectfully with one Indigenous community. However, I acknowledge that our learning journey continues, rooted as it is in our lifelong struggle to decolonize ourselves as well as facets of the society that surrounds us.[42]

RESEARCHING RESPECTFULLY WITH FIRST NATIONS COMMUNITIES

In the past two decades, researchers have come to recognize the many ways that scholarly inquiry has tended to disadvantage First Nations communities.

Traditional research approaches have bestowed "expert status" on non-Indigenous researchers while failing to acknowledge Indigenous expertise.[43] Until the 1990s researchers were able to enter Aboriginal communities and leave with information and artifacts that they did not own but from which they benefited through publication, sales, and heightened career status.[44] The individuals and communities whose knowledge and belongings had been taken seldom benefited in the same way as the researcher.

In recent years a shift has occurred toward more ethical, participatory research methods. Ethnohistorian Donald Fixico frames this shift in terms of three distinct phases in the evolution of American Indian history. The first phase focused on third-person descriptions of Indigenous peoples. The second phase included snippets of quotations from speeches of both colonized and colonizer pertaining to key events such as wars or treaties. The final phase has involved the recent shift toward giving centre stage to Native voices.[45] This shift has helped "to diffuse the power relations inherent in the production and dissemination of knowledge."[46]

University boards of research ethics, journals, and publishing houses are much more vigilant about ensuring that proper community-centred research protocols have been followed before allowing research to proceed and manuscripts to be published. By adopting respectful research approaches, non-Indigenous research allies help to advance decolonization efforts, defined as the "deconstruction of ideological, legal, legislative, operational, textual and other institutionalized structures sustaining unequal and discursive relations of power between non–First Nations and First Nations citizenries."[47]

Most of the literature on conducting research with and for – rather than about – Indigenous communities resides in disciplines other than history, such as anthropology, literary studies, and Indigenous studies. An excellent example is the most recent collaboration between anthropologist Leslie Robertson and the Kwagu'l Gixsam Clan. The focus of their 2012 book is Ga'axsta'las (Constance Jane Cook, 1870–1951), a Kwakwaka'wakw leader and activist immortalized through written accounts by anthropologists like Franz Boas. Such accounts of Ga'axsta'las present a story of "betrayal based on her support of the potlatch ban" and opposition to other traditional Indigenous practices.[48] Her resulting marginalization from her own people had far-reaching consequences for the well-being of her descendants, who were "publicly called down, told they couldn't dance or shouldn't wear regalia or that they didn't understand what they were doing in the cultural realm."[49] Robertson and the Kwagu'l Gixsam Clan collaborated

to contextualize Ga'axsta'las's actions and honour her memory by highlighting her advocacy for Indigenous rights, particularly those of women
and children. In so doing, they established a positive social and cultural
identity for formerly shunned family members, while illustrating the
devastating consequences of written accounts that have traditionally es-
chewed the voices and interpretations of the researched in favour of those
of the researchers.

Given researchers' historical legacies of disrespect, misrepresentation,
and unwillingness to acknowledge Indigenous voices, the research literature
now contains numerous guides that help non-Indigenous researchers to
work respectfully with Indigenous communities. I was heartened by Cree
scholar Shawn Wilson's belief that non-Indigenous researchers, such as
myself, can work successfully with Indigenous communities by adopting
an "indigenist" paradigm, the main tenet of which is the establishment of
respectful relationships.[50] This process includes honouring the role of the
Indigenous participants and recognizing that the information researched
belongs to the individuals and communities from whom the material is
collected.[51] This understanding is echoed by Cora Weber-Pillwax, who
contends that "deconstruction and decolonizing discourses or practices
on their own will not lead ... Indigenous researchers to where [they] want
to be."[52] Research practices must align with Indigenous values, such as
the importance of establishing respectful relationships and working to
serve the community within which the research occurs.

Working with the Māori in New Zealand, non-Indigenous researcher
Augie Fleras has developed a cultural safety model for non-Māori researchers that stipulates two requirements. First, researchers must learn to be
culturally self-aware in order to avoid the potential negative effects of their
"unwitting imposition of their cultural beliefs, values and norms" on the
research participants.[53] Second, researchers need to inform themselves
about the cultural, historical, and structural circumstances of the participants. These two aspects of awareness allow researchers to "suspend values
and assumptions in interpreting other people's culture or behavior" and
to foster mutual respect by sharing in the production of knowledge.[54]

Furthermore, it is considered mandatory that the project informants
participate in all decision making right from the start and that either
memoranda of understanding or research protocols be drafted and signed
before any information or artifacts are collected. Another foundational
aspect of working respectfully with First Nations communities is enabling
participants to review and correct transcripts and stories so that both re-

searcher and interviewee co-construct and mutually agree upon the knowledge to be used.[55]

To simply state that all of these prescriptive guidelines were followed for this project would be to understate greatly the intricacies of working respectfully with and for Indigenous communities. As a non-Indigenous researcher, I encountered more complexities than anticipated as my research assistants and I prepared for eventual contact with the former students by following the literature on working respectfully with and for First Nations communities.

As suggested by Fleras, we informed ourselves about the "cultural, historical and structural circumstances"[56] of the Tsimshian. We read extensively from the works of early twentieth-century anthropologists such as Diamond Jenness, Franz Boas, Marius Barbeau, and Viola Garfield, whose findings inform descriptions of traditional Tsimshian education contained in Chapter 2. We also consulted contemporary works, the most useful of which included Margaret Seguin Anderson and Tammy Anderson Blumhagen's "Memories and Moments: Conversations and Recollections," Kenneth Harris's *Visitors Who Never Left: The Origin of the People of Damelahamid*, Kenneth Campbell's *Persistence and Change: A History of the Tsimsyen Nation*, James McDonald's *People of the Robin: The Tsimshian of Kitsumkalum*, Jay Miller's *Tsimshian Culture: A Light through the Ages*, and Christopher Roth's *Becoming Tsimshian: The Social Life of Names*.[57] With a solid introduction to the "cultural, historical and structural circumstances"[58] of the Tsimshian of Port Essington, I reflected on my own cultural beliefs, values, and norms and wondered how I might refrain from unwittingly imposing these on my participants and their stories. Having been raised as a bicultural child of immigrants, I took some solace in knowing that my early exposure to multiple worldviews might be of help. Nevertheless, I still worried about whether the members of the Kitsumkalum community would accept me or my research proposal. Would they dismiss me and my research team as what Margaret Kovach calls "smash and grab" (i.e., self-serving) researchers who seek to benefit from others' stories?[59] Why should they trust us? At the base of all these questions were the two most important ones: who is this research for, and why should it be done?

It would be disingenuous to argue that the purpose of this research was solely to benefit the community with which we wished to collaborate. Of course, as a university-based researcher, I was genuinely curious about the situation at Port Essington. For years, I have argued that historians have generally neglected the schooling of Indigenous pupils who attended on-reserve day schools.[60] Indeed, most of the history of Indigenous education has focused on the horrors of the residential schools.[61] However, conflating residential schooling with Indigenous education is problematic since Indigenous children attended residential schools in lower numbers than they did day schools.[62] Equally problematic is the dearth of research investigating the transition that many Aboriginal children made from segregated, federally controlled day schools to integrated, provincial public schools in the decades following the Second World War. Narrowly historicizing Aboriginal education in terms of residential schooling tends portray Native peoples as one monolithic culture resistant to change. At the outset of this study, then, the story of Tsimshian education at Port Essington and Terrace presented an opportunity to fill a legitimate research gap.

On a more personal level, I also acknowledge that as a citizen of Canada it is impossible to be ignorant of colonialism's tragic legacy for generations of Indigenous peoples. Here was my chance to be part of a reform movement that seeks to build bridges between Indigenous and non-Indigenous Canadians. Could I learn to be an ally to Indigenous peoples, or was I destined to remain a perpetrator of the shameful legacy of colonialism?[63]

As I wrestled with my own motives, I had to face an even more difficult question: what did the former students of Port Essington stand to gain from such a research project? I concluded first and foremost that since histories of northwest British Columbia ignore the fact that the children of Port Essington integrated into public education prior to the laws that enabled such a move, the "grand narrative" about Canada's shift to integrated schooling fails to account for their experiences. Former students' stories have the potential to enhance a historical record that has not served Indigenous people well. Furthermore, local histories of the region have generally ignored Indigenous voices. As the research of James McDonald and others has indicated, the Tsimshian were important to the economic development of British Columbia's northwest coast largely through their participation in resource industries such as fishing, logging, and canning. Thus the research presented here benefits the participants by enabling them to take their rightful place within the province's social and economic history. As Indigenous law professor James (Sa'ke'j) Youngblood Henderson has noted, reconstructing history through Aboriginal experiences is important for conceptualizing Indigenous realities.[64] In addition, I hope that former pupils' integration stories will provide inspiration and guidance to their offspring and future generations. Initially, I suspected that their stories had been shared orally with younger generations, but I hoped that by recording and disseminating them more widely, a greater number of youngsters – both Aboriginal and non-Aboriginal – might be inspired. I later learned that their stories had not been shared either among members of their own generation or across generations of Tsimshian.

With some trepidation but clear motives, my assistants and I next tackled the task of locating the former pupils whose names appear on the 1947 class list. Having learned that Port Essington had been abandoned since the 1960s, we turned to Canada 411 to attempt to match the names on the list with names and addresses in towns surrounding Port Essington. With numerous matches, we concluded that many of the former day school pupils might reside either in Terrace or Prince Rupert. As noted above, Shawn Wilson argues that the foundation of working from an "indigenist" paradigm is the establishment of respectful relationships with Indigenous individuals and communities to whom information and artifacts belong.[65] Cognizant of this and aware that Western standards of research do not consider it appropriate to contact individuals on a class list directly, I knew we had to find another approach. So in the spring of 2009, I consulted my colleague Dr. Anne Marshall, who has spent decades working with Indigenous communities on the north coast of British Columbia. She suggested that we meet with her graduate student Judith (Edosdi) Thompson, who is Tahltan by ancestry but works at Northwest Community College in Terrace. We arranged a breakfast meeting at a local restaurant. After examining the class list, Edosdi confirmed that many of the former students resided at Kitsumkalum, west of Terrace. She gave me contact information for Dr. James (Jim) McDonald, an anthropologist at the University of Northern British Columbia who had been a researcher with the Tsimshian at Kitsumkalum since the 1970s. Jim passed away last spring. Along with the list, I sent a letter of introduction to Jim, who confirmed that most of the people on the class register did live at Kitsum-kalum and would likely be amenable to an oral history project exploring their transition from the day school to public schools. Jim McDonald advised me to send a detailed letter of introduction to Kitsumkalum chief Don Roberts Junior and to band manager Steve Roberts. Jim also agreed to talk with them in advance about the project.

Several researchers have stressed the importance of "situating oneself" to establish respectful relationships with Indigenous communities. According to Margaret Kovach, Indigenous researchers almost intuitively adhere to the pan-Indigenous "protocol of introductions," which pays respect to elders and enables the community to situate the researchers.[66] "When we self-locate, we represent our own truths."[67] This made sense to me and evoked one of my earliest crosscultural memories. When I was ten years old, my mother took me and my three siblings to Greece, her country of birth, to connect us more solidly to our language and heritage. We spent two and a half months in a small village where we were immediately recognized as outsiders.[68] My siblings and I quickly learned that in response to the question "whose are you?" we were to state our names and identify our parents and grandparents in addition to our current country of residence. At the time, I would mindlessly recite the words that my mother provided me: "My name is Helen Raptis, daughter of Theodore and Angela Raptis. My mother's parents are John and Stavroula Laliotis, and we all live in Canada now." It was only as an adult that I came to understand more fully the meaning of this exchange of words and the feelings that it evoked in my interlocutors, who would usually burst into emotion when they stated their relationship to my family and told me and my siblings who we resembled.[69]

My letter of introduction to Don and Steve contained quite a bit of detail in the hopes that "situating myself" would help me to establish a relationship with the people of Kitsumkalum. I described the trajectory of the research and how Anne Marshall, Judith (Edosdi) Thompson, and Jim McDonald had guided me in making contact with them. I then explained that I was interested in Indigenous history because, as a child, I had learned to walk in two worlds: the mainstream Canadian culture most significantly embodied by the schools that I attended and the Greek culture of my home life. I outlined my prior experiences with Indigenous peoples. The first was a close relationship with a high school friend whose father was not Indigenous but whose Haida mother had lost her status upon marrying him. Later, while living in Montreal, I became deeply troubled by the 1990 Oka Crisis and acknowledged then that my understanding of Indigenous "issues" was shallow at best. So in 1991, when one of my professors at McGill University asked me to teach at the Kahnawake Reserve near Montreal, I accepted the opportunity to enhance my understanding of Indigenous peoples.

I explained to Don and Steve that I had the financial support to undertake a research project probing the experiences of former Port Essington students and would very much appreciate the opportunity to discuss the idea with them further. In keeping with respectful approaches to working with Indigenous populations, I stated my preference that project participants be involved in all decision making from the start and my desire to create a protocol, or memorandum, of understanding prior to any interviewing.[70] I finished the letter by indicating that I would call them both a few weeks hence to follow up.

My follow-up phone calls resulted first in a conversation with Steve, the band manager. From Steve, I learned that he, Jim, and Don had discussed the pros and cons of a research project of the kind that my letter proposed. Steve invited me to visit the reserve, and we secured plans for July 29 to August 2, 2009. As I waited apprehensively for my trip to Kitsumkalum, my husband received a phone call from his doctor's office indicating that the knee surgery for which he had been waiting years was being fast-tracked to July 28 due to a cancellation! I was elated for my husband but gripped by fear for my fledgling research project. How could his surgery have been rescheduled to the day before my planned departure? To leave so soon after my husband's surgery would be too hard on him and my children, aged ten and fourteen at the time. So I phoned Steve and explained the situation. Steve informed me that in preparation for my arrival, the Kitsumkalum Band Council had organized a reunion for former Port Essington residents, scheduled for July 30! Hundreds of people were slated to attend the day-long festivities at the Kitsumkalum Community Hall, with many arriving from across the province. As my hands turned cold, I remembered Jim McDonald's article indicating that community feasts, such as this upcoming reunion, were traditional Tsimshian vehicles for conducting community affairs ranging from the transfer of names within clans to the establishment of crosscommunity relationships.[71] What was I to do? Failing to show up for the reunion was definitely not an ideal approach to establishing a "good relationship" with the community. After a frank conversation with my husband, we both decided that I had to honour my travel plans. I left for Terrace on July 29.[72]

The next morning, I made my way to the Kitsumkalum Band Office. In keeping with the guidelines for respecting cultural knowledge, I arrived first at the office of Chief Don Roberts Junior. We spent a couple of hours together, during which he talked at length about his concerns over the dispossession of land, language, and culture experienced by his community. He also reminisced about his childhood, painting a picture of Port Essington as an idyllic place to grow up. Throughout his recollections, he wove in stories of key community members, past chiefs, and activists: Louis Starr, Mark Bolton, John Wesley, and others. He talked of the generations of Tsimshian who have struggled to regain control of their ancestral lands, culminating most recently in lengthy and frustrating treaty negotiations.

Don's memories were also peppered with episodes from his own school experiences, and he talked about his disillusionment with formal education, the details of which are fleshed out in Chapter 5. At one point, I felt tears welling up in my eyes and fought desperately to hold them back. Was the intense emotion I was feeling a response to Don's negative experiences, or was it a show of solidarity for all children – myself included – who had struggled to navigate the transition from the comfort of our home cultures to the foreign world of schooling? I was swamped with emotion and uncertainty. Should I suppress the tears? Should I allow them to flow? Would Don see them as an authentic show of sadness, or would he perceive them to be the inauthentic "cover" of someone attempting to secure a relationship with his community for personal gain? Deciding that I had to be true to myself and suffer the consequences of his possible judgment, I surrendered to my emotions and let the tears roll down my cheeks. After a moment of silence, Don asked me what I wanted to know and why I wanted to do the research. Against the backdrop of the concerns he had just described, my research plans seemed trite, and my throat tightened. Could anything I had to say strike Kitsumkalum's chief as worthy of his community's attention? After a moment, I stated that my concerns paled in comparison to those facing the community but added that the integration events at Port Essington were curious because they predated legislation that would enable Indian children to attend provincial schools. I explained that I was interested in learning from the former students' experiences how and why integration had occurred as early as it had in Port Essington. Understanding that Indigenous peoples "remain attached to an area of land over an extended period of time,"[73] I suggested that recording a slice of life at Port Essington might benefit the town's former residents and their offspring by highlighting the happenings of a place that is no longer regularly inhabited. As argued by the National Indian Brotherhood in their 1972 policy paper, *Indian Control of Indian Education*, "unless a child learns about the forces which shape him: the history of his people, their values and customs, their language, he will never really know himself or his potential as a human being."[74] I closed by reiterating that my interests were not as pressing as treaty negotiations, efforts to secure adequate housing, or concerns about students' educational achievement. I told him that I would understand completely if he decided not to proceed with the project.

Chief Roberts affirmed his interest but stated that a "slice" of life at Port Essington would not suit the needs of the community since it restricted

the experiences of one group of learners to a single point in time, which
is contrary to the Tsimshian worldview, which conceives of an eternal
cosmos without start or end.[75] He noted that Tsimshian ways of knowing
were holistic and always acknowledged the continuity of time. In particular,
he felt that it was important to include information about traditional
Tsimshian learning from time immemorial alongside a discussion of the
day school era and the later experiences of learners who first attended
the schools of Terrace. I agreed that his request could certainly be ac-
commodated. He then listed the names of contacts to whom I should
begin speaking and said that I would find them at the festivities in the
Community Hall. We agreed that I would not derive any financial benefit
from the project and that at the end of our work together, all research
materials would be turned over to the Kitsumkalum Treaty Office. We
also agreed that it was appropriate to draft a written protocol to be approved and signed by the Kitsumkalum Band Council. Given that I had
to return to Victoria so quickly, we agreed that I would make another trip
to Kitsumkalum to work out the details at the earliest convenience of the
council.[76]

After our conversation, Don led me to the Community Hall, where he
formally introduced me to the reunion attendees and handed me a micro-
phone. I introduced myself briefly and indicated that I looked forward to
meeting people and hearing their recollections of life at Port Essington.
For the remainder of the day, I circulated throughout the hall, looking at
photographic displays, introducing myself, hearing peoples' stories, and
asking whether they would be interested in participating in a formal research project. I was fascinated by the stories I was hearing and awed
by the reunion attendees' willingness to share. At the same time, I was
burdened by what Margaret Kovach calls the dilemma of "dual accountability to the Indigenous community and to mainstream Western research."[77] That is, to obtain ethical clearance from my university's Ethics
Review Board, I needed to provide a copy of the research protocol co-
constructed with the community. Since this had not yet been done, no
"official" research could take place. I noted people's names, listened in-
tently to their stories, and assured them that I would return to the community as soon as I could to record their stories "officially."

I then learned of the problem with attempting to "serve two masters":
it cost the project valuable information. For instance, numerous people
had suggested that I speak with someone whom I identify as "an elder."
Many community members considered this elder to have been a leader
during their school days. Although she was not at the reunion, I caught

up with her the next day. She freely shared her memories of Port Essington and the day school with me. Her stories were insightful, and if I had not been bound by my university's ethical guidelines, I could have recorded them. But being caught between two masters, I thanked the elder for her willingness to speak to me and assured her that I would return as soon as possible to capture her insights. In the summer of 2010, after signing a research protocol with the Band Council and securing ethical consent from my university, I returned to Kitsumkalum and contacted the people who had indicated their willingness to participate in the study.

Each participant – except this particular elder – read and signed a consent form prior to being interviewed. When I returned to Kitsumkalum and presented her with the form to sign, she told me that she no longer wished to participate since using such a form "was not the Tsimshian way." I took this to mean that she had given her word verbally and did not recognize the authority of the university. I was deeply disappointed but did not press the matter. I told the elder that I appreciated her frankness and thanked her for teaching me a very good, but difficult, lesson. As I gathered my belongings and left her, I told myself that if respectful approaches to working with Indigenous communities meant that "the power lies with the research participant, the storyteller,"[78] then I had to accept what had just transpired. As sad as I felt about losing a key informant, I felt worse thinking that I had insulted this elder by essentially adhering to Western procedures in an attempt to "serve two masters."

In addition to feeling sadness about the loss of the elder's insights and guilt for potentially having insulted her, I was also perplexed. Having read and adhered to prescriptions in the literature about working respectfully with First Nations communities, I had thought that I was proceeding in a good way. This incident caught me completely off guard. I had read and understood Margaret Kovach's statement that "engagement with Indigenous knowledges means engagement with Indigenous communities" and her advice about "taking direction from Indigenous communities"[79] at the moment when "tellers are prepared to share."[80] But what did this mean in practice? Could I have disregarded the ethical guidelines that were approved by my university? Was it simply – as one of my colleagues suggested – a matter of amending the project's ethics approval? Would the elder have reconsidered if I had pressed the matter?

Although difficult, this elder's withdrawal from the project presented me with a good learning opportunity not only with regard to the question of researcher accountability. Her refusal to sign the ethical consent form highlighted for me that learning to research respectfully with Indigenous

communities is not a linear process – nor is it free of challenges. My research assistants and I found much written in the scholarly literature
about best practices for working with and for Indigenous communities,
but the terrain was bumpier than I had expected given the somewhat
straightforward guidelines found in the relevant scholarship. What has
become clear to me through this incident is that much about learning
how to work respectfully with Indigenous communities inevitably takes
place when researcher and participant first encounter one another in a
crosscultural space, a moment that can evoke tension and emotion, while
requiring careful, spontaneous decision making. Hopefully, in the future
more non-Indigenous researchers who have sustained respectful research
relationships with Indigenous communities will share their stories not
only of successes but also of challenges encountered in order to help both
Indigenous researchers and allies move to a better place.

PARTICIPATION AND REPRESENTATION

The project's contributors varied with regard to the extent of their participation. Some preferred to be tape-recorded, whereas others did not.
Most participants requested that their stories be presented under their
own names, with their words attributed to them directly, not blended
into general thematic discussions, as is typically the case with academic
writing. As historian Wendy Wickwire notes, research on Indigenous
communities has been restrained by the "Boasian paradigm," which privileges the notion of single, communal accounts of Indigenous "life."[81] As
Emma LaRocque points out, however, respectful approaches to conducting
research with Aboriginal participants require that each voice be considered
unique.[82] It would be highly unusual for an Indigenous person to speak
on another's behalf, and people usually preface their stories with the
proviso that "they are expressing only their own experiences and opin-
ions."[83] For these reasons, the participants' stories of their educational
experiences are presented under the names of each individual in Chapters
4 and 5.

Nevertheless, conventions of the academy dictate that scholarly inquiry
include an interpretive component. I have achieved this dual accountability
in two ways. First, the participants' stories are annotated in spots that were
deemed necessary for academic elucidation but in ways that were considered acceptable by the speakers themselves. In some cases, annotation
appears in the body of the texts; in others, additional details, explanations,

and analyses appear in endnotes. Full interpretive treatment of the participants' stories is provided in Chapter 6, which also includes a discussion of the dilemmas of interpreting other people's stories. The decision to hive the bulk of the analyses into a separate chapter was difficult to make. In the end, this was considered the best approach since my understanding of each generation's views on the nature of Tsimshian education hinged on the notion of stability and change over time. Isolating my analysis of each of the two generations' stories within the specific chapter in which their narratives appear would necessarily have precluded the ability to note changes in Tsimshian education across two generations at Port Essington and Terrace. Since this study was framed around questions pertaining to stability and change across time and place, each generation's narratives needed to be analyzed in comparison to the other's.

It is important to reiterate that the interpretations of the participants' words are mine as the principal investigator and not necessarily attributable to the participants, although they read, corrected, and approved the chapters. In the words of Margaret Kovach, the very act of "sharing one's own story is an aspect of co-constructing knowledge from an Indigenous perspective."[84] Thus the participants' willingness to approve their stories for publication, as well as their selection of the book's title and dedication, constitute their main contributions to the co-construction of this work.

As stressful as the procedures leading up to and during the interview process were, no element of the research project was as difficult to tackle as the question of representation. Would I be able to tell someone else's story without substituting my voice for theirs? At the heart of the matter was the notion of "giving back" to the community knowledge that would be useful to the individuals and to the collective from which the knowledge was drawn. This dilemma was exacerbated by the fact that, as an "outsider" to the community, I had no way to gauge – on my own – what was of value to my participants.[85] To ensure "authentic, ethical representation," all interview transcripts and multiple drafts of stories were provided to the interviewees for review, revision, and correction.[86] Individually, participants corrected and approved their stories. Nevertheless, representation not only includes considerations of accuracy but also pertains to the elements of a participant's story that are left in, what is removed and why, as well as how the diverse strands of thoughts and anecdotes are woven together into one coherent, meaningful story. As identified by Coast Salish researcher Robina Thomas, the challenge was "to compile all the stories into one story while at the same time not losing the intent of the many stories"; the task was essentially to "find the story to tell."[87]

The participants made corrections of fact, removed elements of their stories that they felt were not useful for wider viewing, and added elements that they felt were crucial to their stores but that I had not deemed necessary. In January 2012 I sent copies of the entire manuscript to all of the participants and invited them to read the draft and attend a group conversation and luncheon on February 18 at the Bear Country Inn in Terrace. At this session, participants discussed the manuscript, drafted a title and dedication, provided their final feedback, and approved its binding and submission for dissemination to a wider audience. At this meeting, I learned that none of the participants had ever discussed their educational experiences with the other participants. I was also happy to discover that the Tsimshian of Kitsumkalum have reclaimed their presence at the former site of Port Essington by holding summer camps where Tsimshian adults train their youths in traditional fishing, hunting, gathering, and food preparation techniques similar to those described by Verna at the opening of this chapter. Thus one of the unanticipated outcomes of this book is that the interwoven documentary and oral sources came together to form a highly textured story that is a useful resource not only for scholars but also for First Nations communities.

2

Indigenous Schooling
as Assimilation:
From Segregation to Integration

To UNDERSTAND THE history of Indigenous education in Canada, it is important to recognize how the relationship between Aboriginal peoples and government authorities changed over time. The relationship between Canada's Indigenous populations and the British Crown was initially one of inter-nation cooperation. That is, European newcomers relied on Indian peoples to provide fish and fur, which fuelled international trade. Native people also exercised physical and geographic prowess in staving off incursions from Americans with expansionary aspirations. Canada's First Peoples, in turn, benefited by expanding their trading partners. This mutually beneficial relationship changed during the late nineteenth century with the decline of the fur trade and Canada's shift to an increasingly agricultural economy.[1] By the time of Confederation in 1867, not only were Indians being increasingly dispossessed of their lands due to growing European settlement, but their populations were also being decimated by the introduction of infectious diseases. Concerned about the ability of Indigenous populations to sustain themselves, policy makers began to explore approaches for assimilation. It was felt that Indians would never enter the Canadian mainstream as long as they continued to speak their languages and perpetuate their traditions and values. Education was considered a key plank in the Canadian government's strategy for assimilating Aboriginal peoples, as it would hasten the replacement of their languages, traditions, and worldviews with those of Anglo-European settlers. Mi'kmaq scholar Marie Battiste, for example, has noted that as early

as the 1700s, Christian missionaries and British government officials used
literacy "as the sword of assimilation" against the Mi'kmaq of Nova Scotia.[2]

Under the terms of the 1867 British North America Act (now the
Constitution Act, 1982), the Dominion government inherited jurisdiction
over Indian affairs from the British Crown, but the provinces maintained
authority over non-Native schooling. Federal government officials felt that
it would be more efficient to build on existing educational institutions
than to start from scratch, so they agreed to finance schools' capital and
operating costs but entrusted management and staffing to various religious
denominations that had already established day schools among Indigenous
peoples.[3]

DAY SCHOOLS

Although little scholarly attention has been devoted to Indian day schools,
they have a long history. Until the late 1870s, government officials relied
mainly on church-run day schools to transform the lives of Native children
and to influence entire communities to adopt "Western ways."[4] During
the late 1700s Methodist missionaries had begun preaching among the
Aboriginal people in the territories that now comprise Canada. By 1821
various communities had converted to Christianity, and by 1830 Native
converts accounted for 1,000 (7 percent) of the Methodist Church's 14,000
members.[5] By the time Canada became a nation in 1867, Roman Catholic,
Anglican, Methodist, and Presbyterian religious had developed a vast infrastructure of missions and schools for Indian peoples.

Some researchers have argued that day schools had more in common
with rural schools than with Indian residential schools.[6] Like their rural
counterparts, Indian day schools tended to be sparsely furnished one-room
wooden structures heated with a wood-burning stove. Like most rural
schools at the time, the day schools' greatest challenge was recruiting and
retaining teachers.[7] Rural conditions were difficult for teachers, who
faced loneliness, isolation, danger from the environment, insufficient living
facilities, few resources, and a lack of connection to other teachers.[8] Given
the unfamiliar cultural norms of reserves, day schools tended to attract
teachers who were poorly qualified and lacked experience.[9] However, as
Chapter 3 illustrates, this was not entirely the case at Port Essington, where
all but one of the day school teachers were certified and experienced. With
so little empirical research on the day schools, only future research can
confirm whether Port Essington's teachers were anomalous or not.

Day schools were also challenged by irregular pupil attendance, as children often accompanied their families during the hunting and fishing seasons. High absenteeism resulted in a high number of dropouts after only a few years of schooling. Rather than adapting the school calendar to align with seasonal economic cycles, government officials chose instead to blame parents for "indifference" and "apathy" toward education.[10]

RESIDENTIAL SCHOOLS

Historians of Indigenous education have focused almost exclusively on residential schooling. As a result, we know a good deal more about residential schools than about other forms of Aboriginal education. As early as the 1870s, the federal Department of Indian Affairs considered day schools to be "a very imperfect means of education" because children returned daily to their Native languages and customs in their communities.[11] Prime Minister John A. Macdonald dispatched Nicholas Flood Davin to the United States to explore the existing boarding school system. Davin found merit in the American residential schools and, in 1879, after consulting with various church officials, presented a report to government recommending their widespread establishment in Canada.[12] Support for boarding schools soon spread, as illustrated by the comments of Edgar Dewdney, Canadian minister of the interior and former Indian commissioner, who stated that he

> never had much opinion of these day schools ... Where those children go to school for a few hours and then return to their wigwams or houses, there is not much chance to improve them ... The sooner we can close the day schools and send the children to the boarding schools, the sooner we will be able to do something with them.[13]

By the 1890s the Canadian government had embraced both the notion of boarding schools, which taught a general academic curriculum to children aged eight to fourteen, and the notion of industrial schools, which trained fourteen to eighteen year olds in practical skills such as carpentry, cabinetmaking, and shoemaking.[14] But two decades later, the federal government began to close industrial schools, having deemed them to be financially and pedagogically inefficient.[15] By 1923 federal authorities had officially phased out the terms "boarding" and "industrial" and had adopted "residential" to describe schools where children boarded away from their families for ten months or more up to the age of sixteen.[16]

Despite their appeal, however, residential schools were costly to run, as the government provided food, clothing, and shelter – in some cases year round – for their Aboriginal charges. As expenses outstripped the level of funding that legislators were willing to allocate, the schools had to rely to a large extent on the human resources of the churches and the children who attended them. Church authorities devised a "half-day system" whereby students spent only half of their day involved in academic pursuits and the remainder of their time doing chores to sustain the schools. In some cases, the entire "student body was out of class for long periods at critical times such as harvest."[17] Girls were taught domestic duties, such as cooking, doing laundry, or scrubbing floors. Boys were trained in carpentry, as well as farming and – depending on the school – tending cattle.[18] This resulted in slow academic progress, leaving many Indian children one or two grades behind their public school peers.[19] This age-grade lag jeopardized students' abilities to enter high school or postsecondary school and relegated them to manual labour and the whims of the resource-based economy. In some cases, the children's farming skills were too rudimentary to make them competitive in the economic marketplace of the dominant culture. At the same time, the pupils' reintegration into their home communities was hampered by their lack of appropriate knowledge and skills to contribute to community sustainability.[20]

Nevertheless, the legacy of the residential school system was even more damaging than the students' inadequate academic and life skills suggest. Individual students were taught that their families and cultures were inferior to those of their colonizers. This attitude led to physical punishment for alleged transgressions such as speaking one's language. Indigenous ways of learning were rooted in communitarian "principles of respect, generosity, and a willingness to help others."[21] By contrast, residential schooling was grounded in the discourse of liberalism, with its emphasis on individual attainment. Thus siblings were purposely segregated to discourage linguistic and cultural retention and to promote each child's absorption into Canadian social mores. Many children developed a hatred for their families and, consequently, for themselves, making return to their homes difficult.[22]

Perhaps most disturbing of all are reports of both physical and sexual abuse meted out to many of the students. As was the case in all Canadian schools until the 1970s, corporal punishment, or the "strap," was frequently administered on the hands and the backside. But a "wide variety of other sadistic punishments have been reported, ranging from choking to having heads shaved to being forced to eat regurgitated food."[23] Many former students experienced "fear of caretakers. Loneliness, knowing that elders and family were far away. Loathing from learning to hate oneself, because of repeated physical, verbal or sexual abuse suffered at the hands of various adult caretakers."[24]

Unbeknownst to many Canadians, the flaws in the residential system were evident by the early twentieth century. Dr. Peter Bryce, chief medical officer of the Department of Indian Affairs, produced his first report on the high mortality rates among residential school students in 1907, arguing that almost one-third of discharged boarding school students in the regions of Manitoba and the Northwest had perished.[25] In 1922 Dr. Bryce condemned the government for failing to safeguard residential school students from tuberculosis: "A trail of disease and death has gone on almost unchecked by any serious efforts on the part of the Department of Indian Affairs."[26] And although government bureaucrats lamented children's poor progress, chronic underfunding resulted in many children not attending school at all.

In light of such facts, historian Jean Barman – among others – has argued that the Canadian government's assimilation policy was a "dismal failure" because the results of residential schooling were completely contrary to its intent. Rather than preparing Indigenous youngsters to enter the Canadian mainstream, residential schools provided them with poor levels of education and estranged them from their communities, leading to their marginalization from both home and society.[27] The legacy of the ill-conceived residential system is evident everywhere in Canada today as former student "survivors" grapple with social maladjustment, abuse of self and others, and family breakdown.

It is unclear to what extent Canadian policy makers in the early twentieth century were apprised of the failings of the residential system. What is clear, however, is that the Canadian government preferred residential schools for "Canadianizing" Indian children. Nevertheless, it also continued to support day schools largely because they required meager human and material investments. Although attendance and achievement were allegedly poor at the day schools, the federal government continued to finance them. By 1951 British Columbia was home to seventy-one such institutions enrolling some 2,094 students, whereas twelve residential schools enrolled 2,186.[28]

INTEGRATED SCHOOLING

Despite its intentions, the Dominion government never fully achieved its goal of completely segregated schooling for Indigenous children. Since no industrial schools had been established in the Okanagan region, some Aboriginal children attended local schools. In 1914 public school teacher Miss A.M. Easton taught up to twelve Indian students in her integrated class. She found the Indigenous pupils' "behaviour and aptitude to learn" to be impressive.[29] Miss Nettie Walker, at Hedley Public School, taught nine Indian children ranging in age from ten to seventeen. According to Walker, the Aboriginal students' "writing and drawing books showed marked aptitude."[30] Miss K. Lawrence of Larkin School taught two promising Indian students, and Miss Minnie Smith of Wood Lake School reported five Indian students to be achieving well.[31] Indian Affairs expenditures for 1915 indicate that the Dominion government paid the province $165.34 in total tuition fees for educating on-reserve Aboriginal students in public schools. Legislation making schooling mandatory in 1920 led to increased student enrolment and an almost fivefold increase in federal tuition fees by 1925 to $738.40.[32]

During the early decades of the twentieth century, the decision to integrate or segregate Aboriginal children depended on many variables. As indicated above, availability of segregated facilities was one consideration. Another critical factor was the number of settler children needed to run a provincially funded school. In Telegraph Creek, for example, Indigenous people considerably outnumbered settlers throughout the first half of the twentieth century. In 1906, with only a handful of school-aged settler children in town and no denominational Indian day school nearby, school trustees welcomed the attendance of local Tahltan children and those of mixed ancestry to meet the province's minimum requirement of ten children to sustain a school. In addition to helping defer costs for the school and the teacher, both the provincial and federal governments provided books for "free to the Indian as well as the white children, while the progress made by the pupils, both white and Indian, has been excellent."[33] From 1912 until the late 1940s, Telegraph Creek Elementary School functioned as an "un-officially" integrated school receiving partial funding and administrative oversight from both provincial and federal authorities.

Local residents' willingness to have their children educated with Indigenous students was another factor that determined segregated or integrated schooling for Aboriginal children. In 1928, for example, lower Vancouver Island's Saanich School Board voted to exclude Aboriginal children from the local public school, citing overcrowding and poor academic achievement. Education Minister Joshua Hinchliffe supported the vote, arguing that the education of on-reserve Aboriginal children fell under Dominion government jurisdiction.[34]

Economic factors also played an important role in schools' willingness to integrate or not. By the mid-1930s integrated schooling had become a more pressing policy issue due to the Depression, which was crippling the Canadian economy. In 1933 the number of Aboriginal children attending public schools throughout Canada jumped to 230 as the federal government reduced expenditures for residential and day schools.[35] That year, British Columbia's education minister negotiated with Canada's minister of Indian affairs for a flat tuition fee of $20 per annum for the public schooling of on-reserve children. Federal tuition payments to the province climbed to $1,747.19 in 1934–35.[36]

By the mid-1940s Canadian officials were reconsidering their segregation policies pertaining to Native schooling. After many years of grieving their living conditions, Aboriginal peoples' discontent peaked after the Second World War given the disproportionately large number of Indian men who fought overseas but who were still denied the right to vote in Canada.[37] In 1946 the Canadian government struck a Special Joint Committee of the Senate and the House of Commons to gauge concerns over Indian well-being.[38] Although most educational briefs and presentations to the committee concerned residential schools, the committee's recommendations for reform also impacted day schools. Following the publication of the committee's 1949 report, the federal government adopted a policy of integrated schooling that was legalized in 1951 with revisions to the Indian Act enabling the minister of Indian affairs to enter into agreements with provincial governments, territorial councils, school boards, and religious or charitable organizations for the schooling of Aboriginal children living on reserves.[39] Across the country, officials began winding down both residential and on-reserve day schools that had previously been managed by church denominations and entered into agreements with provinces and local boards to enrol Indian children in public schools.

Unfortunately, very few scholars have investigated the postwar era, during which the Canadian government shifted from a policy of segregated to integrated schooling for Indigenous youngsters. Among the few historians who have discussed the Canadian government's 1951 policy shift from segregated to integrated schooling, most have tended to examine federal and provincial policy development, while neglecting how policies affected individuals in communities.[40] For example, *Shingwauk's Vision*, James R. Miller's seminal work on Canada's residential schools, attributes the impetus for integration to national economic issues.[41] That is, integration provided a convenient alternative to financing a separate system of education for a growing Native population attending dilapidated schools in need of upgrading and expansion. Historian John Milloy supports Miller's view, arguing that the rationale for Canada's shift from segregated to integrated schooling was twofold: policy makers' longstanding goal of assimilating Native peoples into Canadian society and "mundane financial considerations."[42]

Even less research has examined the integration experiences of former pupils who made the shift from segregated to integrated schooling, with the result that this aspect of Indigenous education has been undertheorized. Michael Marker is one of the few scholars to study the impacts of integration on Aboriginal children using historical methods. Marker has examined the high school experiences of Lummi youngsters in Washington State during the 1970s. He has concluded that "in many respects, and for many Aboriginal teenagers, going to a mainstream high school was worse than going to a residential school" due to the stereotyping and racist views of Indians held by administrators and teachers.[43] Furthermore, Lummi students were exposed to daily violence directed toward them by non-Aboriginal students who perpetuated economic, political, and cultural pressures established in the larger community. The tension-filled school experiences of the Lummi mirrored the conflict that plagued the community due to the Boldt legal decision of 1974,[44] which affirmed the Coast Salish peoples' treaty right to catch half the salmon at their accustomed fishing sites throughout Puget Sound. Marker refers to this as the "most controversial and potent decision in the history of American Indian law," one that led to outrage by non-Native community members and tension for Aboriginal teens.[45]

Diane Persson's research on the history of Blue Quills School in Alberta paints a more variegated portrait of integration experiences, suggesting that sociopolitical contexts may be important factors in understanding the impacts of the integration policy. For example, a student integrated in the 1950s characterized his experiences favourably, noting that "there were about 15 of us who went into St. Paul to school. The kids really didn't give us a hard time ... So we made friends easily."[46] One decade later, however, another student reported less favourable experiences, stating that the students "were not prepared for it at all. We were so used to being with our Native peers that we were not used to being around white people ... And all of a sudden you're thrown in with a bunch of white kids that laugh at you because everybody is wearing coveralls."[47] These largely unexplored components of Indigenous educational experiences present significant gaps in our collective historical understandings.

3
Tsimshian Education versus Western-Style Schooling

THE TERRITORY OCCUPIED by the Tsimshian peoples spans from Port Simpson in British Columbia's northwest to Kitselas in the east and Klemtu to the south.[1] Archaeological sites suggest ongoing occupation of the region by highly advanced human societies for well over five millennia.[2] The ancient Tsimshian were composed of multiple groups whose mobility was facilitated by coastal waterways, such as the mighty Skeena River, which stretches 560 kilometres inland from the British Columbia coast.[3] No discussion of Tsimshian education would be complete without first acknowledging the complex social systems that regulated Tsimshian behaviour patterns, including the inheritance of goods, titles, economic resources, and cultural rites such as dances, stories, and ceremonies.[4] Like all Indigenous peoples, the Tsimshian developed an elaborate system for handling their relationships with the natural environment, known today as "traditional ecological knowledge."[5] This incorporated knowledge about how to manage and sustain food sources, including harvesting and hunting sites, as well as how to use the resources for nutrition and health maintenance.

Since the beginning of time, the Tsimshian have organized themselves around four exogamous matrilineal *pteex,* translated variously as "clans," "tribes," or "phratries." These include Laxgibuu (Wolf), Laxsgiik (Eagle), Ganhada (Raven), and Gispudwada (Killer Whale).[6] Each pteex regulated spousal selection, which was not a matter of individual choice until approximately the third decade of the twentieth century.[7] Members of the same pteex are not permitted to marry despite not necessarily being from the same *waap,* translated as "family" or "house." Traditionally, marriages were socially negotiated alliances to ensure the continuation of social status.[8] Tsimshian society also consisted of four hereditary social classes: royalty, nobility, commoners, and slaves. Marriages were to be arranged from within social classes, although instances of crossclass marriage did exist. Children of crossclass marriages could regain status only through extensive gift-giving festivities, such as the *xalait* (potlatch).[9] The potlatch was the means through which Indigenous peoples of the northwest coast ensured their social rank and hereditary privileges. "Complex and highly formal," the potlatch followed strict protocol, as it was an integral part of the west coast Indigenous economy.[10]

Each pteex consists of several *waaps* (house groups), which represent both a building and those who abide in it. The waap has stewardship over artifacts and privileges that are inherited through the mother's lineage and that usually pass from a man to his sister's son. Objects include – but are not restricted to – house posts, paintings, beams, ceremonial costumes, feast dishes, utensils, and crests designating pteex membership.[11] Privileges include the rights to certain ceremonial dances, songs, and *adaawx* (histories), as well as the use of specific territories for hunting, fishing, and harvesting resources for food, clothing, shelter, medicine, and ceremonies.[12]

A foundational tenet of Indigenous thought is the belief in a world of knowledge that exists beyond the "immediate sensible world of perception."[13] For Tsimshian peoples, this belief was particularly manifested in the notion of reincarnation, although it lost prominence after contact with European settlers. More specifically, it was thought that characteristics of a member within a certain lineage could reappear in their grandchildren, a point illustrated by the fact that the word *wo* is used for both cradle and grave box.[14] This notion was codified through the practice of inheriting names and through formal rituals such as the xalait. "Tsimshians," notes Christopher Roth, "are embedded in cycles of transmigrating souls" in that "names and not their wearers are the true members of Tsimshian lineages."[15] Much like the view of Western philosopher Plato that ideas – not material objects – are universal, the Tsimshian belief is that souls are eternal and reappear with each successive generation through the bestowal of universal names. The conferring of names links "a preexisting biological individual and a preexisting immortal individual"[16] so that Tsimshian knowledge and culture – such as names, lineages, crests, and stories – remain perpetual.

According to the European worldview, names are fleeting since their bearers are mortal. In contrast, Tsimshian bodies, which are mortal, wear "immortal social personages" who transcend time to link "ancient historical events" describing the "origins of the name, of the house lineage, and of the lineage's right to territories and resources."[17] That is, names signify to both wearer and community members one's history as well as one's contemporary place in society. Careful consideration is allotted to determining who receives a name since the next bearer is tasked with upholding the characteristics of the name as well as the stories and regulations pertaining to possessions and privileges.[18] A single name, through what it says and through what people know about where it fits into a system of names, registers ongoing participation in a web of relationships among lineages, histories, wealth, and territories.[19] Names are "social actors" that provide social stability and continuity amid societal change and are allocated through ceremonial feasts.

Another critical aspect of traditional Tsimshian culture was an economic cycle that was intimately tied to resources abundant in the environment. It began in early spring with the harvest and trade of oolichan, known for their rich and versatile oil. Their Tsimshian name was "saviour" since oolichan prevented starvation among the people after many winter months of subsisting on preserved foods. Oolichan that were not immediately consumed were carefully covered in pits to enable decomposition and were then boiled and pressed to extract their oil.[20] The month of May was usually dedicated to gathering and storing seaweed as well as halibut fishing. June was the season to collect abalone, shoots and greens from freshly blooming foliage, and eggs of shore birds, such as seagulls. Fruit picking marked the summer months, a harvest that began with salmon berries and ended in the fall with crab apples. Fall was devoted to fishing and to preserving chum and salmon. Autumn was also the season to hunt and preserve deer, elk, mountain goat, sheep, bear, ducks, and other wildlife. In late autumn the Tsimshian feasted at sites such as Port Simpson and Port Essington, known among the Tsimshian as Spaksuut (pronounced "Spokeshute").[21] In the winter, most Tsimshian returned to their inland villages, such as Kitsumkalum and Kitselas near the contemporary towns of Terrace and Kitimat. Others remained on the west coast.

A child's education began at a very young age and was usually overseen by family members from the mother's lineage. Children were usually enlisted to assist with family chores as early as age five. A girl learned household tasks such as weaving, fruit picking, and food preservation from her maternal grandmother. Boys were taught fishing and hunting skills by their maternal uncles, from whom they inherited trap lines and hunting territories.[22] During the winter months, boys were taught to carve and to repair tools, whereas girls learned how to weave clothing, mats, and baskets.[23] These tasks suggest that the education of young Tsimshian was largely anchored in practical skills for sustenance derived from the land.

Without the pressures of hunting, gathering, and food processing, Tsimshian families spent winter evenings playing games, solving riddles, and telling stories – both formal histories and *adaawx* (house-specific stories). The former were more universal, historically significant accounts that were told widely by many.[24] House-specific histories could be told and received only by members of specific family groups. These recounted such historically significant facts and events as ancestral lineages and family territories, crests, and privileges.[25] Stories tended to culminate with important sayings and proverbs that taught "the ethics of living" – particularly off the land – to younger generations.[26]

Because Sm'algyax, the Tsimshian language, was oral rather than written, stories were told and retold to ensure that details were not lost with time. It was generally the house chief or matriarch who taught children their house history. Among the most important lessons recounted to youngsters was the importance of behaving respectfully toward all things, both animate and inanimate, since all creations were considered to possess souls.[27] Knowledge, according to this Indigenous worldview, expresses "the vibrant relationships between the people, their ecosystems, and other living beings and spirits that share their lands."[28] Less formal *'txal 'ya'ansk* (anecdotes) conveyed lessons about personal qualities and maintained the memories of individual ancestors and family friends.[29]

Although most people worked collaboratively within their waap, there were exceptions for members who held specialized knowledge.[30] As was the case throughout Indigenous societies worldwide, Tsimshian elders traditionally recognized children's unique capabilities and talents as manifestations of the child's inner spirit. According to Indigenous worldviews, all individuals are endowed with unique gifts with which to fulfil their life's purpose. Over the course of a lifetime, a person's "learning spirit" "knows its path and becomes attracted to certain learning experiences, gravitating toward those elements that it needs to complete its learning journey."[31] As a result, certain individuals would be selected to train for specific roles. For example, *gwildmniits* (shamans) were practised at reading how the moon and stars regulated tidal movement. These group members, who studied separately, would use their expertise to advise on proper conditions for fishing and harvesting. Others who possessed specialized expertise were woodworkers, who created storage boxes, bows, canoes, and totem poles. Medicine men, or shamans, used their extensive knowledge of local plant extracts to heal illness.[32]

Interestingly, shamans worked on both the physical and the spiritual levels. Whereas some physical ailments could often be healed with plant extracts, others were thought to derive from a spiritual imbalance and were rectified through specific rituals to "cleanse" the patient's soul.[33] However, shamans were not the only community members tasked with overseeing the spiritual well-being of the community. The *sm'oogyet* (chief) also played a role as a spiritual leader. First and foremost, he modelled respect for all of creation, both animate and inanimate. This was done by honouring or paying tribute to animals and spirits not only during birth and death rituals but also before hunting and fishing expeditions. Prior to feasting, the hunted or harvested bounty would be honoured by the sm'oogyet clad in ceremonial robes and headdresses.[34] Intergenerational festivities, such as *luulgyit* (feasts), prepared children for the cultural rituals they would assume as adults.

One of the most important concepts in Tsimshian education was the principle of sustained observation as a prelude to demonstrating mastery. Like other First Nations groups, failure was not a concept commonly held by the Tsimshian.[35] As a children moved from the observation stage through to mastery, they were usually assisted one-on-one by someone older and more skilful.[36]

During the mid-1700s, Russian, Spanish, and English explorers disrupted social, cultural, and economic stability among the Tsimshian residing on the northwest coast of what is now British Columbia. The arrival of Catholic missionaries during the 1830s was predated by contact with Russian Orthodox officials who had settled in Alaska from the late 1700s. The Hudson's Bay Company set down roots in the area in the 1830s, and in the 1850s William Duncan, a lay preacher with the Church Missionary Society of England, began preaching at Port Simpson after having learned Sm'algyax. By 1862 Duncan had managed to baptize or obtain consent for baptizing fifty-eight Tsimshian from the region.[37] However, following a smallpox epidemic, Duncan moved his community to Metlakatla. The new community was self-sufficient and included houses as well as a church, courthouse and jail, town hall, museum, and reading room. Community members contributed to industries such as a salmon cannery, forge, sawmill, and soap house.

Religious conversion was greatly facilitated when Catholic, Protestant, and Methodist missionaries established schools among the Tsimshian population. Methodists made widespread, permanent inroads with the coastal Tsimshian in the early 1870s after Alfred and Kate Dudoward were converted to Christianity. Born of white fathers and Native mothers, the Dudowards had a high rank among their people and became integral to the mission at Port Simpson. When Methodist missionary Thomas Crosby took up residence there in 1874, the community flourished.[38] Within five years, Crosby and his wife had established a boarding home for Tsimshian girls, followed by a home for boys in 1890. Methodists in the lower Skeena region had begun to experience competition from both the Anglican Church and the Salvation Army by the late 1890s. First founded in London, England, the Salvation Army was "organized on a quasi-military basis" and characterized by its uniforms, flags, and brass bands, which the Tsimshian of Port Essington found particularly appealing.[39]

PORT ESSINGTON INDIAN DAY SCHOOL

In 1877 the Methodist Church founded a mission at Port Essington to be presided over by the region's first missionary: William Henry Pierce, a converted Tsimshian.[40] Pierce's influence was powerful, and within a year many Tsimshian had permanently left their traditional inland villages and resettled at Port Essington. By 1879 Methodists had erected a church and school on the reserve, over which Pierce initially presided.[41] Pierce was replaced by the Reverend Dennis Jennings, who taught until 1889, when Miss Margaret Hargreaves, also a Methodist missionary, assumed teaching duties at the school. A year later she resigned when she married Pierce.[42]

Teacher transiency, which had plagued British Columbia's rural schools since their inception in the 1870s, was particularly problematic at the Indian day schools due to the poor salaries offered by the various religious denominations that managed the schools.[43] By contrast, teacher retention did not present a challenge in the early years of Port Essington Indian Day School when abundant numbers of missionaries were willing to make the town their home. Over time, however, staffing the schools became problematic.

With the formation of Canada, authority over public schooling was conferred upon the provinces as outlined in the 1867 British North America Act (now the Constitution Act, 1982), which also granted the Dominion government jurisdiction over Indian affairs.[44] Thus the Government of Canada assumed responsibility for educating First Nations children. Operating within a political framework of classical liberalism, Canadian

Port Essington Indian Day School, 1890s. *Courtesy of Royal BC Museum, Image B-05843 c, British Columbia Archives.*

officials preferred not to deal directly with the day-to-day matters of individual Canadians' lives. Given that religious denominations across the nation had already established missions and schools in outlying Aboriginal communities, the government found it more administratively expedient – as well as cost-efficient – simply to fund existing schools while leaving the on-the-ground management to the churches. The Indian Act, first formalized in 1876, established the administrative apparatus for schools financed by government but operated by the churches. By 1880 the bureaucracy charged with overseeing Indian livelihood consisted of a large civil service, housed in Ottawa's Department of Indian Affairs, as well as an even larger contingent of fieldworkers who were responsible for putting federal policies into practice at the local level.[45]

Although Indian Affairs officially employed day school teachers, the Indian Act stipulated that a reserve's chief and councillor had the right to determine a teacher's religion. "In practice," states historian E. Brian Titley, "a church that claimed a reserve as its terrain based on a record of missionary activity in the area assumed the right of nomination."[46] In Port Essington this arrangement worked out well from 1879 to 1925, with the day school employing only four teachers over that forty-six-year period. Over the next twenty-two years, however, eleven more teachers passed in and out of the school until its closure in 1947.

Although historians have acknowledged the difficulties that day schools had recruiting and retaining qualified teachers, the phenomenon has not been well researched. The remainder of this chapter explores teacher turnover for several important reasons. First, the pages that follow clearly illustrate that teacher transience at Port Essington Indian Day School had less to do with teachers' unwillingness to stay on the reserve than with the petty dealings of self-interested church officials and neglectful government authorities. Second, the closure of the day school in 1947 was directly linked to the inability of school officials to secure a teacher. Third, the high rate of teacher turnover prevented children and teachers from establishing long-term relationships. This phenomenon contrasted significantly with traditional Tsimshian education, where children's primary caregivers from their mothers' lineage were also their main educators.

From 1879 to 1947 fifteen teachers taught at the Port Essington Indian Day School. Initially, Methodist missionaries presided over both church and school. This ended with the arrival of Miss Catherine Tranter, a Methodist missionary who taught at the school from 1890 to 1910 at a yearly salary of $75.[47] Tranter was well respected in the community, having learned Sm'algyax well, which she used with the children. She also followed a flexible calendar, keeping the school open eleven months of the year and scheduling one month's vacation for fall rather than summer.[48] When Tranter left in 1910, Ernest H. Pierce briefly taught school until January 1911, when church officials appointed Miss Hilda Bland. Unfortunately, Bland opened the school for only twenty-one of the sixty days of the spring term.[49] When provincial inspector A.M. Tyson visited the school in March, he found twenty-two "children of school age that had been home all winter" with parents "very much aggrieved" by the situation. Tyson reported to J.D. McLean, Canada's assistant deputy and secretary of Indian affairs, that the closure had resulted when Indian families travelled up the Skeena River, where they were employed in railway construction. Although they returned within several months, the Reverend T. Ferrier – superintendent of Indian education for the Methodist Church – had already informed Miss Bland that there were insufficient funds to pay her and had essentially dismissed her. There is no indication in the historical records of what was done with the money allocated by federal officials to pay her salary. Nevertheless, in April 1912 Pierce again temporarily assumed the teaching position, further frustrating federal Indian Agents who had complained to authorities in Ottawa on several occasions that teachers' salaries ought to be paid via the Indian Agent rather than through the church.[50] Meanwhile, Methodist officials made no secret of the fact that they preferred missionaries to lay teachers.

In October 1912 Miss Fanny Noble was appointed to teach at the day school.[51] Miss Noble – who graduated from Port Essington Elementary School and had assisted Miss Tranter at the day school at the turn of the century – proved to be a competent teacher who remained at the day school for thirteen years.[52] Both provincial and federal Indian Agents admired Noble's "scrupulous cleanliness," the neatness of the school register, and her "deep" interest in the children's work.[53] Although she was a "successful teacher" who "won the favor of the Church and Government officials," her tenure was not without difficulty. When visiting the school in late August 1913, Indian Agent C.C. Perry found that Miss Noble had not opened the school. Upon further investigation, Perry learned that the Reverend George H. Raley had "forgotten to mail instructions" to Miss Noble, causing the school to remain closed into September and clearly illustrating the church's aversion to nonmissionary instructors.[54]

Raley's "memory lapse" was but one reason for the Methodist ministry's growing frustration with the day school's perceived lack of progress. In October 1916 W.H. Pierce wrote to Duncan Campbell Scott, Canada's deputy superintendent of Indian affairs, suggesting that the government construct a residential school to replace the day school. Pierce was concerned by the poor levels of attendance among the children, who often accompanied their parents on seasonal fishing and hunting expeditions. According to Pierce, "no real progress is ever made and both teacher and pupil are discouraged."[55]

Whereas Pierce emphasized the negative, Noble strove to highlight the positive. In her 1916 quarterly report, she informed Perry that Ethel Nelson and John Spencer were deserving of prizes for their attendance, which had been overall very "regular" at the school. She also noted that thirty-three of the children had taken part in a Christmas "entertainment" that was well received by the "white population."[56] Despite Noble's positive spin, Indian Affairs officials ordered Perry to "put forth every effort to increase attendance, at once" since fewer than eight out of thirty registered students attended on average in 1916.[57]

Dennis Jennings, Fanny Noble, and the students of Port Essington Indian Day
School, December 1916. *Courtesy of Prince Rupert City and Regional Archives.*

Few records exist from which to determine the curricula that day school
teachers followed. As early as 1919, federal officials mandated the use of
provincial curricula.[58] Limited evidence suggests that teachers imparted
the rudiments of reading, spelling, grammar, history, arithmetic, music,
drawing, and Scripture with the goal of assimilating Native peoples into
the Canadian way of life. Some fine arts were taught, depending on the
teacher's personal interests. Many day school instructors supported extra-
curricular learning in the form of agricultural pursuits and domestic science. As well, special events such as sports days, Christmas concerts, and
Empire Day were all observed.[59] Students were able to complete Grades
1 to 8 at the day school, at which point they had to decide whether to
attend high school at Prince Rupert or transfer to a residential school.

Miss Noble left Port Essington in 1925 partly due to financial concerns.
The cost of living in Port Essington was high given that all supplies had
to be transported into the community by boat. In 1920 Miss Noble requested a raise to $800 yearly, a figure approximately two-thirds of the
average salary for rural teachers of her tenure in the province's public
schools.[60] Although she did not possess a teaching certificate, Noble
had completed high school in Victoria and had proven, after almost eight
years, that she could teach reading, spelling, writing, and drawing to her

twenty-two pupils, of whom thirteen attended on average.[61] After five years of negotiating with church officials, she was finally granted a pay increase to $800 per annum in 1925 – the year that she resigned.[62]

Noble's immediate successors did not prove to be as resilient and resigned after two years. In 1927 Miss Helena Hare, who had one year's experience at Kitimat, succeeded Miss Annie Roode at a salary of $950 annually.[63] When Hare resigned in 1929, Miss Louise Fakeley was appointed at $1,000 per year but stayed in Port Essington only a month. In her sharply worded resignation letter, Miss Fakeley noted that for the month of September, she had opened the school for only two days due in part to a measles epidemic. But more importantly, she found it impossible to secure suitable accommodation. Initially, she was told to live (alone) in the hospital, which opened only during summer months with the arrival from Prince Rupert of Dr. Large, a visiting physician. She found it "too large and barn-like for one person," and the kitchen was "horribly dirty." When Dr. Large permitted her to live in the nurses' home, she found that there were "drunken men ranging around this town and fighting every night," with "the worst offenders" living next door. She recommended that a policeman be stationed in the town to "get the place cleaned up." Refusing to open the school, Miss Fakeley took refuge at the home of a friend in Hazelton, 290 kilometres away.[64]

In spite of the troubles that Miss Fakeley endured during her stay at Port Essington, there is evidence to suggest that teaching and learning were taking place at the school. In 1929 she submitted nine pupils' artwork and poetry to the Prince Rupert Exhibition. Several of the children won prizes for their work, although their names were not noted.[65]

Although church authorities were generally charged with appointing teachers to day schools, the situation at Port Essington during the 1920s became dire enough for the Canadian government to intervene. On November 5, 1929, A.F. MacKenzie, acting assistant deputy and secretary of Indian affairs, took charge of the situation and replaced Miss Fakeley with Dorothy Deane at a salary of $1,000 per year.[66] Miss Deane held a second-class teaching certificate and had several years of experience teaching public school. But the situation at Port Essington proved too much for Miss Deane as well, and by the end of December, she had tendered her resignation. The teacher with the longest tenure was Mrs. Elizabeth Pogson, appointed by MacKenzie in January 1930.[67] Pogson taught at the school for twelve years in total, but her time there was broken into two different periods: from 1930 to 1937 and from 1942 to 1947. Pogson's experiences are worth describing in detail, for they illustrate – more than

Where go the Boats?

Dark brown is the river,
Golden is the sand;
It flows along for ever,
With trees on either hand.

Green leaves a floating,
Castles of the foam;
Boats of mine a boating—
Where will all come home?

On goes the river,
And out past the mill,
Away down the valley,
Away down the hill.

Away down the river,
A hundred miles or more,
Other little children
Shall bring my boats ashore.

Prince Rupert Exhibition Entry A, Port Essington Indian Day
School, girl aged ten. *Courtesy of Jim McDonald.*

the other teachers' – the extent to which church and government officials
deterred teachers from working at Port Essington. Indeed, Pogson was
caught in the centre of neglectful church officials, disinterested government officials, and an ideologically driven federal school inspector.

Pogson possessed a second-class teaching certificate and came highly
recommended after eight successful years in Manitoba's public schools.
Her salary was set at $1,000 per year, but she had to supply her own fuel
and light. Contrary to customary practices, Pogson was permitted to reside
on the reserve given that her husband was an "invalid" and that she had
a five-year-old daughter to care for. MacKenzie noted that this was clearly

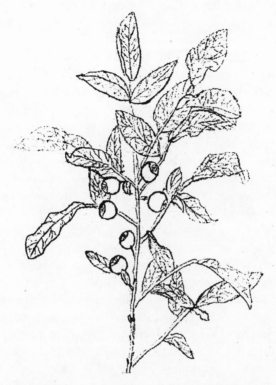

Prince Rupert Exhibition Entry B, Port Essington Indian
Day School, girl aged thirteen. *Courtesy of Jim McDonald.*

an exceptional case since Indian Affairs officials did not support having a
man with "no duties in connection with Indian work" residing permanently
on the reserve.[68]

Mrs. Pogson's work at the school initially proceeded smoothly, with
her students making adequate progress. One of them, Edward Bolton, the
"first native scholar in BC to have been successful in passing his [high
school] entrance examination from an Indian Reserve day school," had
enrolled in King Edward High School in Prince Rupert in 1935.[69] Nevertheless, Pogson annoyed federal authorities in the spring of 1930 by requesting that a suitable teacherage be built on the reserve. She complained
that the house she had rented for several months was abruptly withdrawn
to accommodate someone else. She and her family were forced to reside
in an uninsulated building that required extensive repairs to render it
habitable.[70] MacKenzie was either unaware – or chose not to apprise

himself – of earlier letters of complaint from former teachers, for he refused to fulfil Pogson's request, erroneously stating that prior to her appointment, "unmarried teachers were employed at this school, and they were able to obtain suitable board and living accommodation."[71]

In 1936 Pogson's situation worsened when District Inspector Gerald H. Barry began filing unfavourable teaching reports with Indian Affairs officials. Inspector Barry noted that the children – particularly the first graders – were making poor progress. This he attributed to "too many children for this rather elderly [forty-six-year-old] teacher." Barry arranged for the ten mixed-heritage students plus Pogson's own daughter to transfer to the local public school. Nevertheless, Barry's assessment of Pogson's teaching may have been more ideological than substantive and certainly did not reflect the glowing reference she had received from School Inspector Hartley after many years of service in Manitoba. Barry lamented that Pogson was "rather too old to make much use of 'Demonstration and Type Lessons.' Her knowledge of the Psychology of Teaching is … very limited, hence she does not get the best results."[72] As elsewhere in North America, by the mid-1920s educational psychology had become well entrenched in normal school curricula, covering topics such as "General Modes of Human Behaviour."[73] Having received her teaching certificate in the early 1900s, it is likely that Pogson used more "traditional" methods of which "modern" educationists, such as Barry, disapproved.

In June 1937 Pogson resigned from Port Essington Indian Day School. Historical records do not indicate whether she was forced out or left of her own volition, but she would appear again in the school's records, as discussed below, and former students have reported that she remained in Port Essington, where her husband was appointed postmaster. Between 1937 and 1942 five teachers passed through Port Essington Indian Day School, two of whom remained for only six months each.

It is also apparent that Inspector Barry preferred not only more modern approaches but also male teachers. By September of that year, Barry had appointed Mr. Benjamin Severson, who had four years of experience teaching in Saskatchewan's schools. Like Mrs. Pogson, Severson came highly recommended. According to Mr. Stillwell, director of training and supervision of Saskatchewan's Department of Education, Mr. Severson was a "highly promising teacher" who aimed "to provide purposeful work that interests and satisfies. His method of teaching has a very strong tendency towards the projects idea. His questions are well selected and require considerable thought. His classroom manner is pleasing and his discipline is good … He is well liked by the pupils and ratepayers."[74]

In spite of these accolades, Inspector Barry soon found fault with Severson too. In his report of October 1937, Barry rated Mr. Severson as "fair" to "poor." He criticized Severson for assigning the younger children to make cut-outs from old catalogues while the older children completed a silent reading test. Barry recommended that Severson attend summer school in order to "settle down and teach definite lessons to all grades."[75] By June 1938 officials were again in search of a teacher for the day school.[76]

Mr. Andrew Rutherford, a fifty-two-year-old Methodist missionary, replaced Mr. Severson in September 1938 at a yearly salary of $1,000. Rutherford had earned a bachelor's degree from McMaster University and held two first-class teaching certificates – one from Saskatchewan and one from Manitoba. Three of his seven years of teaching had been done at mission schools in Japan. He also had administrative experience, having been vice-principal of a seven-room public school.[77] Inspector Barry was pleased with Mr. Rutherford, stating that he worked "hard for the children," who were "happy and clean."[78] But Rutherford proved problematic for Indian Affairs officials. Some of the Native boys were leaving the reserve to play games or attend extracurricular classes with non-Aboriginal children under the tutelage of Catholic reverend Father Champlain. Rutherford disapproved of Natives mixing with non-Native children, and conflict arose between him and Father Champlain. As historian Keith Smith has noted, "sectarian discord" was commonplace, as various denominational groups vied to win the hearts and souls of Indigenous community members.[79] Barry and Indian agent Collison intervened, reminding Rutherford that although he "had a perfect right to give his congregation any advise [sic] he thought right," he had best "pay little attention to the fact that the Indian boys mixed with others in the Port Essington village."[80]

When Rutherford resigned a year later, the position was filled by Mr. Francis W. Chilton, a married, forty-two-year-old missionary with a first-class professional certificate from Saskatchewan.[81] Chilton appealed to church and government officials alike due to his twenty years of teaching experience and because his father had been a Methodist minister. Nevertheless, Chilton suffered from chronic bronchitis due to gas exposure while serving abroad during the First World War. By December 1940 Chilton had resigned. Although his ill health contributed to his resignation, other factors also came into play. According to his letter of resignation, Chilton sought to be reimbursed for the janitorial expenses he had paid, having learned that Indian Affairs had allocated funds to the Methodist Church to cover sweeping, scrubbing, and fire lighting.[82] Since there are no follow-up letters on record, it is not clear whether

Mr. Chilton ever retrieved these funds from church officials; nor is it clear where the funds ended up.

In January 1941 thirty-two-year-old Ruby Lau was temporarily appointed to the school while church officials sought a male missionary to teach at Port Essington. Lau held a second-class teaching certificate from Brandon Normal School in Manitoba and had five and a half years of experience.[83] By July of that year, church officials had replaced Miss Lau with Mr. Roy B. Vannatter, a missionary from Klemtu, British Columbia.[84]

Vannatter proved to be a very poor choice, despite the fact that Indian Agent James Gillett initially found that he "had good control over the children," who "appeared keenly interested" and made good progress.[85] In the spring of 1942 some of the parents had informed Indian Agent Gillett that the teacher "was corrupting the morals of the school children." When Gillett visited the reserve on May 4 to investigate, he found only two children in attendance. When Vannatter admitted to having "committed sexual interference" with one boy aged eight and two aged twelve, Gillett advised him to resign immediately and notified the police. In spite of Vannatter having admitted his guilt, the local police were not prepared to press charges and eventually disregarded the incident since, after further investigation, they found enough evidence to charge Vannatter on another unrelated matter.[86] This incident sadly reflects government and church officials' lack of care in dealing with their Indigenous charges. More importantly, however, it contradicts the commonly held notion that Indian day schools were less harmful for pupils than residential schools.

By the 1940s the situation at the day school was desperate. With the onset of the Second World War, Canada was gripped by a severe teacher shortage as many men and women left the profession to assist with the war effort. As early as 1940 church officials lamented the shortage of money and of personnel willing to commit their lives to rural mission work.[87] By 1943 it appeared that their missions were "depleted of experienced leadership to an extent unparalleled in all their long history."[88] Indeed, beginning in 1940, Port Essington was without a minister to guide a congregation that had dwindled to forty-one members by 1947, a year when no baptisms, marriages, or burials were performed.[89] Unable to find a suitable teacher in 1942, officials nominated none other than Elizabeth Pogson on a temporary, one-year basis at $1,000 per year. Church officials argued in Pogson's favour to Indian Affairs, stating that "while the Department was not quite satisfied with [Pogson's] work as a teacher, she is quite satisfactory from the standpoint of character and personality, and has a good influence among the Indians."[90]

The other factor working in Pogson's favour was the retirement of Inspector Barry. As had been the case during the Depression, the Second World War had forced Indian Affairs to cut costs by reducing its complement of federal school inspectors and arranging for provincial school inspectors to lend a hand.[91] Provincial inspector Bergie Thorsteinsson, who had replaced Gerald H. Barry late in 1942, was much more tolerant of Pogson's techniques, which he characterized as "not the most modern" but "effective."[92] Given Pogson's satisfactory standing, Indian Affairs granted her a permanent position in September 1943. This arrangement suited R.A. Hoey, superintendent of welfare and training at Indian Affairs, as he found "nothing on file" to indicate that Mrs. Pogson had ever resigned.[93] Hoey's actions illustrate again the "arms-length" attitude that government officials in Ottawa adopted with respect to the school's daily workings.

In November 1944 Inspector Thorsteinsson reported that Mrs. Pogson was "carrying on in her usually conscientious and efficient manner." Unlike Barry, Thorsteinsson found that primary-level children were particularly good at reading. However, of the nineteen students enrolled, twelve were making fair or bad progress, largely due to poor daily attendance.[94] Absenteeism frustrated government and church officials alike, who blamed parents for taking their children with them during fishing and logging excursions.[95]

On May 30, 1947, Indian Agent F. Earl Anfield regretfully accepted Pogson's resignation from Port Essington Indian Day School. After over twenty years of teaching, twelve of which were at Port Essington, Pogson moved to Victoria, where she died in December 1952 at the age of sixty-one.[96] Pogson's resignation came three years after her husband's death and coincided with Port Essington's overall declining social and economic vitality. The final quarterly school return that Pogson filed with Indian Affairs listed only ten pupils enrolled and an average daily attendance of only four.[97]

Likewise, Port Essington's public school, which had enrolled eighty-two pupils at its zenith in 1933, was also becoming unsustainable. This was due, in large part, to the federal government's decision to remove Japanese Canadians from coastal areas. As a result of their removal, enrolment at Port Essington Elementary School dropped from forty-five in 1940 to thirteen in the spring of 1942.[98] With only fourteen children enrolled in the public school by 1947 and little likelihood of finding a teacher for the day school, Indian Agent Anfield requested that the Prince Rupert School Board "consider admitting the Indian children of Port Essington to the 'white' [public] school" on a "cost per pupil per year basis less provincial grants."[99] Although no agreement was officially signed, Indian Affairs agreed to pay the board $65 per year per Indian child.[100] On the first day of school in September 1947, Mrs. Pogson accompanied the day school pupils over to Port Essington Elementary School, where she left them in the hands of their new teacher, Miss Olynyk.

PORT ESSINGTON ELEMENTARY SCHOOL

Port Essington Elementary School was located on the corner of Cascade and Lorne Streets. Although it origins are unclear, it was established as a public school during the 1890s and was large enough to accommodate forty children.[101] Between 1895 and 1947 it employed twenty-two teachers, the first of whom were a husband and wife team, T.A. and Belle Wilson, who later became physicians.[102] Even more so than the day school, the public school had trouble attracting and securing skilled teachers. In his memoir of life at Port Essington, Ernest A. Harris says that some teachers were more memorable than others. He recalls that Miss Gower, employed during 1916, gave out chocolate bars for class prizes. Her successor, Miss Mayovski, introduced the students to school gardening, and Mr. Dominie, who taught during 1918, overused the strap.[103] Miss Johnson, who immigrated from England in 1920, possessed a third-class certificate, whereas Robert Gordon from Pictou County, Nova Scotia, hired in 1921, possessed a university degree.

When District Inspector R.F. Davey visited Port Essington Elementary School in April 1948, he found thirty-eight pupils enrolled, all of whom were "of Indian or mixed origin." He noted excellent progress and an average attendance well over 90 percent, which necessitated the opening of a second classroom.[104] Local inspector E.E. Hyndman's assessment was equally glowing. "Considering the large enrolment the control is very good … Community-school relations are excellent … Improvements that have developed this year under difficult conditions have given a basis of hope for the future." Hyndman closed his report by commending Miss Olynyk, the teacher, "for the manner in which she has met the challenge of this difficult situation. The progress of her pupils and the high regard of the community are deserving rewards for her efforts."[105]

Former students who attended the school during the 1950s recall learning from Mrs. McDougall. Her school records from 1957 to 1962 indicate that the average school day included lessons in spelling, arithmetic, reading, geography, and history. For reading, most students studied passages from the Friends and Neighbours series and worked through the Jolly Numbers mathematics series. One student, Edna Bolton, was studying science in the book *Wonder World of Science*. As well, Mrs. McDougall exposed the children to square dancing and ring games as part of the physical education curriculum. Art lessons included "calaedescopic" [sic] designs, stencil designs, finger painting, pastel work, cutting and pasting flowers, seasonal cards, and baskets. Records indicate that the class belonged to the Red Cross and held parties for Halloween, Valentine's Day, St. Patrick's Day, and Father's Day. Christmas was celebrated with a concert and a decorated tree. At the end of the year, eight of the twelve children passed into the next grade, whereas four were advised to repeat their studies from the previous year.[106]

In 1949 – two years after integrating the day school pupils into the elementary school – federal authorities agreed to pay 60 percent of the costs of constructing a second schoolhouse in addition to pupil operating costs.[107] This arrangement solved two dilemmas for the district. First, Port Essington Elementary School needed renovation, having suffered from a chronic lack of funding during the Depression and the Second World War.[108] Second, Prince Rupert school trustees had long been angered that some of their public schools were educating Indian children, whom the board believed were the responsibility of the Canadian government.[109] In particular, some trustees believed that Indian Affairs ought to educate children of mixed marriages who had found their way into local schools – as was the case at Port Essington Elementary School. That same year, British Columbia amended its School Act to formalize cost sharing between the federal government and individual districts.[110]

This arrangement – whereby federal authorities simply paid the bills but offloaded the day-to-day dealings of the school onto others – was entirely fitting for the day school. It certainly maintained the federal government's longstanding policy of (under)funding Indian schools while entrusting others with their management, which had first been established in the nineteenth century through agreements with various religious denominations.[111] But the willingness of Indian Affairs officials to provide Port Essington with financial support could not stem the tide of the town's demise. Being built entirely of wood, the town had suffered from several fires over its short history. The fires of 1961 and 1965 destroyed most of the homes and buildings and finally left the town uninhabitable.[112]

The majority of families who left Port Essington during the early 1960s relocated to Terrace, where the burgeoning logging industry promised steady employment. Initially, most children enrolled in Kalum School.

When that proved not to be appropriate to the students' learning needs, many of them transferred to Riverside.[113]

TRADITIONAL INDIGENOUS education has been defined as daily processes occurring in natural settings that maintain a group's cultural, mental, spiritual, and physical well-being.[114] Such an approach to education differs from formal Western schooling in various ways. The first and most important difference is the early recognition of the place of specialized knowledge. Although all children were taught important values and skills, they were not all required to master the same knowledge or skills to the same level of ability. Adult members of the community determined which youngsters were most adept at using which kinds of knowledge and skills.[115] Adults would then mentor the children to assume specialized roles, such as those of the gwildmniits or a moon and star reader. This approach contrasts with Western conceptions of education, where all learners are expected to display a certain level of mastery over a common curriculum until roughly age sixteen, or the end of Grade 10.[116]

The second key difference between traditional Tsimshian education and formal Western schooling is the extent to which Tsimshian learning was integrated into the life of the community. Like other Indigenous communities worldwide, the skills and knowledge for which children were being educated were visibly relevant to the harmonious functioning of the social group. In the words of Inuit scholar Sheila Watt-Cloutier, "learning and living were the same thing, and knowledge, judgment, and skill could never be separated ... [Yet] in the institutional way of learning, these things are frequently pulled apart and never reassembled."[117] Indeed, in traditional Indigenous communities, it was unlikely that one would hear the age-old complaint voiced by many a schoolchild: "why do we have to learn this stuff?" For K. Tsianina Lomawaima and Teresa McCarty, Native communities would be better served if scholars and educators were to "explode the narrow schooling paradigm" in favour of a broader, more comprehensive view of education *as* and *for* life.[118]

Finally, Tsimshian education differed from formal Western education in that all of the children's "lessons" were delivered by adults whom they knew well and who played important roles in their lives: parents, aunts, uncles, grandparents. As a result, children were able to establish caring relationships with their primary "teachers" – their family members. As cultural psychologist Reuven Feuerstein has found, a child's initial learning experiences within the family set the pattern of "learning how to learn." This is due to the important mediating role of the experienced adult who mentors the child in a safe and caring environment. In short, traditional Tsimshian education was holistic in that the spiritual, emotional, intellectual, and physical capacities of the child were nurtured together by close family members. By contrast, Western approaches to formal schooling are premised on the separation of mind and body.[119] Furthermore, the establishment of close student-teacher relationships in formal school settings is hampered by high teacher turnover. Teacher transiency was particularly acute at Port Essington, prompted by low pay, lack of adequate housing, and poor working conditions.

4

Walking on Two Paths: Education and Schooling at Port Essington among the Pre-1950s Generation

THE STORIES AND EXPERIENCES of Mildred Roberts, Wally Miller, Sam Lockerby, Verna Inkster, Clifford Bolton, Harvey Wing, and Charlotte Guno reveal, first and foremost, how they manoeuvred through and benefited from two educational spheres: the traditional hunter-gatherer world, through which they took their places in Tsimshian society by acquiring knowledge, skills, and values as ancient as their ancestors; and Western-style Anglo-Canadian schooling, which emphasized numeracy and literacy. Their voices are grouped together because they were born prior to recommendations made by the Special Joint Committee of the Senate and the House of Commons and changes to the Indian Act in 1951 that permitted Indian children to be schooled with non-Indians. Sadly, like the residential school literature, their stories also illustrate encounters with discrimination as well as the enormous latitude that government officials exerted over their livelihood. Unlike residential school narratives, their stories clearly illustrate that the church wielded far less power over the lives of children and their families at Port Essington than did government officials.

Notably, this generation's stories are not restricted to their experiences with and perceptions of schooling. Although there has been a tendency among non-Indigenous scholars to equate education with schooling, the elders' stories reveal broad, multifaceted views of education that cut across all of their journeys through time and space.[1] These views are in keeping with a worldwide Indigenous perspective that "education is a lifelong continuum of experience gleaned from interaction with one another, with all of nature (seen and unseen), as well as with all of the cosmos."[2] Indeed, one of the main themes running through the stories of this generation's members is their view of their experiences as multirelational. Their links to the land, culture, language, families, and friends at Port Essington helped them to develop a strong sense of place and belonging, which shaped their notions of self and agency, two critical elements that enhanced their transitions from childhood to adulthood.

MILDRED ROBERTS

Mildred Roberts was born in the hospital at Port Essington in the early morning of August 20, 1931, to James Bolton and Selina Gosnell.[3] She is a member of the Killer Whale Clan. As a young person, she learned much about traditional Tsimshian education from her parents and grandparents.

> They educated their children by showing them how to do things. Showing them how to work. [They] didn't learn one and one, didn't learn A-B-C's ... But they learned by watching what their parents did – or their grandparents, their aunts and uncles. Their whole family would take part in what they do – how they teach them, how they train them. But they didn't call it training, just teaching them ... *Suwilaaẏmsk* is "to teach"; *suwilaawks* is "to learn."

Tasks were allocated by gender.[4] For example, Mildred's mother was

> educated to do the food. Like processing the fish ... how to preserve them. Drying them. Salting them. I don't know when salted food came in. I guess, after European days. But what my grandmother said about how people used to preserve years ago was: They'd get oil from seals and bears and they'd dry things – almost dry. Then they'd soak them in the oil. They'd leave them in there ... in containers, the bent[wood] boxes then. That's what they used years ago before tin cans came in and buckets. Today we just put them in jars. Put salt in. That's the most important thing. You have to add salt and then seal them. If it is fish, you don't put water in it. If it is meat, you don't put water in it. You just fill the jars and remember to salt it. [To seal it] you have to put the lid on and put them in the boiler and boil them for three and a half hours, four hours. It all depends on what it was. Everything is preserved that way. Seafood, like clams, cockles, abalone, I think the younger

people past me do not know what abalone is. Anything that we can jar, we do it. Berries, jams, we have to seal them.

Mildred noted that among her ancestors, the men were tasked with building the bentwood boxes, and only recently have women begun building and carving with wood. In contrast,

> women made baskets. They used baskets too for storing things. But there's a way to keep them water- and airtight so that they don't leak. They used pitch [from trees] on the outside … My grandmother said that cedar didn't rot as fast as other things … They could make ropes out of that [too]. And that's what they used to tie things for anchoring.

Because of its durability, men also preferred cedar for making dugout canoes. Although the Tsimshian buried their dead, they did not use coffins.[5] "Instead of coffins, they made mats of cedar bark and just rolled them in there" before burial.

In addition to the skills she learned, Mildred credited her family with teaching her important values that she considered in some ways to be similar to those of non-Tsimshian people. As historian Susan Neylan has argued, the boundaries between Christian and Tsimshian spiritual systems were not "impermeable" but "elastic." Missionary incursions into the region did not result in a rapid termination of Tsimshian spiritual practices, but rather the two systems complemented each other.[6] According to Mildred,

> There must have been a God because my grandmother always used to tell us a story in our language about how the enemies came and chased these people, and the big tide came up and they drowned. And when I read the Bible and it said about the Red Sea, that's where she got it from. But she didn't mention that she got it from the Bible. So where did she get that story from? There's other stories that she'd tell us, [and] then when you read the Bible, you see it. But then I heard some First Nations people talking on TV one time … Their grandfather told them about what's going to happen and what happened … and they didn't have Bibles then. So where did they get this from? It's the same thing as what's in the Bible. But there were no Bibles. They got their information the same way that Abraham or somebody else got it.

Among the many stories passed down orally across the generations was that of the great flood.[7]

Fish drying in the sun. *Courtesy of Wrathall Collection, Image JRW1867, Prince Rupert City and Regional Archives.*

Everything was almost wiped out. And they started a new world. Just like my father-in-law told me: there was only one language around this area. All the people lived by Damelahamid. That's around by Hazelton area, Gitxsan area. There's a story that Ken Harris, and his mother wrote about that.[8] All the people lived there before the flood, I think, and then they scattered. Some came down this way, some went out the Nass, some went out to the coast. And there was only one language then. [Now] that's a dialect they have in the Gitxsan area. And things started changing after.

One of the most important values Mildred felt that she learned from her elders was respect. Once, during a funeral, Mildred's elders warned the children that Death would take their breath away if they did not show respect for the deceased by crying like the adults. So Mildred and her peers began to howl loudly, showing that they too were respectful. She advised the young people of her community

to respect themselves, respect their community, respect life, respect people that tell some stories. Respect the stories and believe that maybe it did happen. There's a lot of things we used to be told but scary things … And we had to think twice before we did things, like making fun of animals. We have to respect the animals ... because of something that might happen. [Mildred's elders] always told about the time this bear took this woman. He took her to his den and married her, and they actually had two bear cubs until the woman was rescued. That's supposed to have happened back here in Kitsumkalum. That's the Xbishuunt story. [The bear took her because] she stepped on bear poo and she made fun of the bear. She was mad, [so] she called the bear some names – making fun of it. So the string, the rope on her pack, kept breaking, and she told the others walking with her to go on and sent her brother to come help her. And then they went up the hill, and it was the bear that took the shape of her brother. That's what they call *naxnox* – a supernatural thing [normally an animal or a person] that you can disguise yourself as.[9] Then the bear took her in this cave and he married her, and she had two babies. And bears hibernate, but she was up and she heard the dog bark. She had a dog named Maask. And then she heard somebody, and she made a snowball and rolled it down the hill. And I think it was her brother that found her [handprints on it] and [saved] her and the bear cubs.

Whereas listening to elders tell such stories was commonplace when Mildred was growing up in Port Essington, it is less common today due in part to the influence of television, movies, and published books.

Remembering her life at Port Essington had always left Mildred with a good feeling, particularly calmness. When she dreamt of her husband and children in Port Essington, "it's always a nice day." Among her fondest memories were those of camping with her immediate family and her father's parents. Mildred's father considered the family's survival to be their main priority.

> He always moved us from camp to camp. From the end of August, we'd move up Ocstall [River], drying coho for the fall fishing season. And they'd get mountain goat. Cranberries, wild crab apples ... were used in jams and dried in the sun to be eaten in the winter. I don't think [my father] even thought of education because we were out of school.[10] We hardly ever went to school because he tried leaving us behind with relatives ... It didn't work out. We weren't happy.

Children were generally five years old before they could assist with family chores.

> When I was five years old, they already started training us to do those different things that we could do. They were training my sister Irene then to

Tsimshian women, 1930s. *From left to right:* Miriam Temple (née Nelson), Jemima Gosnell, and Selina Gosnell (Mildred's mom) as young women. *Courtesy of Richard Roberts.*

filet. And they'd do the little tail part first and whatever we could do. I can remember pulling the heart out of the fish and putting them in a pot to boil them, and we'd eat them. They're pretty big. They call it *k'oopn*.

It is important to note that even while at camp Mildred experienced activities that helped to develop her English skills.

We didn't [often] go to school, but we did learn things. We always sang. Any new song that comes out, we listened to on the radio. [In addition], we'll make our own [playing] cards. They used to have those little cards to separate eggs [in storage boxes]. We'll pull them out and put your own numbers on them. And my aunts Cecelia and Josie, when they were living with us, they'd bring Sunday school papers.[11] [The church] used to hand out Sunday school papers every week so we could read them ... and the Bible. If it was nice enough outside, we'll have our "church" outside.

In addition to procuring and preserving their own food, Mildred's parents also supported their family through employment in the local economy. In the early 1930s her mother worked at the Anglo-British

Columbia Packing Company, one of three fish canneries in the Port Essington area at the time. Mildred remembers the cannery operating until 1936, when her "brother Billy was a baby ... That was the last time I remember because my mom had to get a babysitter. She had to keep running home to nurse the baby." In the late 1800s and into the early decades of the twentieth century, northwest coast canneries relied heavily on Native women's labour.[12] Like many of her female peers at the time, Mildred worked at the Cassiar and North Pacific Canneries between the ages of twelve and twenty.[13]

Although much of their time was occupied doing chores to sustain the family, the children of Port Essington enjoyed childhood pastimes too. Mildred and approximately fifteen other children constituted the Port Essington Happy Gang, whose members performed regularly at the Port Essington Band Hall on the northwest side of the reserve.[14] Mildred explained that the

> group was started by Bill [Willy] Spalding with Christmas carolling ... We went carolling on Christmas Eve. You go to the church and [Willy would] play the organ. And then Christmastime they loaded the organ on the big sleigh and the gas lantern, and we went door to door. The last house we went to was my grandmother's house, and they had their refreshments. My mom and dad were down there with them. They had coffee and sandwiches and cakes. When anything [went] on in the hall, they'd invite the whole community of Port Essington. They'd send out invitations. There was never anything off the reserve. Everything took [place] there on [the] reserve.[15]

One of the most popular events held on the reserve was the day school's Christmas pageant, which people looked forward to every year. Mrs. Pogson, the day school teacher from 1930 to 1937 and from 1942 to 1947, was particularly skilful at coordinating plays and concerts.[16]

> The things she used to do were really neat. She always had someone play the piano. They would do drills. The one thing that really stuck out in my mind was that one time when all these teams, they had tinsel – the silver – and they did a drill and then they handed [off] one end of the tinsel and the other, and then some got down on their knees, and it ended up in a star ... it was a great big star. All the girls in white dresses. The boys in black pants, white shirts, and ties. Their headpieces were gold tinsel. [Then] they sang ... "Oh Star of Wonder."

Walking on Two Paths   63

Aside from the concerts, much of the children's school time was spent learning routine subjects: math, spelling, writing, English, and history – which Mildred enjoyed most. Art work consisted of drawing, tracing, or simple crafts such as making straw baskets out of grass. As was the case in rural schools across the country, the older children would help the teacher to care for the younger ones, but in most cases individuals worked at their own pace.

In the morning, fifteen minutes were allocated to recess. On sunny days, the children spent their recesses playing games, such as kick the can and hide and seek. "Old Tom" was a kind of "one-base baseball" where a child would hit the ball and then run to the base and home again while trying to avoid being hit by the ball. If your playmates hit you with the ball, you were "out." Most people would go home for lunch, do a few chores, such as dishwashing, and then return to school by one o'clock.

Mildred recalled most teachers with some degree of fondness, although school itself initially posed a challenge, as she spoke no English.

The very first teacher that I had was Mr. Severson ...[17] He was a good teacher. [But] I used to cry because I didn't understand what he was saying. He used to take me home to play with his children ... a boy and a girl. I remember the boy's name was Brian, but I don't remember the girl's name. We would have tea and things. They spoke their language. I spoke mine. They took me home so I could learn.

Not everyone, however, was as kind as Mr. Severson. Mr. Chilton[18] apparently used to tease Mildred in an attempt to make her smile but instead made her cry.

Ms. Lau, who taught at the school during 1941,[19] insisted that only English be spoken during class time. But Mildred had difficulty shedding Sm'algyax, her first language.

Even if I used English, I will say, "Look at that big *mak'ooxs* [salmon berries] over there." I'd mix them up. Then, somebody writes my name on the blackboard. Five minutes [detention] for using my Sm'algyax word. I used to write, "I must not speak Indian." Start with 25 times. Then 50. Then 75, 100, right up to 500 times. And then there're times that I had to stand in the corner ... I was the only one that was stubbornly using my language ... But I still mixed it because I did not know the English word for "salmon berries." I knew it by the Tsimshian word, but even now there's some birds

that I know the Indian name, but I don't know what the English name is.
I don't know if I was angry or getting frustrated because I had to do it so
many times. You think I'd learn, but maybe I didn't mind. That's why I kept
doing it. I just had to learn not to use Sm'algyax. But how do you learn?

Indeed, how does a child "unlearn" the language of her home?

Mildred recalled that Mrs. Pogson was a "good teacher" but that she
seemed too old, as she had also taught Mildred's father. In addition,
Pogson allegedly favoured students who attended school more regularly.

> I don't think she really liked us because we dropped in and out of school.
> We could never really take part in [the Christmas concert] because we would
> come in late, but she let us stand there [to sing] the songs. We [all] got
> along, but then this one time my brother [Billy] was sitting behind this kid
> that was always turning around and doing things to him. And then he
> would never fight back, but this one time he did his written assignment – he
> had it all finished – and this kid turned around and tipped the bottle of
> ink. And this time [my brother] punched him. [Mrs. Pogson] didn't stop
> to find out what was wrong. She just ran and started hitting my brother
> with that hickory stick. And my younger brother [Clifford] jumped out of
> his seat and ran crying. And I told him [in Sm'algyax] to sit down, or she
> was going to hit him too. And then she came running to me and she started
> hitting me. I think she just sort of lost it ... And I held on to the stick and
> it broke, and she ran and she took the strap and she was just hitting me all
> over my arm. And I grabbed the strap and held on to it, and she told me
> to leave. I didn't want to leave because of my brothers. I didn't want to leave
> them there. Because she sort of seemed like she was singling them out. But
> I left and I didn't really go into detail why I was sent home.

Nevertheless, Mildred's parents learned of the incident from others in the
town. Although her father did not raise the matter with Mildred directly,
he and others expressed their dissatisfaction with the school to the Indian
Agent. Due to incidents like this and the alleged abuse perpetrated by
former teacher Roy Vannatter in 1942, parents began agitating to close the
school.[20] Interestingly, different perspectives about childrearing had long
been a point of disagreement between Indigenous and non-Indigenous
peoples. As historian James R. Miller points out, non-Aboriginal settlers
felt that Indians indulged their offspring. By contrast, Aboriginal peoples
in central Canada "were aghast at the firm discipline Europeans exercised

on their children, to the point that they called French mothers 'porcupines' because of their apparent lack of tenderness."[21]

Life at Port Essington presented its share of other hardships as well. By December the Skeena River would often be icy.

> A bunch of people drowned being caught in the ice one year, three families ... altogether seven people on February 4, 1947. The Bennett, the Spalding, and the Wesley families. The Spaldings ... married to the Wesleys and the Wesleys' father. And the Spaldings' sister married a Bennett. Peter Spalding's two little boys, Kenny and Andrew. His wife, his father-in-law, his sister, and brother-in-law. Jacky, who was left behind, survived. He was sent to the TB hospital two years later and drowned down there.

And then there was the trauma of the Japanese internment in April 1942.[22]

> They loaded them up on the barge and took them to Haysport and loaded them up on the freight box cars. That was sad. Really bad. There was a lot of people ... like my mother. She had a best friend, a good friend, that was a Japanese lady. And the Kameda's store – they were quite good friends with them. When my sister was really sick – she almost died – Mr. Kameda used to come down every day. He would bring grapefruit, or lemons, or any fruits. He'd kneel beside her bed and pray. When he finished, he was gone.

When Port Essington Indian Day School closed permanently in 1947, Mildred decided not to transfer to the "white" school because she felt she was too old to mix with the younger children. Mildred noted that there were very few "white" children in the supposedly "white" school.

> By then, it was mostly First Nations that were under the White Act[23] that got passed. So their children had to go to the public school, and there was a few from Finntown and there were no Japanese left. There were the Wings ... well we took them as Natives. Their mother was Native. They were all family ... family and friends. So they're the very same people they deal with outside of school, so it wasn't any big change ... not like from Port Essington [when] they went from a six[-pupil] classroom to a six-hundred-[student school] in Terrace. That was quite a big change.

After the 1961 fire, the Canadian government decided not to rebuild the town's infrastructure because of declining employment prospects in the region. Most of Port Essington's inhabitants moved to Kitsumkalum just outside of Terrace and entered the local economy through the logging industry.[24] After a second fire in 1965, the town was abandoned.[25]

Mildred found the move to Kitsumkalum difficult. In the vicinity of Port Essington, travel was mainly by boat, and most townspeople owned one for fishing purposes. But in the Terrace area, one needed a vehicle simply to go anywhere off the reserve. In Port Essington, families could also be more or less self-sufficient by hunting for deer, mountain goat, or bear, fishing for seal or seafood, and gathering fruits or berries. In the Terrace area, costly licences were needed.

The move to Kitsumkalum was difficult for other reasons as well.

> We moved August 22, 1963. My children heard about Terrace ... We made one trip up to Kitsumkalum maybe about two weeks before we moved. Then we moved. Like my son Don said, it's just like stepping out in Mars or something. The change ... I would sooner have moved down to Prince Rupert way than up here. I was more familiar with down that area [and] the climate. Up here it was so hot, really hot. And really cold in the winter-time. In Port Essington the snow ... will go fast. In Essington my children left for school at eight thirty, quarter to nine. They never walked down alone. [My sister-in-law] Vicky will come all the way over to walk down with them. And she'll walk them home. When Don was going to school, she will take him down, and then he didn't come home for lunch. He went to my uncle's. And after school, Vicky will walk them home. So there was always family around. And they were in class with cousins ... and they'll be home by three o'clock, a little after three, and Saturdays they were home. I was able to teach them things. The three older ones had learned how to make bread. [At Kitsumkalum], they left home before eight in the morning [to get the school bus into Terrace], and we don't see them until about after four. And they had a lot of problems on the bus with the other children. A lot of problems ... It used to hurt me to send them. I wish I could drive them, but we had no vehicle.

Another problem was that Mildred's children had, until then, been schooled all together in a one-room, multiaged classroom. But in Terrace siblings were assigned to classrooms in different buildings. When her youngest son was sent out in the rain in his socks as punishment for speaking out of turn to a girl in the seat behind him, Kitsumkalum's chief intervened, and as a result, Mildred's children were moved to another school that better addressed their needs.

Reflecting on her education, both formal and traditional, Mildred felt that her most important learning was the training she had at home.

> I learned how to be a mother ... [and] a wife. When you are in a house, you have to work. If you are going to live here, you do your share of the work. Everybody has their jobs. Everybody has to help the mother with the younger ones. The boys help the father with what he has to do. Like my grandmother said, my father – when he started working – he would help his dad with everything ... Help raise the younger children. He would fish with him and things he didn't get paid for. He learned to take care of his family, and the only way that he can take care of his family is to move us to a camp where we can get food. And he always did a little logging. He always had about two different guys employed. His brother [Eddie] was always there. And his uncle Arthur, or else Dan Brown, one of the bachelors in Essington. He will always have his brother Eddie with him and his cousin ... My father really worked hard, and so did my mother. He'll employ others with his logging and with his halibut fishing. He had the boat, and he always took his brother and his uncle, or his cousin, or brother-in-law.

Mildred felt that the basic skills she learned at Port Essington Indian Day School were somewhat useful to her. However, she found that her most useful formal training occurred in 1991, at the age of sixty, when she attended the Adult Education program at Kitsumkalum to complete the requirements for Grade 12.

> I tell my grandchildren, "You should stay in school and work hard in school. It's no fun going to school when you are old. Nobody wants to play with you!" [laughs] I didn't really push education with my children because I didn't really get educated and I got by in life, but it's different now. You need to have papers to get a job. You have to go to university. You have to get a certificate.

Since 1989 Mildred has worked at Kitsumkalum as a drug and alcohol counsellor and prevention worker. She was first hired for her maturity, years of service to the community, and ability to abstain from consuming alcohol. "I tried to get a youth group going. I was trying to get a ladies' club going ... And I'd go visiting at the old folks' home. I would go visiting down at the hospital. I had to do things ... So that helped me get my job." Once she secured the job, she underwent two years of focused training.

Mildred Roberts, Kitsumkalum,
February 18, 2012. *Photo by
Helen Raptis.*

Because of teachers' efforts to eradicate the use of Sm'algyax, Mildred
is one of only a few residents at Kitsumkalum who speak it. Sadly, due
partly to her own painful experiences, Mildred never taught the language
to her own children. She is now part of community-wide efforts to revitalize the Tsimshian language and culture. During the 1990s she co-taught
Sm'algyax at Northwest Community College with American linguist
Emmon Bach as part of a credit program sponsored by the University of
Northern British Columbia. "I used to go everywhere with my grandmother, and she'd be telling me stories [in Sm'algyax]. Nobody seems to
have time now." Mildred acknowledged that life at Port Essington was
tough at times; nevertheless, she felt that the richness it offered in terms
of learning opportunities more than made up for the hardship.

WALLY MILLER

Wally Miller's mother and father parted ways not long before he and his
twin sister were born on September 18, 1931. Consequently, Wally took on
dangerous adult responsibilities at a very young age.[26] At age four, he
began gillnet fishing with his uncle Louis Starr. Once, his uncle was

> doing about four, five miles an hour at the mouth of the Skeena River. I
> was hand loading the net. I was standing, piling it in ... four years old and
> I was hauling it in. We'd go down and a wave would wash right over the
> boat ... We were soaking wet but we had to keep going to get the net in.

By the time Wally was ten and a half, he was cooking for six men on a seining vessel captained by his uncle.[27]

Wally's early commitment to fishing didn't afford him much time to attend school. Nevertheless, he has memories of attending the on-reserve day school for Grade 1 and later the off-reserve public school.[28] Like so many of his contemporaries, his experiences were not entirely positive. Since Wally's father was non-Native, his mother had lost her Indian status by marrying him. This posed problems for Wally with respect to formal schooling.

> We went to the day school for a short time until we were told [by the Indian Agent] we had to move off the reserve and the school because it was ... on the Indian part, eh, and we had to go to the public school ... We weren't allowed to live on the reserve then because we were white! ... Until Bill C-31 came in ... and they made Indians out of us!

Wally's comments refer to the situation for Indian women prior to the passage of Bill C-31 in 1985. The Indian Act was characterized by a patri- archal bias stipulating that a woman who married a non-Native immedi- ately lost her Indian status, as did her children. Yet, if a non-Native woman married a Native man, the non-Native woman was granted Indian status. In 1985 Bill C-31 finally ended this discrimination.[29] Although Wally's mother and sister moved to a home off the reserve, he refused to go. Wally chose to live with his uncle's family on the reserve, thus maintaining Tsim- shian tradition, where young men are prepared for adulthood as hunters and providers by their maternal uncles.[30]

Wally remembered enjoying some aspects of the public elementary school, where his first teacher was Mrs. Donaldson.[31] The school's chil- dren hailed from diverse ethnicities, including Chinese, Japanese, Finnish, and nonstatus Natives who were offspring of mixed marriages. According to Wally, the children "all got along ... but got into a scrap every now and then." He recalled doing the "usual" schoolwork, such as arithmetic, writing, and reading, but did not remember doing any artwork. "I was in a few plays, but I can't remember them. I remember I was in them, but what kind of plays they were I don't know."

Wally spoke of his childhood pastimes with fondness. In addition to participating in school performances, he belonged to the Happy Gang group, which performed plays and sang for the entire community at the Port Essington Band Hall.[32] Other memories from his youth remained vivid.

We used to go up to the lake in my hometown, behind my hometown. The lake is over a mile long or half a mile wide, and the whole lake used to freeze. We used to skate against the wind ... and then get a branch from the other side and just hold it up with the wind pushing down ... There was a log there, and all of us would get on one end and start swinging the log, and whoever can hang on hangs on. And you go in a circle, you go real fast, and you have a hard time to hang on. You fall off as it's going round ... We had a lot of parties at the lake [with] the fire going all the time. We used to leave at two o'clock in the morning [with] the full moon ... It used to be cold in those years. Not now, not so cold anymore.[33]

At school Wally experienced a fair bit of punishment for his allegedly poor behaviour.

Oh yeah, I got the strap lots of times. I got the strap the first day I went to school there in public school. I built these little barns [out of paper] in Grade 1, and I was rolling them back and forth and juggling, and I got a strap for doing it in school. You see, I wasn't supposed to. So I got strapped but ... it never did hurt me. They couldn't hurt me at all with the strap ... 'cause these were working hands.[34] I was taking wood all the time – chopping wood and everything. So it never hurt me at all. "Let me know if you're tired," I said. [Mrs. Donaldson] sent me down to [Mr. Jones] to get a strap, and he would put his whole heart into it, strapping me ... And he couldn't hurt me either. So he hit me across the face with the strap, and I went home and my uncle [Chief Louis Starr] saw that, and he went up and [dealt with him]. My uncle said, "You ever touch him again, I'll be here to see you." I used to get in a lot trouble, without even half trying.

This anecdote illustrates well the different views on childrearing espoused by non-Indigenous and Indigenous peoples. Despite his misbehaviour, Wally completed Grade 7 at Port Essington Elementary School, and then for Grade 8 he enrolled in correspondence learning provided by the British Columbia Department of Education.[35]

English was the language of the school, but Wally spoke only Sm'algyax with his family. Although his elders relayed stories to him during his childhood, Wally regretted that he "didn't pay much attention. I'm kind of sorry that I didn't listen because it's one of the things I could have learned at that time if I'd have listened." As an adult, Wally became more inclined to talk with the elders about Tsimshian traditions, but his long spans out at sea left little time for leisure: "We were always fishing."

The Happy Gang, February 1946. Wally is the third boy seated on the left. Mildred is the second girl standing on the left. *Courtesy of Prince Rupert City and Regional Archives.*

Wally was proud of his fishing, which had sustained him and his family until his retirement in 1996. During the mid-1960s, he had travelled to Canada's east coast, where he fished until the 1970s, after which he was able to buy his own vessel and return to the Pacific Northwest. During this time he fished south along British Columbia's coast as well as north to the Bering Sea. Like so many Tsimshian men of his generation, sustaining his family was his first priority. "I was working and fishing, and then I turned around and put my brothers and sisters through school [in Prince Rupert]. I bought a house for my mother." When the regional Indian Agent came to his home to discuss welfare for the family, Wally was not afraid to tell him exactly how he felt about government "assistance": "I told the Indian agent, 'Don't step foot in my house again.' I said, 'We don't need your help at feeding twelve kids at $26 a month.' I didn't care for the Indian Agent. I didn't like him."

Wally felt that the learning that was most influential in his life was what his uncle had taught him about how to survive at sea.

> I travelled on water all the time, and I used to read the sun [with a] sextant. That's what I had to go by when I was learning boats. Going out back then, we headed up Forrester Island to the Bering Sea. Nine days. The guys figured we missed Alaska altogether. I says, "No." I says, "You won't see land until noon tomorrow." It's a long run. Fourteen days to get to the Bering Sea. It was tough weather.

Wally Miller at home,
Kitsumkalum, August 2010.
Photo by Helen Raptis.

Wally travelled the Bering Sea seven times. One particularly memorable trip found him and his crew of eight caught in a storm with a wind blowing over a hundred miles an hour. In such a situation, "you just have to ride it out. You can't do anything. You just drive into the waves and pray that the cruel one don't come – that's one that's three times the size of an ordinary wave – and crush the boat." Wally and his crew survived it, but a nearby boat went down. "All the crew was gone, and we couldn't do anything to help. We were barely staying afloat ourselves." Another life-threatening storm hit while Wally and his crew were off the coast of Alaska.

> I was up for eighty-five hours with no sleep, and I went to bed and I could hear the guys talking ... and they said, "Here comes another one, here comes another one, another cruel wave with wind over a hundred miles an hour." And the thing is they didn't even call me when it started. We could have got out of it. But we were caught in it, so I got up and I looked and I said, "Oh my goodness, I can't believe it." If I didn't hear them talking ... And then I only had two hours sleep out of that eighty-five hours and then another twenty-six hours before I got to bed again ... We anchored up. Wave come over and hit the side of the cabin and cleaned the whole deck off. [Thankfully] we had all our gear in the water. If we didn't have all the gear in the water, we would have had to pay for it all. [The wave] would have taken it all off. It took everything else off. But we got all the gear back, so we didn't have to pay for it. The insurance paid for the damage to the boat.

Despite the danger, Wally wouldn't trade life at sea for anything: "It's good clean air. Beautiful. I've seen scenery that you can't imagine. People call everything that they look at ... *beautiful*. You don't know what beauty is until you get out in the water and see it. Then you see what beauty is."

Despite the natural beauty he experienced while at sea, he still believed that the region around Port Essington ranked as among the most breathtaking. Throughout his fishing travels, he told other fishers' stories about Port Essington. "I used to look forward to going home. To me, it was still the nicest place in the world. Doing a lot of travelling all over, I still missed Port Essington." Wally is the proud father of two children, thirteen grandchildren, and nine great-grandchildren. He has retired to Kitsumkalum, where he appreciates the peacefulness and the natural beauty of the surrounding environment.

SAM LOCKERBY

Sam Lockerby was born on November 6, 1935, at his maternal grandmother's home in Terrace and belongs to the House of Old Raven.[36] In addition to raising Sam and his biological siblings, his parents, Cecelia (née Nelson) and Sam Lockerby Senior, also raised other children from the community. Sam's parents "adopted" his niece Laura and his second cousin Reynold – in the "Indian way" – and raised them as their own. Whereas adopting someone outside of a *pteex* (clan) or *waap* (house group) was traditionally undertaken through ceremony with elaborate protocols, adoption of extended family members was much less formal, as was the case with Sam's parents' "adoptions."[37]

Soon after his birth, Sam and his family moved to Port Essington, where his parents had been raised. He expressed fond childhood memories of Port Essington, including playing games such as "Old Tom" as well as hiking and rowing while admiring the beautiful landscape surrounding the town.[38] He also recalled numerous community-wide events where adults would participate in competitions such as rowing and foot racing. "New Year's Eve [people] would all paint up their face, and they had a good [brass] band there too. Very good band."[39] In his youth, Sam also belonged to the Happy Gang, which performed plays at the Port Essington Community Hall. As a young adult, he taught himself to play an accordion that a cousin from Port Simpson had given him. Together, Norman Brooks, Gus Collins, and Irene Collins provided the music for dances held at the Community Hall.

There was a lot of fishermen those days and used to be quite a lot of [fishing] branching off from the river down further and through the slough. Bunch of canneries there: Cassiar … Sunnyside, Inverness, Port Edward. [People] used to all come up [to Port Essington] during the weekend, and people would put on a dance [there] in the hall.

Survival was a priority for Sam's family, which had lost its hereditary trap lines, formerly situated along present-day Kalum Road, when George Little founded the town of Terrace in 1905.[40] Consequently, formal schooling was not considered vital. He began attending Port Essington Indian Day School in 1942 and was taught by Mrs. Elizabeth Pogson, whom the children allegedly nicknamed "onion head" due to the tight bun into which she pinched her hair. When Sam was eleven years old, the day school closed, and he and his classmates transferred to the public school under the tutelage of Miss Olynyk.

Sam found school a struggle. He attributed his inability to progress beyond Grade 5 to the fact that he rarely attended, as he was most often engaged in hunting and fishing to ensure his family's subsistence. "Everything I tried to do was tough for me. Because my parents weren't … educated either. I was just brought up [mostly camping] with them until I was a teenager." On the rare occasions when Sam attended school, he seldom paid attention. For his inattention, Miss Olynyk often strapped him and made him sit under the table. Despite his largely negative experiences, Sam remembered enjoying some aspects of formal schooling, particularly art.

Sam believed that the knowledge and skills that served him best throughout his life were those his father had taught him about survival.

> I didn't go to school often because my parents, they camped a lot. They just come home for a little while, and I'd go to school … We harvested seaweed and abalone and [did] halibut fishing. [We'd go] out … away through Granville Channel, where we lived [in little log houses] to trap. Dad fished in high or low tide – kept fishing.

Seafood, including crab, cockles, clams, abalone, and fish, was plentiful, as was game such as mountain goat, deer, and bear. A garden of potatoes, onions, and carrots – maintained by Sam's mother – supplemented the family diet. Although his mother preserved much of their food to sustain them over the winter, Sam's father also shared their harvest with needy

Port Essington families. As a result, Sam learned the important Tsimshian value of helping those who are less fortunate.

Sam began formal employment when Jimmy Donaldson hired him at Brown's Mill, located up the Ocstall River.[41] There, he first worked transporting crews of "slashers," men who cleared away trees in preparation for the installation of power poles and lines carrying electricity to Prince Rupert and beyond. Later, he worked with a crew that repaired the poles. It was during this period that he spent his leisure time hiking and overnight camping up in the mountains surrounding Port Essington. He and his nephew made their way up into the woods to Big Lake by following the wooden flume that once supplied the town with fresh water.[42] At other times, Sam and his nephew would

> go way up ... further up Ocstall River ... out hunting. One time we got nothing. Didn't see anything up the mountain. Come back down, we were going home in the gas boat. But standing on the [boat's] deck, I look through the trees. Boy! I spotted them. Goats! ... Five. One big, big one, but he's smart and took off before we can get closer. We dropped the anchor – in fifteen minutes, [we] go in, got four goats. Had them on the boat in fifteen minutes. How close they were down to the water. [We also] hunted deer ... geese ... mallards ... lots of bears and wolves around ... [and] seals there on the ... sandbar. When the tide falls, they just lay there.

By the time Sam was in his early teens, economic shifts had already begun to impact life at Port Essington. "Everything was shutting down," he noted. "Used to be canneries there. After a while, everything changed. They locked it down." During the 1960s, when fires all but destroyed Port Essington, Sam relocated to Prince Rupert and began commercial fishing for Nelson Brothers, located at Port Edward. The Nelson family, who had immigrated from Norway in 1909, ran several canneries around British Columbia but set up shop in Port Edward in 1943.[43] When operations closed there, Sam shifted briefly to logging but soon found work as a packer for the Cassiar Cannery at Prince Rupert.

> They hired me there to pick up fish from the fishermen. Yeah. Hired another deckhand helper who would steer. Before they used a fish cue ... a long stick with a hook ... A fish cue they call it, and that's how we used to deliver ... [Put them in] the side hatch, or the hatch where you throw your fish in. You used a fish cue. But then not too long [later], we had to pick the fish

Remains of water flume, Port Essington. *Courtesy of Frank Freiburg.*

up by hand. No more fish cue. They outlawed it. Because you poked [the fish] … damage the meat when you do that, three [or] four fish on there [at a time].

Sam spent most of his adult life in the fishing industry. Whereas Port Essington had lost its stature as an economic hub, fishing at nearby Prince Rupert was still profitable. "Yeah, in those days, boy you'd make your money fast. Every fisherman made their money." A high, stable salary had many benefits, including enabling Sam to provide his parents with modern amenities, such as an electric washing machine. The downside of having more than enough to live on was that he spent much of his salary treating himself and his friends to drinks at the local beer parlour.

Sam's penchant for sharing his earnings continues a longstanding pattern among Indigenous wage earners. As historian John Lutz notes, by the late 1800s Indigenous labourers had entered the paid workforce in high numbers and were using their earnings to improve their social status. Until its ban in 1884, the potlatch – where hosts gave away vast amounts of material goods as well as cash – had traditionally been the vehicle for enhancing one's prestige.[44]

Sam Lockerby,
Kitsumkalum, August 2010.
Photo by Helen Raptis.

Nevertheless, Sam acknowledged that the years of stable, high-paying, seasonal employment had all but evaporated: "Now you can hardly fish anymore. They won't even open the Skeena [River] anymore. You can't even fish. Maybe [for] one day. That's about all [for the] summer the way it works out now. And the workers, they can't even live through work ... They get stamps, eh ... but not enough hours for [employment insurance]." Acknowledging how difficult it is to work in the natural-resource sector today, Sam has advised young people to get good job training.

Verna Inkster

Verna Inkster was born in Port Essington on July 3, 1936, to Herbert Spalding and Elizabeth Bolton.[45] Her Indian name, Wii'nluttk, means "big nest," and she is a member of the Raven Clan. When she was growing up, her father, a fisherman and sawyer at Brown's Mill, advised his children to be self-reliant. Following Tsimshian tradition, Verna and her siblings would accompany their parents out to camp in their traditional territories, where they learned important life skills, such as procuring and preserving food. Like her ancestors, Verna's Tsimshian education consisted of observing and learning traditional skills and knowledge passed down over the millennia.[46]

We learned from our parents and grandparents ... For example, we'd go to Arthur's Island for seafood, Baker's Inlet for halibut and clams. We'd be out

at camp up the Ocstall River from about September to the end of November.
When we got back, we'd go to school again – until the Family Allowance
cheque policy forced us back to school. The government threatened to
withdraw Family Allowance [payments] if we didn't attend school ...[47] The
men would usually do the hunting from spring to fall and fishing in the
summer ... Usually, the women would prepare and preserve the foods. For
example, we'd dry seaweed in squares by placing it over rocks in the sun.
Then we'd chop it up. We'd line containers with newspaper and then put it
in to preserve it. In the old days, we used oil cans but now people use big
plastic pails like the ones that restaurants get filled with potato salad, etcetera.
I've taught some of these skills to my children, such as preserving seafood.

When not out at camp, Verna's family resided at Port Essington. Children kept themselves busy with self-generated leisure activities and with
tasks to assist their families and community members.

I miss my hometown. For a small town, there was always a lot to do. And
there was no TV. On Sundays we'd rush down to the Salvation Army church
so we could beat the minister [Ben Brown] to bang the drums to call people
to attend. What attracted me most to the church were the hymns. There
was also an Anglican church and a United church, but I don't remember a
United Church minister.[48] We had lots to do. In the winter, we'd hike up
the valley about two hours and go ice skating on a frozen lake. We'd pack
lunches and bring wieners to roast in a bonfire. We'd get back late in the
day. There were no problems with drugs and alcohol back then. We kept
busy. For example, one of the men at Port Essington was blind. He lived
alone, and so we'd go and cook and clean for him once a week. We'd provide
him with everything he needed for the week and make sure it was all within
reach. That's what we were taught: to look out for each other.

In addition to these activities, Verna recalled attending traditional
Tsimshian naming and adoption ceremonies until the early 1940s.
Festivities were held in the Salvation Army's Band of Workers Hall on the
northwest corner of the reserve but had dwindled by the late 1940s.

Verna attended the Methodist-run Port Essington Indian Day School
from 1942 until it closed in 1947. She spoke of her time at the school with
mixed emotions.

The school was long, one room. We had a wooden stove that warmed
it. We'd stand around it to keep warm in the winter. We did reading and

Verna Inkster at home,
Kitsumkalum, 2010.
Photo by Helen Raptis.

writing. We learned about *Jack and Jill*. I think everyone memorized it. We did a lot of drawing for art ... We mostly drew buildings and things around Port Essington. We did lots of singing and there were Christmas concerts, where we sang songs such as "Silent Night." At recess and after lunch, we'd play outside, mostly baseball. We'd also go around and pick berries and eat them with our lunch.

But I remember one time Mrs. Pogson [the teacher] hit one of the students. It was very frightening and I ran out of the school all the way home. I hid in the attic I was so scared. I don't know why it happened, but it was the only time. I was so scared it would happen again, but my parents talked to me and convinced me to go back.

When the day school shut in 1947, Verna and her schoolmates were transferred to the town's public school: Port Essington Elementary. She recalled learning a lot at the public school and from Miss Olynyk, the teacher: "She taught the Grade 5s to 8s in the grey school. I really liked her. She helped us a lot. She was a good teacher – strict enough but not mean. All the kids got along with her, so it was good. Miss Isaac had the Grade 1 to 4 students in the red school." English was the language used in the school, although some of the children spoke Sm'algyax at home. Verna could not recall any rules regulating language use, but she stated that the children "just spoke English at school. It was understood [that they would]." The school seemed well supplied with material resources: "We got the books given out to us at the start of the year, and then we had to return them. But my parents always had to buy supplies – pens, paper, scribblers – in Prince Rupert at the start of the year."

Both Verna and her parents were satisfied in 1947 when she attended what was commonly referred to as the "white" school. However, despite being referred to as "white," the school was not entirely "white."

> It was hard in the beginning because the other kids teased us. The kids who regularly attended the public school teased us when we arrived because we were Indian. But the strange thing is that they were mostly all Indian too. They were just kids whose parents were enfranchised or came from mixed marriages.[49] So they didn't attend the Indian school but the public school. We were even related to some of them! We played together and everything, but they still teased us. I talked to my mom about that. She said, "Don't get mad. You're all the same. They probably just think they're better." Miss Olynyk also talked to us all and told us we were all family – just some were status and some nonstatus. We were all the same, so we needed to get along. After that, no one teased us and everything went well.

That the Indian children of the allegedly "white" school would "other" the children of the day school – many of whom were family members – attests to the power that racial discourse exerted in early twentieth-century British Columbia.[50]

Verna completed Grade 8 at Port Essington Elementary School at the age of thirteen. She then attended Port Alberni Residential School for a year, during which she finished Grade 9. But her education was cut short due to her father's gendered attitude toward the value of formal schooling.

> I enjoyed [school]. But then we moved to Terrace, where Dad found work as a sawyer in the sawmill. I was upset with this because I wanted to go to school. Dad sent my brothers to school but not the girls ... and when we moved to Terrace, I found a job at a café in town. Later, I went back to school to the Adult Education program on the [Kitsumkalum] reserve to complete my Grade 12. I missed the score I needed in math by two points, so I couldn't get into college. I had wanted to be a nurse, like my mom ... My mom went to school in Port Essington, and she was trained to be a midwife/nurse by the doctor who ran the hospital over the summer months.[51] She delivered many babies. This would have been around the 1920s.

In 1957 Verna married Richard Inkster. Ever resourceful, Verna decided to pursue her second passion, cooking.

Richard and Verna Inkster with wedding party, 1957.
Courtesy of Verna Inkster.

I also liked cooking, so I was able to do that too. I spent twenty-three years working at a poultry farm. I also worked at Gims Restaurant [in Terrace] … For the past nine years now, I have been running a catering business – Tsimshian Catering – with my daughter. We cater for meetings for out-of-town groups as well as weddings [or] funerals for people in town.

Her catering company is a family-run business that hires students who need to finance their studies in higher education.

Reflecting on her educational experiences, both formal and traditional, she advised young people to value and actively seek out education: "Whatever you like, pursue it. If you want to, go to college or university. Mining

Four generations, Kitsumkalum, July 2011. *From left to right:* Verna Inkster's daughter Lori Marion, great-granddaughter Mikaiya Duncan, Verna, and granddaughter Millie Duncan. *Photo by Helen Raptis.*

is important these days; fishing and logging are out. But today it's easier to go to school than in our day. There's financial help available. Take the opportunity."

CLIFFORD BOLTON

Reflecting on a childhood without electricity, running water, telephones, or insulated buildings, Clifford Bolton concluded that living in Port Essington "made a tougher person out of you."[52] Clifford was born at the Prince Rupert Hospital on January 4, 1939, a time when steamships no longer ferried passengers through the waters around Essington. Instead, people usually crossed the turbulent mouth of the Skeena River in individuals' fishing boats to seek medical care for the sick, the injured, and women in labour: "On a good day it took well over two hours [to travel to Rupert]. In the wintertime there was ice. It would be an all-day adventure trying to get through. I know there were some people that died on the way to Prince Rupert ... There were children that were born on the way."

Nevertheless, the environment's physical hardship helped to foster one of the values that the Tsimshian people hold most dear, communal thinking.

You had to hang together to survive. I remember when there was a boatload of a family. They hit ice and sunk; they all drowned. [But] everybody went out there looking for them, even though it was dangerous. I always remember my dad going out because he always was the one who had a real good sea boat ... His boats were made for working.

And so, it seems, was Clifford's father, James, whose efforts provided not only for his family but for the well-being of others as well.

We had different camps down on the coast where you went to get seaweed and abalone. Different places where they camped to fish halibut and cod and salmon ... clams and cockles ... We had one main camp [at] Baker's Inlet and that's where my dad logged and ... had traplines ... I always remember my dad coming in with a boat full of seafood or something. Whether it was a big sea lion or seals or a boatload of oolichans, people just came down and [dad said,] "Take what you want." He never ever sold it or asked for money.

By sharing his bounty, James instilled in his children the importance of communalism.

As a child, Clifford participated in Tsimshian traditions associated with procuring and preserving food. Nevertheless, ceremonial aspects of the culture had long been suppressed, and he did not witness any dances, naming festivities, traditional carving, or potlatches, the latter having been officially outlawed since 1884.[53] According to Indigenous practice, grand-parents "hold the stories of their families and their people," which they bestow upon the community's children.[54] The oppression of traditional Tsimshian culture, says Clifford, was precipitated by missionary work, schools, and government legislation. He supported this view by noting that traditions were sustained until the early 1900s, when, as a young woman, his grandmother attended the Crosby Home for Girls in Port Simpson:[55] "The culture came up to my grandmother's time [and should have been] passed off from her to her eldest daughter and eldest son, but it stopped with her ... Of course, she wouldn't break the law. She was a God-fearing person right till the day that she died."

Despite efforts of several generations of missionaries and teachers in the Skeena region to suppress Tsimshian culture, certain traditional values and practices survived into Clifford's generation. The following anecdote illustrates how Clifford's grandmother subtly perpetuated the fundamental

Tsimshian values of a strong work ethic, a sense of spirituality, and respect for elders.

> I always remember when my grandma looked after us ... My mom and dad went to [Prince] Rupert, so she came to the house to look after us for the day and the night ... She was cooking breakfast, so we ate ... And then when I finished, she said, "I want you to fill everything up in this house with water. *Everything.* Kettles, pots ..." And the stove had a reservoir on the side and I filled that. Any tubs around, I had to fill them. Everything. I had to drag that sleigh most of the day, and she said, "You never know, the house might burn and we need the water." I thought, "Oh, the house isn't going to burn." I hauled all the water. I finished my last load and I took the boiler off and I sat on the front porch on the steps and I'm sitting there. There was a little bit of snow on the road. And I probably was thinking, "Why in the heck do I always have to haul the water?" And then I see black snowflakes coming down. And then all of a sudden it dawned on me that there's a fire somewhere. I ran out in the road and [saw] our house was on fire. I went to the church just down the road from us and sounded the alarm.[56] Everybody came down and in ten minutes all my water was gone.

Clifford believed that his grandmother had a vision, which was not an uncommon element of Tsimshian spirituality prior to the twentieth century. He felt that, increasingly, people had lost their spiritual nature, which he attributed to the assimilative legacy of religious missionaries and restrictive government policy dating back to the early twentieth century: "During that time everybody was trying so desperately ... to be like white people. And to be like an Indian and to speak Indian and to do Indian things was considered backwards. And nobody wanted to be backwards. After all, [a lot] was against the law ... to carve a mask, sing the songs, do the dances."[57]

Clifford had mixed emotions about his experiences with formal schooling. When he entered Grade 1 at Port Essington Indian Day School in 1945, he already knew how to read and do simple arithmetic. Therefore, he was perplexed when his teacher, Mrs. Pogson, did not promote him to Grade 2.[58] Clifford recalled that his teacher was strict and didn't hesitate to use both the pointer and the strap to discipline the students. Although Mrs. Pogson apparently understood Sm'algyax, she would not tolerate its use in the classroom. The reading program she used followed the adventures of Joe and Ruth, allegedly Indian children, and their dog, Billy. Mrs. Pogson began class each morning by lining up the children in front of the

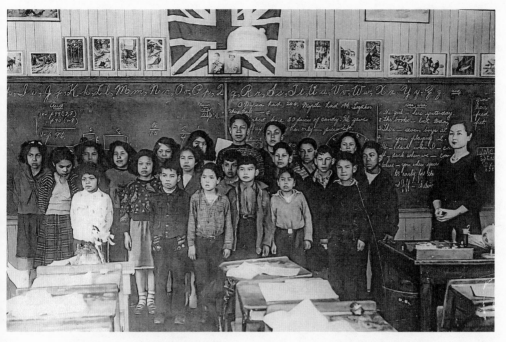

Port Essington Elementary School, 1947–48. Clifford is in the checkered shirt in the front row. On the right is Miss Olynyk, the teacher. Wally Miller is the second boy of three in the back row. *Courtesy of Cynthia Bohn.*

"Joe and Ruth" posters mounted on the walls around the classroom. She would point to a poster, pose a question, and one by one ask each student to answer.

Clifford recalled well the day that the children of Port Essington Indian Day School transferred to the public school.

> I don't remember [Mrs. Pogson's] exact words, but she was telling us that we were going to all go up at the grey [public] school. I remember we all marched up there and … then we all came in lined up. We were being introduced and the [new] teacher [Miss Olynyk] was asking questions. But [Aunt] Vicky was the [only] one that spoke. Vicky was our spokesperson.

Like so many others who made the shift to the allegedly "white" school, Clifford was surprised to learn that the "white" pupils consisted of his own cousins or offspring of Indian parents who had become enfranchised.

In 1954, when Clifford had completed Grade 8 at Port Essington Elementary School, he faced the decision of whether to attend public high school in Prince Rupert or residential school. Since his parents had separated by that time, he opted for the Anglican-run St. George's Residential School in Lytton, where his brother Alec and sisters Laura and Shirley also studied. Clifford described his residential school experience in generally positive terms, although he had encountered difficulty adapting to Lytton's arid climate after growing up on the temperate northwest coast. In addition, he found it challenging to adjust to the loneliness. To make matters worse, shortly after arriving, he blew off his thumb, index, and middle fingers with a dynamite cap.

> I spent a month in St. Paul's Hospital all by myself. I spent Christmas in hospital, my birthday, and New Year's. It all happened in the hospital. But we had to grow up quick there. We had to learn how to survive [among roughly] 200 boys and 200 girls ... There had to be some rules. And you either chose to obey them or not obey them. And if you choose not to obey them, then you can live in hell. And I'd seen boys who chose not to obey them, and they lived in hell.

Clifford credited his residential school training with teaching him things he could not have learned at Port Essington, such as how to farm and work with dairy cattle. Every day, year round, St. George's pupils were out on the farm, where they milked cows, helped to harvest produce, and cleaned and maintained equipment and fences. Although the pupils resided at the school, Clifford and his peers rode a bus each day into town to attend Lytton High School with non-Native students. Clifford found his studies to be a welcome break from the physical chores for which the students were responsible at the residential school. "It was nice to get out, and then at lunchtime we could walk downtown and go to the café and have a pop or whatever." He remembered his teachers encouraging him to pursue academics. For example, the principal of St. George's had promised to pay his fees if Clifford chose to attend university. But Clifford doubted his abilities, and for reasons he couldn't articulate, he convinced himself that he was unable to do it.

During his stay in Lytton, Clifford found the other pupils to be amiable, and he participated fully in school life. In addition to participating in school dances and other festivities, Clifford excelled at sports.

Clifford Bolton's National
Rifle Association medals and badges,
awarded for competitions in Bisley,
England. *Photo by
Helen Raptis.*

We had a basketball team. And we'd have [track and field] runoffs and [they'd] pick out the best one, and then they competed against Ashcroft and Lytton's best. Then we went to Kamloops ... where everybody met. The Indian kids were long-distance runners. I trained with my friend from Aiyansh. He was a long-distance runner, so I just ran with him.

Clifford also trained to be an expert marksman with St. George's army cadets, "the only all-Indian army cadets in the country." The boys practised on a 600-yard rifle range that he and his classmates built under the guidance of Vice-Principal Ron Purvis. Mr. Purvis and his wife took a liking to Clifford and encouraged him to follow his interests.

They pretty well raised me. They called me their son and I lived with them ... We built a home up there ... Before [Mr. and Mrs. Purvis] retired from residential school, they started building a place up at Lillooet. So on the weekends, if any of us wanted to go up there and earn a bit of extra money, then we went. We wheelbarrowed cement and put a basement together and helped the carpenter as he built the house. We built a swimming pool at the residential school. Then we built our own rifle range.

Clifford attributed Ron Purvis's determination to the fact that the vice-principal had fought at Dieppe and therefore found "nothing else on this earth too great of a challenge." Mr. Purvis assembled and trained the St. George's boys in a cadet squad that ranked third in British Columbia upon its first inspection. By its third inspection, the group had improved its ranking to first in Canada among the army, navy, and air force cadets. Given his shooting expertise, Clifford was chosen to represent Canada at several international competitions held by the National Rifle Association in Bisley, England.[59]

At an early age, Clifford had expressed interest in the arts, with drawing, painting, and carving being his preferred pastimes. During the 1955–56 school year, Mr. Purvis introduced him to cutting and polishing rocks, a pursuit that soon branched into jewellery making. In 1959 Clifford had the opportunity to present Queen Elizabeth with a jade brooch in the shape of a tomahawk when she passed through Lytton on a royal tour of Canada.[60] A jade pole he carved was valued at $20,000 in 1978. Since that time, many of his ornamental carvings have been displayed at public festivities and have graced private collections across the country.[61] During the 1990s Clifford and ten other applicants were selected to train with Tlingit master carver Dempsey Bob. Clifford was commissioned to carve a cedar canoe for the people of Kitselas in 2010 and to create a jade piece to form part of a BC government mace in 2011.

Clifford was the only Native in his high school graduating class, a statistic anticipating the poor graduation rates that continue to vex educators today. He later regretted not pursuing postsecondary education since, after graduation, he drifted through several unfulfilling jobs: "I did odd jobs with George Brown [in Port Essington] ... renovation work and stuff like that. I knew enough about carpentry to do that. [Then] I got a job with the [Terrace] co-op store. At the time, I was one of the very few, if not the only, Indian working in a business in Terrace." He attributed this distinction to prevailing discriminatory attitudes at the time, although he noted that he also met many "good people." In 1969 he joined the Central Marketing Service at the Department of Indian Affairs. The purpose of the service was to employ provincial buyers to purchase Indian art and send it to officials in Ottawa, who in turn would market the items to

Clifford Bolton's graduating class, Lytton. He is the first boy on the left. *Courtesy of Clifford Bolton.*

different outlets. Clifford noted that although the idea was a good one, it was managed by "bureaucrats" who "just bungled everything."

Reflecting on his experiences, Clifford felt that what he gained from his traditional Tsimshian education was equally as important as his formal schooling. He described his Tsimshian education as foundational for having essentially shaped the qualities of his inner character, namely "sharing and respecting and working and being dependable. We had to be dependable because we started working on the boats when we were little." Nevertheless, Clifford also considered himself lucky for the learning opportunities that St. George's Residential School had afforded him. Unfortunately, not all of Clifford's teachers were as supportive as Ron Purvis. Clifford felt that over the years some of his instructors had implied that "white" culture was superior to that of Indians. Although he believed that his teachers were generally well intentioned, he did not think it was right for his people to be "shot down. [We] were made to believe that our people, our parents and grandparents, were inadequate people."

In 1981 Clifford was elected chief of Kitsumkalum. In this role, he procured the first grant dispensed from the provincial First Citizens Fund to construct an Indian arts and crafts store, known as the House of Sm'oogyet

Clifford Bolton
with the canoe
he carved for
the village of
Kitselas, August
16, 2010. *Photo
by Helen Raptis.*

Pole-raising ceremony, 1981. Initiated under Clifford Bolton's tenure
as chief of Kitsumkalum. *Courtesy of Clifford Bolton.*

(meaning "Chief").[62] This initiative set the stage for future projects to revitalize and sustain the Tsimshian language and culture at Kitsumkalum through feasting, pole raising, and naming ceremonies, in addition to the teaching of Sm'algyax offered to both Native and non-Native residents of the Terrace region. Clifford passed away on April 12, 2012.

HARVEY WING

Harvey Wing was born in Port Essington on March 18, 1941, to an Indigenous mother, Eileen (née Wesley), and a Chinese father, Lee Wing.[63] Harvey's father was a fish packer, whose role was to purchase fish from fishermen and transport it to canneries. Lee also ran the Skeena Café, located on Dufferin Street north of the Port Essington Indian Reserve, and later acquired a general store with a pool room.[64] In 1946 Harvey's parents divorced, and by 1951 Lee had moved the family to Port Edward so that his children could attend high school in Prince Rupert.[65] According to Harvey's sister Charlotte, Lee was cognizant of the discriminatory sentiments of the era and chose not to remarry: "Dad was a loving father ... He always made sure we had enough of everything. [But] because we are children of mixed blood, he was afraid that we would not be accepted and treated well by another woman."[66]

Harvey began school in 1947, the year that officials closed Port Essington Indian Day School and transferred the children to Port Essington Elementary School. He recalled arriving at the day school in September to be informed by the teacher, Mrs. Pogson, that the children would be integrating into Port Essington Elementary, a public school. The teacher marched the children to their new school and left them under the charge of their new instructor, Miss Olynyk. Aside from helping to transport desks and resources from the day school to the public school, Harvey did not remember much about his first year. A few weeks into the term, Harvey's older brother and his friend were heating the fire poker in the school stove in order to use it to carve their initials into a desk. But the poker "got caught. They couldn't get it out." So the older boys blamed Harvey, who was expelled.

Harvey had few memories of formal schooling but noted that it was a fun place to make friends. He recalled reading *Dick and Jane* and being strapped almost every day for allegedly talking out of turn. When the family moved to Port Edward, he enjoyed the social aspects of attending Port Edward Elementary School, where the basketball team he played for won most games. Nevertheless, he also discovered that not much learning had taken place at Port Essington: "Math we didn't do too much of that ... arithmetic. And spelling ... I just couldn't spell at all, so I didn't really learn too much ... when I was going to school in Essington. When I went to Port Ed, half the things I didn't know nothing because I never learned it in the classes before that." Harvey's observations support many parents' longstanding critiques that the schooling of Aboriginal children was inferior in many ways to that of non-Aboriginal children.[67]

School did not always interest Harvey as much as working outdoors. He spent most of his time assisting his father with fish packing. After the family moved to Port Edward, schooling worsened for Harvey. The turning point came in Grade 9, when he attended Booth Memorial Junior Secondary School in Prince Rupert. During the first three weeks of school, no one could seem to tell him which class he belonged in – possibly due to his mixed heritage.

> I was upstairs and then downstairs, and the next day, again I was upstairs. I never learned nothin' the first three weeks because all I was doing was going up and forth. They just couldn't tell me what room I was supposed to be in. They'd tell me, I'd go up there, and then, I don't know, one of the teachers or somebody else would tell me, "Well you don't belong in this one." So I'd go back downstairs again.

When Harvey was finally assigned to a classroom, he quickly learned that his teacher was not fond of him.

> Six weeks I think I was in school [and] the teacher just told me, "I don't care how smart you are or anything else. You're not passing. I'm your homeroom teacher. You could have all grade A's but you're not passing." So what the hell was the use of me even trying to learn in school? [The teacher] hated me for some reason ... I guess he must have read my report card from the other school. But I was the only one he really picked on in the class too because ... the other kids, they were just as bad as I was and they never ever got their name mentioned or put up on the blackboard or [got] detentions or anything else, but I got one every Goddamn day I was in school in Booth.

That year, Harvey dropped out of school. He felt it was his only option given the teacher's declaration of imminent failure, illustrating not only the powerful effect that teachers' expectations had on children[68] but also the impact of the discrimination that continued to characterize teachers' views about children of mixed heritage. By the second half of the nineteenth century, social scientists were increasingly influenced by naturalist and geologist Charles Darwin's theory of evolution, which had introduced the idea that plants and animals adapt through natural selection. The notion that only the hardiest individuals survive and thrive was inappropriately applied to entire races that were deemed inferior to whites. With the apparent confirmation of a human pecking order that placed whites at the top of the hierarchy, offspring of mixed race unions were considered to be among the lowest.[69]

Although Harvey believed that some of his teachers were prejudiced, he did not say this about the children of Port Essington: "Oh the kids just got along together good up there. There was no bickering between them or anything else. If it was, it was just because they did something to one of them ... before or some darn thing. Otherwise, we got along all good. Never ever had to lock the doors or anything in our house."

Harvey felt that his formal education was less than ideal, having had little impact on his overall life. In contrast, he believed that his informal learning, both from the communities in which he lived and while on the job, was indispensable. Among the important values modelled by his elders was the notion of helping others. Although Port Essington did not have electricity during the years that Harvey was a child, his father ensured that the schools had power. The family lived at the back of the family store, where Lee Wing kept two generators.

> I guess for the lights. He had one small one and a big one. And [for] the big one, he made people put up poles so he could string wire from there to the school. He [also] gave some to my auntie and I guess the other two Chinese guys that lived across [from] the store. I guess he was giving them a bit of light power too.

Harvey also noted that he developed diligence and a strong work ethic while growing up in Port Essington. Since there was no indoor plumbing and the town's flume did not operate during the winter, most families carted water from creeks on hilltops several hundred metres away.

> [We] would have three five gallon [jugs] ... [and each] would have a small little spout here and a handle on it, so five gallons it would carry. And three of them ... we'd put it on the sleigh and we'd have to push it home, and I was always in the back. And the spout would be pointing in the back, and my feet would just get soaked, and by the time I got back home again, my

Fishing, Port Essington. *Courtesy of Jim McDonald.*

feet were always almost frozen. I'd have to go in there and sit right by the
fire. And … I remember we used to have to pump oil all the time from
down in our basement, up [to the kitchen stove]. Two of us would have to
do it. If that drum up on top was empty, then it didn't matter. We just kept
pumping until the drum we were pumping from was empty. But if we tried
to fill it up while it was half full, then somebody would have to be up on
top to watch so it wouldn't spill out.

On other occasions,

all the older kids – say sixteen, seventeen, eighteen years old – they would
have to go out and cut wood and bring it back in for their family. [And]
when they brought it in, they cut it up. Everybody got some. The younger
kids, we used to go up and help them after they dragged it into the snow.
When they dragged it down from where they were cutting it, it would make
a little trough, and we would put water in there to make [the snow] hard.
And if somebody towed in a big log down at the beach, the older people
would cut it up. In those days there was no power saw. It was all handsaws.

They'd do that and we'd play around and try to help them. But being little kids, we couldn't really work the saw very good, but at least we were trying. And then when they cut it up in blocks, and everything else, we packed it up to the road and ... took it to the houses.

Yet there was always time for fun too. For example, the younger children often amused themselves by sliding down the hardened troughs etched into the snow where the logs were dragged. Despite working hard, Harvey felt that Port Essington was a very good place to grow up: "Never, ever mistrusted anybody. You seen somebody doing work, you always went over, asked if you could help. Everybody up there just helped each others. Well ... everybody knew each others up there. It was so small. Everybody knew each others up there."

Nevertheless, Harvey was quick to add, "At that time, you didn't have to be smart to get a job or anything else. You didn't need papers ... All you needed was a strong back." So he set his sights on the world of work. First, he worked for his father, packing fish. Within a year, however, Jack Tasaka, a local boat builder, hired him to haul and pile lumber and to paint newly finished boats. After a few years with Jack, Harvey worked for the Nelson Brothers Fisheries.[70] He began by gillnetting and packing, later becoming a skipper for them. He gillnetted for roughly twenty years and then seine fished until his retirement at age sixty-four.

Over the years, fishing, canning, and logging operations were consolidated by large corporations that increasingly squeezed out family-run and small-scale operations. To survive in the Skeena region today, young people are increasingly in need of more than "a strong back" and a will to work.

That's why I'm trying to tell all my grandkids and every kid that I'm working with now. I tell them, "Get your education man." But ... no I didn't ... at that time .... we didn't need an education. And most of the stuff where I worked, I knew what was happening if they hollered at me to do something. I knew what the heck to do. So I figured that's all I really needed. I wasn't going to go travelling around looking for a job. I was just going to be right where I was.

A strong back, a willingness to work, and other values such as the importance of helping others – particularly family and friends – brought Harvey much success in life. In 2010 he and his wife, Faith, celebrated their fortieth wedding anniversary. They reported that they had successfully

Faith and Harvey Wing, Kitsumkalum, August 2010. *Photo by Helen Raptis.*

raised seven of their own children and two others whom they adopted. They are proud grandparents to twenty-four grandchildren and five great-grandchildren.

CHARLOTTE GUNO

Charlotte Guno had one overwhelming emotion when reflecting on life at Port Essington: loneliness.[71] She was born to Charlotte (née Harrison) and Edward Bolton at the Prince Rupert Hospital on August 13, 1943, by which time Port Essington had reached its zenith and was well into its social and economic decline. When Charlotte was a toddler, the town's canneries had shut down, and many Port Essington residents were drifting away in pursuit of work.[72]

> I can't believe how lonesome I felt ... Everybody was starting to move away ... It was ... empty. I remember ... visiting [my grandmother] at her home and she was telling me, "You know what? I'm going to leave pretty soon. I don't want to leave ... But I have to leave because I'm getting old. And I

need to be near a doctor ... So that's the only reason that I'm leaving." So she did leave ... That was an earth-shaking experience to go through.

With Port Essington's population dwindling, many of Charlotte's early childhood memories revolved around harvesting and eating foods that grew wild in the nearby fields or were cultivated in her grandmother's garden.

We did berry picking ... blueberries, salmon berries, crab apples, and the odd apple tree, plus cranberries. We ate a lot of green stuff. I still eat them ... Young salmon berry shoots, we'd pick them, put them over our shoulders, head out to the boardwalk, and have our little bowl of sugar ... another one of oolichan grease, and dip, dip, dip ... Simple things ... made you happy. My mom harvested our salmon, and our grandmother did the smoking. Grandmother had a garden of black currents, red currents, rhubarb, Saskatoon and gooseberries ... also potatoes, carrots, radishes, and ... peas. My mom harvested clams, cockles, and abalone.

Nevertheless, like so many others, Charlotte too left Port Essington when the opportunity arose. Charlotte's father, who worked as a fish packer and as a member of the British Columbia Indian Commission, believed that the only way to "survive in a white man's world is through getting an education."[73] Thus Charlotte worked diligently at Port Essington Elementary School, a public institution, where she undertook lessons in spelling, reading, math, writing, printing, and recreation. The school year also included square dancing and celebrations for Halloween, Christmas, Easter, and Valentine's Day. When she had completed Grade 8, she wrote to the regional Indian Agent, requesting to attend St. George's Indian Residential School in Lytton, where her cousins Clifford, Alec, Shirley, Laura, and Bobby were enrolled.[74] "I wanted to feel that at least I knew some people there. I knew it was going to be different and challenging [since] I was very shy and I was very quiet."

Charlotte considered her attendance at residential school to have been a good experience, despite repeating Grade 9 to improve her mark in English.[75]

I got ... chosen ... to work in the canon and his wife's home after school. She taught me how to set a table, how to bake biscuits, how to housekeep. Christmastime and at Eastertime ... she would buy us an outfit. A nice top,

sweater top, and skirt. There [were] three girls ... and two guys working
in her home. We didn't eat with them ... [And then] the canon's wife decided
to teach five students how to play piano, and I was one of them. So she
chose me ... Believe it or not, I played Chopin and Mozart and Beethoven,
all that crazy stuff.

After completing Grade 10, an Indian and Northern Affairs official informed Charlotte that she was being transferred to a boarding home
program in Vancouver to complete her secondary schooling, illustrating
the unfettered latitude that government agents exercised over the lives of
Native peoples.[76] Charlotte graduated from Richmond High School in
1962 and enrolled in a one-year general commercial program at Vancouver
Vocational Institute:[77] "We'd dabble in typing and shorthand and filing
... basic accounting. I thought, 'Woa! I'm gonna conquer the world with
this ...' And you know what? I did. I can't believe that I only went to one
year of college, and I've accomplished what I have."

Upon completing her postsecondary courses, Charlotte began a series
of secretarial jobs, commencing with on-the-job training with the Indian
Affairs office in Prince Rupert. She married in 1964, and her former husband's job took the newlyweds to Vancouver, where she secured employment at the Main Street office of business magnate Jim Pattison. Despite
having received a practical education that helped her to secure constant
employment, Charlotte felt that her success came at a cost as well: "The
only thing that ... bothered me about leaving home – yet I knew I had
to do it because I was the oldest and I needed to get an education and I
needed to support myself and the family – was leaving my siblings behind."
Charlotte feels that when children departed for residential school, it
resulted in a split in the family that was never repaired. She argued that
the children who remained in Port Essington were almost like a "separate
family" from those who moved away to finish school. Her guilty feelings
were somewhat allayed when her siblings reported that they loved their
teachers at Port Essington Elementary School. Mr. and Mrs. Harrison, a
husband and wife teaching team, seemed committed to the children of
Port Essington. "They had compassion for our children that were left alone
in [that] empty ... world." Charlotte further encouraged three of her six
siblings to achieve their educational goals: "I always thought that my responsibility after I got my education was to help my mother. To help her
have some ... comforts. To help my siblings get an education ... whether
they came and lived with me while getting an education. That was my
job." Only her youngest brother did not pursue postsecondary studies

since he had begun fishing with his father at an early age. By the time he was fourteen, he was a joint operator of a fish packer, ensuring a steady, well-paying livelihood.

In 2001 Charlotte became the education administrator of the Kitsumkalum Indian Band, a job about which she expressed enormous passion. Her role involves looking after the educational needs of band members at the elementary, secondary, and postsecondary levels. Charlotte is the principal of Kitsumkalum's 'Na Aksa Gila Kyew Learning Centre, where students aged nineteen and over can obtain their "Adult Dogwood" certificate.[78] She liaises with schools in the Coast Mountain School District, helping parents and students to deal with challenges that may arise while their child is at school. She also sits on the boards of the provincial First Nations Education Steering Committee, First Nations Schools, and Northwest Community College.

In contrast to her boundless energy are the young people she encounters who seem to have no sense of direction. Coast Mountain's Aboriginal drop-out rate is fairly high, which Charlotte attributes to lack of parental support and poor school environments:[79] "I intervene if parents allow me. All I ask of parents is that they ensure their child has plenty of rest and a full tummy. I encourage them to support their child by getting involved – homework, parent-teacher meetings, school events." To address the problem of children not completing their school assignments, Charlotte has initiated an after-school homework club that functions on the premises of Kitsumkalum's Adult Education Centre. In addition to addressing academics, Charlotte tries to help the students adopt values that she learned from her elders, such as respect and hard work. She stressed that "you have to work for what you want. You *have* to work for it. It just doesn't get given to you."

Equally frustrating for Charlotte is what she perceives to be poor learning conditions in schools: "Discrimination ... If you talk down to an Aboriginal, well kids mirror what they see and hear. You have to have an environment that is loving, warm, and safe." Charlotte has observed that Indigenous students "flourish in an environment of their own. It really needs to be a caring environment. It needs to be a respectful environment, and it really needs to be where we give thanks to a higher power than ourselves and recognize that. We need to have our elders at the school." To support her views, Charlotte argues that students have experienced more success at Terrace's Centennial Christian School than at public schools. Centennial is an independent school where students observe a strict dress code, bullying is not accepted, and respectful interactions are

Principal Charlotte Guno and 'Na Aksa Gila Kyew Learning
Centre's 2009 graduating class. *Courtesy of Charlotte Guno.*

fostered by a belief in a higher power. Since the tuition fee is out of reach
for many families, Charlotte and several others have been advocating a
"choice school" within the public system. Her dream is to establish a school
within the Coast Mountain School District, accessible to all, that honours
individual learners and empowers them with the knowledge, skills, and
attitudes to succeed. Interestingly, such an environment would bear re-
semblance to the educational setting in which Charlotte found herself
nearly five decades ago, where she developed a sense that she could "take
on the world."

THE STORIES OF THE PRE-1950S generation are framed in broad, multi-
faceted ways portraying education as a wide-ranging concept that exceeds
the narrower western European notion of formal schooling. Each of the

participants from this generation wove their recollections into the larger framework of their entire lives, illustrating the contention that education from an Indigenous perspective is a "lifelong continuum of experience gleaned from interaction with one another, with all of nature (seen and unseen), as well as with all of the cosmos."[80] Whether it be Mildred, who explained that her volunteer efforts were as important as her formal schooling in securing her a position as an addictions counsellor, or Harvey, who learned the value of hard work as a child by delivering kindling to Port Essington residents, this generation learned in many ways across many settings – not just at school.

Given the older generation's inclination to define education more broadly than schooling, their stories provide important counternarratives to the narrow conceptions of education illustrated by the literature on residential schooling. For example, whereas the students of this generation tended to interpret their out-of-school learning as important for the formation of their values and work ethic, scholars of residential schooling have condemned out-of-school chores as wasted time taken away from more valuable classroom learning.[81] The question facing historians is one of interpretation. If the participants in this research viewed family and community chores as character-building and an integral part of their overall educational journey, why have the school-based chores performed by residential students been condemned as unimportant? I suggest that the participants in this study attributed value to their nonschool experiences because of the broad, holistic view of education advanced by the Tsimshian people. I also suggest that the devaluing of non-academic learning presented in the literature on residential schools reflects the Western notion that true learning is cognitive and thus academic. Marie Battiste calls this cognitive imperialism, which is rooted in European ways of knowing. She considers it part of a process of "white-washing" Indigenous peoples' minds, which has occurred through assimilation, monolingual and monocultural European education, and immersion in a "Eurocentric context complete with media, books, laws, and values."[82] This concept is revisited in Chapter 6.

Scholars have noted that since Confederation, decisions and policies impacting the lives of Aboriginal peoples have been oppressive and erratic due to both disinterest and lack of awareness on the part of the Canadian government.[83] Yet, as Wally's resistance to his forcible removal from the Port Essington Indian Reserve reveals, navigating through such disruptive policies enabled this generation to develop a strong sense of agency. It would be wrong to conclude that the participants whose stories appear in this chapter were merely victims of circumstance.

The importance of Port Essington's geographic environment in shaping
the participants' notions of self is also evident in their recollections. More
important still is how the environment's role changed over time in response
to evolving social and economic circumstances at Port Essington. For
example, social and economic changes that occurred during the twelve
years separating Mildred's birth in 1931 from Charlotte's birth in 1943
were profound and yielded very different reflections on Port Essington.
For Mildred, Port Essington and its surrounding territory played an important role in her acquisition of traditional Tsimshian skills and values
transmitted by her family while out on the land. In contrast, Charlotte
characterized her birthplace as lonesome and explained that she chose to
leave at the earliest opportunity. By the time Charlotte was born, the
Tsimshian were no longer able to subsist fully off the land that had once
sustained them. Their relationship to their environment had been permanently disrupted.

Finally, this generation's stories illustrate a sense of relationality that was
not restricted to the land alone, as they also commented on interpersonal
relationships – both positive and negative – among family, community,
and teachers. Interestingly, church officials appear to have played a minor
role in their lives. Here again, the stories from this generation provide an
important counterbalance to the residential school literature, where church
officials and missionaries are shown to have played significant roles as
school administrators, priests, and teachers – even as the system was being
wound down.[84] This is not to say, however, that spirituality did not figure
in their recollections. Mildred, Verna, and Clifford all touched on the notions of formal religion and/or spirituality.

5

Buried Seeds Taking Root:
Dispossession and Resurgence
at Terrace among
the Post-1950s Generation

MARIE BATTISTE HAS ARGUED that European settlers appropriated not only Indigenous lands but also people's lives and livelihoods "like the snow takes the grass."[1] Although the grass disappears temporarily, it does not die but re-emerges after lying dormant for the winter. This metaphor of the buried seed taking root after a period of dormancy is appropriate for framing the stories of the five participants featured in this chapter: Don Roberts Junior, Steve Roberts, Richard Roberts, Carol Sam, and Jim Roberts. These participants are grouped together because they attended integrated schools after the closure of Port Essington Indian Day School. Don and Steve began their schooling in Port Essington and transitioned to schools elsewhere, whereas Richard, Carol, and Jim were schooled in Terrace because of their displacement to Kitsumkalum after fires destroyed Port Essington. Their stories illuminate a time after Port Essington had reached its social and economic nadir. But more importantly, they were all born after the Second World War and after Canada amended the Indian Act to enable Indigenous children to be schooled with non-Indigenous children. The predominant themes that tie their stories together include the dispossession of their Tsimshian language and culture; their difficulties transitioning from Port Essington to Kitsumkalum; and their negative elementary school experiences in Terrace. Although high school was somewhat better for everyone in this group, all five experienced some degree of discrimination. Furthermore, their ability to remain part of Canada's economic fabric was seriously compromised due to global economic shifts that disproportionately affected wage labourers in resource-based industries. Despite their hardships, however, they all managed to transition to adulthood and sustain themselves with paid employment. All went on to raise families, and it is within their children that they have planted the seeds of cultural and linguistic resurgence. Each talked about the importance of education to their offspring and other young people in their communities and beyond – even though only one of the five had graduated from high school and none had completed a postsecondary degree.

Don Roberts Junior

On February 28, 2011, Don Roberts Junior was elected to his third term as chief councillor of Kitsumkalum.[2] Although his family resided at Port Essington, known among the Tsimshian as Spaksuut (pronounced "Spokeshute"), he was born in 1952 on his grandfather's boat in Prince Rupert Harbour before his mother could reach the hospital. Since Don was eleven when his family relocated to Kitsumkalum, most of his childhood memories are of growing up in Spaksuut. One of his favourite pastimes was playing "Old Tom"[3] with his friends and siblings. He recalled that the community was tightly knit and that everyone knew each other.

Don acquired many of his traditional Tsimshian skills and knowledge while living at Spaksuut. He began fishing at age five with his father and uncles and soon understood ocean tides, as well as the habits of many varieties of salmon that populated the waters of the Skeena River. In addition, he learned the best locales to harvest herring eggs, seaweed, clams, and halibut. With the help of his aunt, Don hung his first nets at age seven and caught a spring salmon. His elders helped him to hone his observational skills, which have been useful to him as an adult since he divides his time between overseeing Kitsumkalum's affairs and commercial fishing. From his elders, he also developed hunting skills and an understanding of the plants used in traditional Tsimshian medicine. He and his brother began hunting with BB guns, later graduating to 22-calibre rifles with which to secure marten, beaver, otter, and deer.

By contrast, lessons Don learned at Port Essington Elementary School were delivered mainly through books, such as the *Dick and Jane* readers. He described his teachers at the school as "good" – strict but supportive – and did not recall any of them openly oppressing the Tsimshian culture or language (Sm'algyax). Nevertheless, Don lamented the harmful experiences of his elders at Port Essington Indian Day School. One particularly

Christmas play, Port Essington Elementary School, 1950s. Don Roberts Junior, as "Joseph," stands to the left of "Mary," who is seated. *Courtesy of Richard Roberts.*

painful story that stood out for Don came from an aunt who spoke Sm'algyax in class and was made to stand in the corner, arms extended with books piled on each hand. When the child's hands eventually dropped under the weight of the books, the teacher administered the strap.

After his family moved to Kitsumkalum in 1963, Don's school experiences took a negative turn. He recalled that the people in Spaksuut were cooperative and helpful with one another. He did not witness any prejudice or bullying, and he noted that intermarriage was fairly commonplace. Due to the ease with which the ethnicities mingled at Port Essington, he did not realize that the residents of Finntown were "white" until the concept entered his consciousness at school in Terrace. Once at Kitsumkalum, Don and his siblings attended Kalum School in Terrace, where circumstances were not ideal. The children experienced discrimination not only from the teaching staff but from the students as well, particularly while riding the school bus. When the children were moved to Riverside Elementary (later E.T. Kenney) School, things got worse. The administration attempted to expel Don and his brother in order to prevent them from writing their Grade 7 examinations. Their father, Don Senior, paid a visit to the school to advocate for his sons, at which point the teachers backed down; the boys sat the exams and passed.

Don remembered the odd teacher with fondness – such as his Grade 7 teacher, Mrs. Delaney. But in general, he felt that the climates were very poor at Kalum and Riverside. Out in the schoolyard, there existed what Don referred to as an "imaginary line," with the white children playing on one side and the Native children on the other: "No one dared to cross to the other side. And the teachers didn't help. When fights broke out, the teachers would just watch, but wouldn't step in to stop it." What was equally upsetting was discovering that the children from Spaksuut were academically far behind their Terrace counterparts, due perhaps to the slower pace of learning they had experienced in their former one-room, multiaged school.

Don remembered clearly the event that first caused him to experience hatred. In Grade 6 he was required to write a report on "lightning." He worked diligently on the report and included information taken from an encyclopedia set that his mother had bought for the children. Not only did his teacher return the report with a failing grade for alleged plagiarism, but he also made sure that everyone in the class knew about it. As Don's classmates gathered around to see his score, "the whole class learned what discrimination meant. And I learned what 'hate' meant. I hated [that teacher] for the rest of my life." When Don moved up to Skeena High School, life seemed to improve since students experienced a variety of teachers with different attitudes and teaching styles. "And the kids were good. For some reason, there was no more line. At high school the kids got along."

Don expressed regrets that the federal government would not finance the rebuilding of Spaksuut after the fires destroyed it during the 1960s. According to Don, the demise of the town was difficult for many residents, not all of whom moved to Kitsumkalum. With many people taking up residence in Prince Rupert and beyond, the former community fractured. Don concluded that the decision not to rebuild the town was simply one of the federal government's many policies that negatively affected the Tsimshian, others being the appropriation of important lands and the

Don Roberts Junior, Port Essington, 2010. In the background is what remains of
Port Essington Elementary School. *Courtesy of Don Roberts Junior.*

allegedly poor regulation of the fishing and logging industries on and
around the Skeena River.[4]

Still, Don was optimistic that his people will see a complete revitalization of their language, culture, and economic livelihood. Like Marie
Battiste, he did not believe that these aspects of Tsimshian life have been
completely lost, but having lain dormant for too long, are ripe for rebirth.
He expressed gratitude that he never attended residential school and was
able to learn traditional skills and values from his Tsimshian elders. He
believed that formal schooling had been less valuable to his adult life
both as a commercial fisherman and as chief councillor of Kitsumkalum
than had traditional Tsimshian learning. As part of his leadership as chief
councillor, he has continued to oversee the development of many important initiatives, ranging from the teaching of the Sm'algyax language and
the revival of important Tsimshian customs, such as naming ceremonies
and feasts, to economic development projects, to the management of Kitsumkalum fisheries and right-of-way agreements with BC Hydro and the
Canadian Pacific Railway.

As the community explores new economic initiatives, he has cautioned young people not to lose sight of the importance of the land to Tsimshian people. He noted that without land rights, there is no economy and that without an economic base, the community will not survive.[5] Don also commented that a full cultural rebirth will be possible only through the assistance of elders who hold important Tsimshian knowledge and skills that link the community to ancestors, values, and customs that predate contact with white settlers. Don is somewhat unique among the interviewees from his generation in that he had early exposure to and continues to value land-based traditions as well as the important role to be played by elders. His views align with the work of researchers such as Michael Marker, Marie Battiste, and James (Sa'ke'j) Youngblood Henderson who insist that Indigenous worldviews reflect "vibrant relationships between the people, their ecosystems and other living beings and spirits that share their lands."[6] The route to cultural resurgence, these scholars argue, is to return to the land and the knowledge, skills, and values it engenders.

STEVE ROBERTS

Steve Roberts remembered Port Essington as a peaceful environment where he spent much of his time outdoors engaged in childhood pursuits, such as collecting minnows in the local creeks with his older brother Don. "We used to disappear," he said, "and nobody'd come lookin' for us."[7] Steve was born on March 4, 1953, long after the town's canneries had ceased operations, which had prompted most local business owners to relocate. Empty buildings, including Port Essington Hotel, Brown's Store, and the once-lively Community Hall, dotted the landscape.

Despite its natural beauty, Steve recalled hardships as well. There was no electricity or running water, and he had memories of "packing water" from up in the hills.[8]

> Over a distance from where we lived there was, I thought, a fairly long distance that we packed water. It was a natural spring where we collected water for ... drinking ... and such. [We transported it] in buckets ... But in [1958] my dad bought a house and relocated us from one part of Port Essington to another part [farther away from Finntown]. And he built a little dam on the hillside and ran a water line from the dam to the house, so we had running water in the house. Cold water. No heated water.

Steve's father, Don Senior, was a commercial fisherman who supplemented the family's income by hunting wild game, such as deer and ducks. His mother, Mildred, had been employed in a cannery during her youth but no longer worked outside the home when her children were born. She kept a vegetable garden, but Steve questioned how much of the produce made it to the dinner table. He chuckled as he remembered "raiding the carrot patch ... I don't know if they were able ... to leave them underground long enough to feed us all." In the fall and spring, the family would travel to Prince Rupert to stock up on nonperishable supplies, such as flour and sugar.

Despite the town's declining population, Steve recalled having plenty of playmates. In addition to his siblings and cousins, there were the girls from Finntown with whom he played "school": "We were the students. I must have liked it [since] I stayed there and played with them. The last name was Snellman. And [there was] Elena Heckala's daughter ... Sylvia.[9] [She] lives in Rupert ... I don't know her last name now. [She] and her husband [later] had the Apex Marina in Prince Rupert."

Steve first attended Port Essington Elementary School in 1959. His fondest memories were of Mrs. McDougall, the teacher, taking the children on hikes to explore the area around the town. Steve believed that the teacher wanted to engage the children in the goings-on of the community. She took them to

> where the men were working. She'd bring the class out ... to go see what [the men] were doing ... when they were doing some public-works-type stuff [like] repairing the pipeline ... They were building a support structure to hold the pipeline up where it spanned the creek. Ed Bolton and the crew had built a pile driver ... for driving the pilings into the mud to support the structure that supported the pipeline.

Apparently, Mrs. McDougall would announce the class's arrival by singing, "Hail, hail, the gang's all here." Steve also recalled once being a shepherd in a Christmas play, but he felt that most school time was spent studying language arts. As was the case in most rural one-room schools of the time, the older children were assigned to help the younger ones:[10] "I remember reading with Edna Bolton. All the students were in one classroom, and I was sitting beside her and she was helping me with reading. She was older ... so she would have been, golly ... I think she would have been ten, twelve years old, somewhere thereabouts, I guess. I would have been about five or six."

Port Essington Elementary School students, 1950s. *Courtesy of Charlotte Guno.*

During the 1961–62 school year, when Steve was nine years old, the number of children enrolled at Port Essington Elementary School fell to just nine (five boys and four girls).[11] Given that the province would fund teachers only for enrolments of ten or more, the school was closed the following June.[12] Steve and his siblings continued their studies through the provincial correspondence school for a year before their parents made the decision to relocate to Kitsumkalum.[13] Beginning in 1919, the province began supplying correspondence programs to families in settlements too small to furnish the ten school-aged children necessary for the establishment of a school. For many rural learners, correspondence was the only option for high school graduation, as rural regions seldom offered secondary schooling.

Having been punished for using Sm'algyax in school, Steve's elders did not speak the language to him. Yet he managed to pick up a few phrases by listening to his parents and grandparents communicating among themselves. Steve did not recall his parents attempting to instil in him any ceremonial Tsimshian traditions either: "They didn't teach us a lot of that. They had problems when they were going to school so they – what they told us – they decided they're not going to teach us our culture because they had so [many] problems when they were going to school. They didn't teach us the language, didn't talk a lot about the culture."

The learning he did with his parents was generally related to procuring food to help the family survive. From time to time, he and his older brother accompanied their father and uncles while fishing, and they were put to work counting the fish. Later, when they were older, the boys sometimes hunted beaver: "We used to get beavers, and our mom showed us how to skin them. [She] probably skinned off most of them while she was doing it! And then in the spring our dad would collect them all up and bring them to the fur buyer in Rupert and sell them."

Steve's recollections of being a student at Port Essington were generally positive, but his memories of relocating to Kitsumkalum were less so. For a long time, Steve was unhappy at Kitsumkalum, where he found the summers too hot and the winters too cold. Most problematic was the transition from a multiaged one-room school in Port Essington to Kalum School in Terrace, where students were segregated by grade level.

> Well, my teachers were nice. I don't remember having any problems with any of my teachers. [But in] elementary, I guess learning to cope with other kids … that was a difficult one. Where we grew up [in Port Essington] you knew everybody. In Terrace you didn't know everybody … We didn't grow up dealing with a lot of people. I think that was probably the most difficult … People are different. Some are more aggressive than others. We were really shy … In elementary school, [you] just learned to stay away from [the bullies] … The "aggressive" in me never came out until I was in high school. [Then I] pushed back.

He and his siblings started off at Kalum School but soon after moved to Riverside. When that was shut down, they transferred to E.T. Kenney School. "I didn't start being comfortable [in Terrace] until I hit high school. Then in high school I had tons of friends. Never looked back." Like so many young men of Steve's generation, he quit school at age seventeen

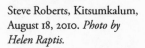

Steve Roberts, Kitsumkalum,
August 18, 2010. *Photo by
Helen Raptis.*

and found work in one of the province's abundant primary resource industries. He began his career with the Department of Fisheries and
Oceans, where he counted fish on the Lakelse River, but his older brother
soon enticed him into logging, where the salary was better. He recalled
that the "money is what drives you. Don't want to be poor." In 1975 no
one would accept a nomination for chief and band manager at Kitsumkalum, so Steve let his name stand and won by acclamation. For three
years, he continued to log by day and manage the band's affairs by night.
But holding two positions became too hard on his family, so in 1977 he
left logging permanently: "I kicked myself for a number of years after that.
My friends that were logging were paying more than double in income
tax than what I earned in a year. Yeah, I missed that part." After fourteen
years, his position was split in two, and today Steve continues to hold the
job of band manager for Kitsumkalum. Reflecting on his own experiences
as a learner and a worker, Steve felt that he had seen "a lot of changes."
Echoing the words of Harvey Wing in Chapter 4, Steve noted,

> In my younger days, [if] you wanted to work all you needed was a desire
> to work. They'll put you to work. They never had any minimum grade
> standing that you needed. Now you're looking at a different economy
> that's driving us. What I see with the younger kids is that if you don't have
> an education, you're going to have a tough time finding work. I see a lot
> of younger people going from one minimum wage job to another. If
> you're looking to move ahead you need to have your Grade 12. You need

to have some college or some university. Otherwise, you're going to have a real tough time. Not necessarily just in our community but right across the Northwest. The economy has changed dramatically. In the Northwest area – and I think most of BC – the economy was driven by commercial fishing and logging. Now that they've basically crashed, there's not an awful lot available if you are unskilled. Even [for] the menial jobs that are available now, you need to have some basic education, some entry level training that will allow you to get into that.

The world that Steve entered in 1953 at Port Essington is distant from Kitsumkalum, both geographically and in terms of day-to-day living. Yet Steve, like most of Port Essington's former residents, has adapted to the changes that he has encountered, managing not only to survive but also to thrive.

RICHARD ROBERTS

On August 7, 1957, Mildred Roberts went into labour with her third child, Richard. She and her husband, Don Senior, a commercial fisherman, quickly boarded his gillnetter at Port Essington and set out for the hospital at Prince Rupert. But baby Richard had other plans. After the couple crossed the Skeena River and tied up at North Pacific Cannery at Port Edward, baby Richard made his untimely appearance on the boat![14]

By the late 1950s, roughly half a dozen families resided at Port Essington year round, most of whom were related to the Roberts family. As a result, Richard and his siblings spent their days playing together and with their cousins. As employment opportunities had all but disappeared from Port Essington, the town's menfolk sought work with fishing companies or canneries on the north side of the Skeena River, whereas the women tended to their homes and children. With the men increasingly away from home, families spent less and less time "out at camp," in contrast to when the pre-1950s generation were children. Thus the youngsters of Richard's generation had little opportunity to learn Tsimshian traditions, such as fishing, hunting, gathering, and food preparation, from their elders. Festivities at which oral histories were passed down from elders to children had also dwindled.

Of the few memories that Richard had of formal schooling, none was positive. In September 1963 he began attending Kalum School after the family relocated to Kitsumkalum that summer. He recalled being strapped

The Roberts family, 1960. Richard is the child in front, held by his father, Don Senior, who is next to his mother, Mildred. *Courtesy of Jim Roberts.*

daily and spending much of his time standing in the corner for allegedly misbehaving: "They made me hate school. They ... I'm pretty sure they didn't like Indians. Right from Grade 1, I was getting the strap just about every other day. Stood in the corner every day, so I hate school and teachers." Spending most of his time banished from his desk, Richard took four years to complete Grades 1 and 2. By Grade 1, he hated school and attended only because it was required.

As the father of four children and grandfather to three, Richard is optimistic that teacher-pupil relationships have generally changed for the better in recent years.[15] Nevertheless, his own children have felt the sting of discrimination, reminding us that "colonialism is not something that existed only at the time that Canada was a colony ... It has continued into the present ... as the primary ideology underlying the education of Indigenous Peoples in Canada today."[16]

> You can find that still, nowadays. There is one teacher ... taught Grade 6. She just about made one of my nieces quit school – as well as my younger brother, along with a few other Native children. Then my daughter is in there. And she'd come home saying, "I think she's singling me out. And she had me standing at the front of the class and made me feel stupid." So I

went in there and tied into her and told her where I'm coming from ...
Told her I don't like teachers and I don't like prejudiced teachers, and [she]
fit both of them. After that my daughter could do anything she wanted in
that class. I'm not going to let anyone mistreat my children because of who
they are.

Richard was pleased to report that after much negotiation, he was able to
secure a spot for one of his daughters at Parkside Alternative School. He
believes that the biggest difference between Parkside and other public
schools is the positive nature of the pupil-teacher relationships. Students
and instructors are much closer to, more familiar with, and more caring
of one another.

I had to fight to get [her] in there. She's so quiet ... She's not a bad kid, so
they didn't want her in there. I had to fight for her quite a bit to get her in.
I have to fight to keep her in there too. But her grades have swung right
around. So the teachers there, they actually look like they want to go to
work instead of [being] forced to. And they'd do anything they can to help
the kids out. This is the only school where all the teachers are called by their
first name. I don't know a last name of any one of the teachers in there. Just
this summer [my daughter] got invited to her teacher's wedding. And she
invited her teacher to her birthday, and she showed up with her family!

Richard said that he would like to have attended a high school like
Parkside when he was a teenager. Instead, he attended a regular public
school, half-heartedly going through the motions. He had good memories
of woodworking and drafting classes, but his interest in these subjects
could not sustain him through the negative experiences, so he dropped
out of school just before his sixteenth birthday, having completed the
better part of Grade 9. He joined many of his friends and relations in the
logging industry, where he spent the next thirty-two years carving out a
living.

In her study of the experiences of twenty-seven Sioux high school students, Peggy Wilson has argued that urban schooling is inherently problematic for Indigenous children raised on reserves. Wilson found that
students were happy, involved, and academically on track while attending
on-reserve elementary schools. But in the urban high school setting, Sioux
students suffered discrimination from both white students and teachers,
as well as significant declines in their academic standings, due in part to
teachers' unjustified prejudgments. Feeling frustrated by not being able

to improve their situation, the students opted to drop out "because that was the most adaptive coping strategy at that time in their lives."[17] Sadly, the institutional racism that took root during the nineteenth century is still entrenched in Canadian schools at the opening of the twenty-first.[18]

Historically, logging has ensured stable employment for young men throughout northern British Columbia. But by the mid-2000s, this was no longer the case due to worldwide competition and declining timber revenues. By 2005 Richard was out of work. He moved throughout British Columbia and Alberta, taking up itinerant logging jobs, but this proved hard on his family, who had remained in Kitsumkalum. In 2006 Richard bid logging farewell permanently and started working as a fisheries enforcement officer for Kitsumkalum, a position he continues to hold. He had seen the writing on the wall in the late 1990s and had begun upgrading his education credentials through adult learning centres around the province. He found these experiences to be much more positive than his childhood schooling: "I found it easier. You want it. Going back when you're older, you *want* it rather than when you're younger and you *have* to do it. When I was upgrading I was always 95, 97 percent, somewhere around there." Although he appreciated the self-pacing of the classes, Richard would have appreciated more intervention on the part of the teacher, who often had too many students to enable one-on-one attention.

> I always tried to have a teacher [help me] just once when I did the [Grade] 11 math in Summerland at this ... adult learning centre. But I didn't like that 'cause they're so busy, and then you hit a snag and they say, "Well the answer's in the back of the book." So you're still looking. Here's the start and here's the end. How do you get to the end? So I think I invented some new ways of doing math!

Richard felt that the most useful course he took was in investigating enforcement, as it helped him to hone his report-writing and photography abilities, two skills he uses daily as part of fisheries enforcement.

Richard acknowledged that the world has changed significantly since 1973, when he quit school and opted for the stability of resource-based employment. Interestingly, as early as 1965, BC historian Wilson Duff remarked that "in some ways it seems to have been easier for the Indians of two or three generations ago to adjust to the simpler white economy of that time than it is for their grandsons to find a place in the more complex economy of today."[19] Since more and more jobs today require Grade 12 schooling and beyond, Richard has encouraged his own children

Richard Roberts, Kitsumkalum,
August 17, 2010. *Photo by
Helen Raptis.*

to undertake as much education as they can. His children seem to be taking his advice: "They're going with it. They've got good goals. The older
one, she wants to go through early childhood development, open up her
own daycare. And then the youngest one, she either wants to be a vet or
a fishery officer." Formal schooling for Aboriginal peoples has indeed
changed considerably since Richard's first encounters at Kalum School in
the early 1960s.

CAROL SAM

Carol Sam (née Roberts) was born on October 6, 1959, in Prince Rupert
to Mildred (née Bolton) and Don Roberts Senior.[20] She belongs to the
Killer Whale Clan. So few people lived at Port Essington by the time Carol
was born that in 1963 her family followed many others to take up residence in Kitsumkalum, just west of Terrace. Although Carol spent most
of her childhood at Kitsumkalum, her mother and grandmother told her
many stories of Port Essington and its people. For example, her great-
grandmother was a midwife who helped to deliver babies.

> Mom always talked about the different elders there that helped deliver
> babies. Like my great-grandmother [Rebecca Bolton], she helped deliver
> babies. And she remembers somebody having a baby, and it was breach and
> [she] turned it [using her hands] ... just on the belly ... Well I guess all the
> older people there, they just did all kinds of things.

One of the strongest images in Carol's memory was of the boardwalk in Port Essington.

> I loved the boardwalks ... The sound, the way [they] felt, everything ... I remember when I was really little, and my mom and all my siblings, they were picking berries just off the boardwalk and my babysitter was a crab, a cooked crab. [Mom] put it in a pie pan and sat me on the boardwalk, and that's where I sat. I was eating away at a crab, and they were up in the bushes picking berries. One of my favourite, favourite memories ever is sitting under the boardwalk, and there's all this broken glass, all different colours, but ... they weren't sharp. They were all worn down [from the ocean]. I liked collecting glass and shells.

Most days were spent playing with siblings and with cousins, who spent so much time with the family that her brother had assumed they were siblings. Without television or organized activities, the children used their imaginations to create their own pastimes. A game that stood out for Carol was "pie tag": "You make like a big pie in the mud ... and you run away from whoever is it but you can only stay on the lines [drawn for the pie]." And much like her ancestors, Carol and her siblings would pick berries for the family as well as visit elderly residents. "We used to go down to Finntown ... and visit this lady Mary Hautenen," one of the town's few remaining residents of Finnish ancestry.

Another of Carol's favourite memories was listening to her mother sing in Sm'algyax.

> I can remember her singing me a song in Sm'algyax. But ... when we went to school, there was just English. And I always blame the day school in Port Essington because Mom always tells us stories about when they went to school. They weren't allowed to speak their language at all, even though when [they] began school that's all [they] spoke. So then when it came time for her kids to go to school, it was like, "All you're going to speak is English." So she learned really well not to speak. [Although] I remember her and my dad speaking it to each other.

As a result of her mother's bad experiences at school, Carol speaks only a few words of Sm'algyax. In addition to her own negative experiences of using her Native language in school, Carol's mother may have been influenced by prevailing notions about language learning of the era. During the 1940s linguists began to hypothesize that problems in second-language

Carol Sam with older sister Stella, Port Essington, circa 1961.
Courtesy of Carol Sam.

learning were mainly attributable to interference from one's first language.
When the "contrastive hypothesis" became popular orthodoxy in the field
of second-language teaching during the mid-1950s, educators often encouraged parents not to expose children to their Native language lest it inhibit
the learning of English.[21]

Although Carol's parents made efforts to sever their children from their
native language, they found it harder to stay away from Port Essington.
Carol remembered making five summer trips to her birthplace. Her father
would board up the family home at Kitsumkalum, and they would travel
by train to Port Edward, before sailing on to Port Essington in her father's
fishing boat. Others who travelled to Port Essington in the summer included her mom's sister and husband. Carol recalled that they were hard
workers who lived and laboured in Port Edward for the winter but fished
for much of the summer season: "[My aunt] was such a strict task master.
We couldn't just laze around and enjoy the quiet. So she had us out there

packing wood, lumber ... Yeah, [she] was a hard worker. She still is.
She never ever believed in just taking a rest and enjoying the day." The
natural beauty of Port Essington and its surroundings was very appealing
to Carol. Sailing up the Ocstall River with family one day, Carol was
impressed by the vast mountains on either side of the river.[22] When she
learned that lunch would consist of sandwiches that she did not like, she
threw one overboard and discovered that the river was clear enough that
she could see the sandwich hit bottom many metres down.

Despite having fond memories of the people and landscape of Port
Essington, Carol felt there were drawbacks too. The town lacked electricity,
running water, and flush toilets.

> What I remember from when I went, when I was there, beside our house
> there was a store or something, an old store that was there and we just used
> a bucket. And then I remember my mom having to take that, and she would
> walk down to the [northeast] end [of town] where the BA [British-American
> Cannery] was ... and that's where she would dump it.

The lack of readily available water made fighting fires difficult. Although
Carol was not quite two years old when the first fire ravaged Port Essington, she swore that she could remember it. Her siblings and cousins
encountered the rapidly spreading flames as they pushed Carol in her
buggy. She remembered seeing the flames and, as a result, has developed
a fear of fire and even candles.

> When the power goes out and we have to light candles, I clean the table
> right off and put them in the safest place possible. I don't like it when
> the kids try to take candles in the bedrooms. If I smell smoke, I kick
> my husband out of bed and make him run around the house. I swear I
> remember it.

For Carol, the move to Kitsumkalum was somewhat traumatic, particularly attending school in Grade 1: "We had to go to the Kalum School,
where the school district buildings are [now], and I remember crying. It
seemed to me every day – it probably was every day ... I hated that
teacher that I had. I don't even remember her name but I didn't like
her. I didn't like the school. It was just ..." Unable to complete her sen-
tence, Carol noted that no one in the family was happy with the children
attending Kalum School. Soon after, a move to Riverside School proved
beneficial.

New teachers ... everything. It was so great. It was a really good school.
They had a different way of teaching. They were really strict and ... I was
scared of anybody and anything. I hid behind my mama's skirts. [But] I
had a really, really good relationship with one of the teachers there. He
was great. I never had him for a teacher. But he pulled me out of myself
and got me to join a choir of all things. And we went and performed out
on the street, and it was like, "Whoa!" I couldn't have done that before
then. And then plus, in Grade 7, I had the most wonderful teacher ever ...
Mr. Sheppard who was the vice-principal ... We all had heard he was so
scary and mean. He was the best teacher I ever had. He was not scary and
mean. He listened to you ... He liked all the students and treated us well.
Well, I think I was kind of his pet ... He was just a really nice teacher. I
truly believe that in the first few years of your life, in school life, if you have
really good teachers, you'll go all the way. But if you don't, oh, you're ...
not gonna wanna go.

Carol recalled the teachers building good relationships with the pupils
and participating in lots of intramural activities such as noon hour staff-
student basketball challenges. Carol was the first in her family to graduate
from high school, after which she spent six months working at a Canada
Employment Centre in Terrace. She married at eighteen and began her
family soon after. She is the mother of six children and grandmother to
eight others.[23]
Reflecting on her education, both formal and traditional, she advised
that young people listen to their mother because "she knows everything."

When I first got pregnant, my mom filled my ears with, "Okay, you have
to do this, you have to do that," such as keeping schedules for napping and
feeding. I did everything she said, and it was so awesome. My kids are really
well behaved, they're really good ... and that was because I listened to my
mother. I did what she told me to do ... [Mom stressed] the importance
of being a family. Not so much in words – just the way she behaved, like
just her actions and stuff. I remember [cousins] coming to stay with us.
They came and lived with us. We had a three-bedroom little tiny house.
Mom had six kids and then [cousins] came and stayed with us too.

Carol spent most of her childhood in Kitsumkalum and Terrace. Yet
her most significant learning came from elders, such as her mother, who
taught her enduring cultural values such as generosity, kindness, how to
mother, and how to make family a priority.

Carol Sam with younger brother Jim, Kitsumkalum, August 2010. *Photo by Helen Raptis.*

My kids, they have their moments and stuff, but when it comes right down to it, they all stick together. [When singer] Buffy Ste. Marie was here, the whole family went and we all sat together, and that's just the way it always happens. If there's a feast going on, if there's something going on, my kids all gravitate, they all come and sit where we're sitting.

JIM ROBERTS

Having spent little time fishing and hunting, Jim Roberts noted that he "wasn't really raised for the traditional parts of the Tsimshian life."[24] Born at Terrace in 1968, Jim felt that when he was a child, his parents shielded him somewhat from the harsher aspects of the traditional Tsimshian livelihood.

My dad used to shelter me quite a bit. I think he'd probably seen the bad side of the Skeena River a lot. Lives lost. A lot of boating accidents, and ... I used to hear stories about people's lives changing because of loss of a life

... People would turn to alcoholism to cope with it. Used to see people when I was a kid who were heavily into alcohol.

As a young man, Jim enrolled in a business administration course hosted by Kitsumkalum in partnership with Northwest Community College. Parts of the course dealt with life skills, such as understanding how people become addicted to drugs and alcohol: "We went to workshops on grieving and healing. That was one of the things that I learnt, how people get into drugs and alcohol. There's usually a reason, don't just judge them ... Usually, it stems from some things that hurt them throughout their life. I guess that gave me an understanding for some people." In addition to helping Jim understand the nature of addiction, these workshops reinforced his cautious views about fishing and hunting in the wilderness of the Pacific Northwest.

Jim did not learn to speak Sm'algyax because although his parents used it to communicate with each other, they addressed the children in English. When Jim was in his late teens, the people of Kitsumkalum had revived some of their long-suppressed cultural traditions, such as feasting, dancing, and drumming. This revival was launched under the leadership of his uncle Clifford, whose story is featured in Chapter 4. Yet Jim considered himself too old to partake fully in these revitalization efforts – although his own children have participated with his strong encouragement.

The gap between Jim and his Tsimshian heritage was partially fostered by his experiences with formal schooling. He entered Terrace's Parkside Elementary School in 1973, the year that British Columbia legislated mandatory kindergarten and abolished the use of corporal punishment, commonly known as "the strap."[25] As a result, Jim was able to evade the types of punishment administered to his elders and siblings. Nevertheless, Jim remembered the pain of being teased by fellow pupils for being a "wagon burner" and having to attend classes with a few teachers who were less than fond of Native children. He said that a turning point occurred for him when he attended a new school in Grade 5. A guest speaker had been invited to address the student body at a whole-school assembly. The topic of discussion was Native peoples, and at one point the speaker asked all those of Native ancestry to stand up. Although Jim initially felt ashamed and was not going to stand up, he noted that others seemed proud to be singled out. From that point forward, he no longer felt ashamed of his heritage.

Jim had somewhat fonder memories of high school, where his teachers put him on an academic route even though he had not selected it: "Well, I used to wonder why they would put me in the academic [track] ... And

they'd say, 'It was because of the test you took at the end of the year.'"
Unfortunately, Jim was unable to imagine how his academic skills could
help him to establish a future career. Since his cousin was a mechanic, this
was the only option to which he gave much consideration. Yet Jim never
pursued this route by enrolling in the necessary classes, partly due to the
discrimination exhibited by school officials.

> Grade 8, I was speaking with the counsellor. It was supposed to be about
> what I wanted to be for my future. And he was asking me if I fish and if
> I hunt ... I said, "Well, no, I don't do that" ... I never really had an interest
> in killing animals ... Just can't do that ... Kind of seemed odd for him to
> categorize me like that.

Some of the discrimination that Jim experienced was more overt.

> A teacher was trying to fight with me one day because in Grade 10 we passed
> each other in the hall, and he stuck his elbow out and hit me. He sent me
> to the office over it ... And he gave them his version of what happened,
> and it didn't really go over so well. I figured that if they're going to try to
> start physically fighting with me, I don't want to be here anymore. And
> then I think, because from that instance, I think it was maybe about a month
> later, the principal walked by and bumped into me pretty aggressively, and
> he was probably almost a foot taller than me. And he was using his size to
> intimidate me.

Jim even recalled experiencing discrimination at high school from fellow
students and witnessing it being wielded against others: "[Terrace] had
two or three arcade pool halls where all the teenagers hung out. And there
was a lot of fighting."
Nevertheless, Jim remembered some teachers who inspired him, illustrating the important role that teachers play in children's lives.[26]

> My kindergarten teacher ... had a good heart. So you could feel that through
> the way she treated everybody. And then I had a Grade 5 teacher [who
> would] push you to use manners. And I felt that was really valuable ... We
> [once] had a PE [physical education] teacher ... I guess he had the mentality
> that if your body was in shape, then your mind was in shape to learn. So
> he used to push us to do exercises. And we'd feel like we were gonna die
> from being tired ... So I enjoyed that and then I got into weight lifting the
> following year with my friends.

As an adult, Jim first found a job helping to construct the fire hall at Kitsumkalum. After a few months, one of his brothers-in-law convinced him to try logging, which Jim described as "the backbone of Terrace at the time."

> I thought I did well ... being a dropout and still making a lot of money. And ... I found out that there were quite a few guys that got a Grade 12 diploma, and they were still logging. It was a hard life, so ... we used to wonder why would someone who graduated go logging? The money, I guess.

Jim logged for approximately five years, after which he assumed work at the Kitsumkalum Salmonid Enhancement Development Project, located across from Pine Lake. But by 2001 the hatchery had shut down, and Jim was taken on at the Kitsumkalum Fishery Program as a catch monitor and technician.

> We travel along the Skeena River from Ferry Island down through Kwinitsa River and down where band members fish. And at that time, nonband members were allowed to fish in the area. So you just travel, interviewing them and compiling the data [on numbers of fish caught] ... and have it generated into reports for Fisheries and Oceans ... And now I'm more involved in the office side of it.

Jim felt fortunate to have learned solid values from a number of role models in his life.

> I think I learned a little from probably a lot of people I know, particularly my dad ... And my uncles. They taught me things throughout the years ... [One] was telling me always [to] pay attention to what other people are doing ... workwise. He said you learn from them. He said, "Pay attention to older people. They always know from their experience. You can learn a lot from them. When they talk, listen to what they're saying."

Jim noted that he also learned good values from difficult life experiences. Without cable television or many childhood diversions at Kitsumkalum, Jim got into mischief in Terrace at a young age.

> I was about seven or eight when I started hanging around with the guys who were about sixteen or seventeen. I got caught shoplifting when I was eight. I was stealing little Matchbox cars, and I had a skin-tight jean jacket

on and I stuck a whole bunch in there ... I guess a guy walked by and
noticed ... They took me in the backroom and they got my name, phone
number, parents' information. Told me go right home or they'll call the
cops on me. I took off. So that put an end to that lifestyle ... The guilt I
felt ... I never stole again. They never told my parents. [But] that was a
valuable lesson. Learning not to steal.

Jim's story of shoplifting illustrates the degree to which children's anonymity in large towns enabled the kinds of behaviour that would have been
prevented in small communities such as Port Essington, where – as Harvey
noted – everyone knew everyone. I return to the notion of anonymity in
Chapter 6 within the context of discrimination and schooling.

Reflecting on his own formal education, Jim believed that the subjects
of math and English had been particularly useful in preparing him for the
fisheries work he does today. He has stressed to his children the importance of getting an education while young so as not to have future regrets.
He felt that schools have changed considerably since he was a student and
expressed satisfaction with the better environments in which his children
are being taught. In particular, he has appreciated the cultural skills that
his daughters are learning at school in Haida Gwaii:[27] "They like doing
things like button blankets, and they're learning to speak Haida at school,
so they're keeping in touch. My son [at Kitsumkalum] ... I don't think he
really has been exposed to much. When he was a kid, he was involved with
the dancing here. But then [the community] stopped [offering] the dancing
... Not sure why." Jim acknowledged the difficulty of influencing young
people's lives once they become teenagers. As is the case with many teenagers across the Western world, when Jim's son reached fourteen, "he had
his mind set" on how to live his life – not unlike Jim himself at that age.

THE STORIES CONSTRUCTED from the recollections of the post-1950s
generation are as significant for what is spoken explicitly as for what is
not. Aside from Don's narrative – and to a lesser extent that of Steve – the
younger generation's recollections were relatively silent on relationships
between land and the Tsimshian people, traditional Tsimshian teachings,
and exposure to the Tsimshian culture and language (Sm'algyax). Interestingly, the younger generation's estrangement from their culture and
language was linked to the spatial and temporal segregation that occurred
after community members moved from Port Essington to Kitsumkalum.
To attend school in Terrace, the students became segregated in time and
space from their elders, a situation that prevented the youngsters from

undergoing traditional Tsimshian learning, including cultural and language practices. In none of the five stories did the interviewees discuss learning Sm'algyax or cultural traditions.

By the twentieth century, provincial game and land laws were increasingly pushing Aboriginal people out of their subsistence lifestyles, as economies of scale afforded fewer but larger companies a greater market share of British Columbia's resources.[28] Tsimshian men increasingly sought full-time (i.e., nonseasonal) work, with the result that fewer fathers and uncles could devote time to initiating their sons and nephews into the traditional pursuits of hunting, fishing, and resource management. Since Don learned these skills from his father and uncles, he continues to use them to provide for the people of Kitsumkalum as both a fisherman and their chief. Born later, neither Richard, Steve, nor Jim learned these traditional skills, and none practises them to this day. Indeed, Jim's observation that his lack of cable television caused him to get into trouble illustrates the extent to which his free time failed to connect to familial or ancestral pursuits.

With fewer traditionally procured foods to preserve, Tsimshian women increasingly engaged in other paid work, which explains why Carol never benefited from her elders' knowledge and skills with respect to food preparation. Without the chance to learn Tsimshian land-based traditions, participants from the post-1950s generation focused their stories more narrowly on formal schooling than on education as a broader, "lifelong continuum of experience gleaned from interaction with one another, with all of nature (seen and unseen), as well as with all of the cosmos."[29] Within one generation, Tsimshian education transitioned from a broad notion of lifelong experiences to a narrower concept focused almost solely on formal schooling.

Although participants from the younger generation reported understanding their parents' decisions not to raise their families "in the Tsimshian way," they were also saddened that their elders' experiences with discrimination had prompted these decisions. Ironically, their parents' choices not to raise their families "in the Tsimshian way" could not protect the children from their own encounters with discrimination.

Carol was the only one of the five interviewed who had graduated and who reported mainly positive experiences in the schools of Terrace. Not surprisingly, she attributed her positive educational journey to two influential teachers who served as respectful role models. Yet Carol was alone in establishing positive relationships with these teachers.

Nevertheless, this generation's stories indicate that today, six decades after the federal government officially implemented a policy of integrated education, school climates are becoming increasingly more hospitable to Indigenous children. A case in point is Richard, who hated school but whose daughter recently found success due to the positive atmosphere established by the teachers at Parkside Alternative School in Terrace. It is important to note, however, that alternative schools can establish more supportive relations between faculty and students due to their small sizes and low teacher-student ratios. Discriminatory acts are more easily perpetrated in the anonymity afforded by typically large public high schools.[30] The importance of teachers building good personal relations with First Nations children cannot be overemphasized.[31] After a century of ill-fated education policies for Indigenous children, it behooves us as a society to make changes to schools' infrastructures in order to allow for more personal settings.

Despite the hardships that members of the younger generation faced, they have transitioned successfully to adulthood while struggling to maintain their places in the wage economy as British Columbia hurtles into a globalized world. Interestingly, their experiences with physical and cultural displacement have influenced them to reclaim their heritage for themselves and for their children. At the same time as they encourage their children to embrace their language and culture, those of this generation have also pressed their children to set high aspirations for formal schooling. In a sense, the generation schooled from the late 1950s into the 1970s occupies a liminal or "in-between" space that bridges two eras: their childhoods, during which they were prevented from inheriting their Tsimshian heritage, and the childhoods of their offspring, who are learning to walk in two cultural and linguistic worlds, much like the elders of the 1930s and 1940s. The younger generation's stories reflect displacement and dispossession leading to cultural and linguistic dormancy, much like the autumn seed claimed by the snow of which Marie Battiste speaks.[32] Yet their negative experiences have helped motivate them to revitalize the language and cultural traditions of the Tsimshian community at Kitsumkalum.

6

Stability and Change: Education and Schooling across Time and Space

THE REFLECTIONS OF THESE two generations of Tsimshian bring to light and highlight the forces of stability and change in education and schooling across time and space and hold answers to the five key questions that inform this book: How has Tsimshian education changed over time and place? What has remained stable? What factors have prompted stability and change? How was education – both informal and formal – experienced by the children who were being educated? What impacts have their educational experiences had on their adult lives overall?

TRADITIONAL VERSUS WESTERN EDUCATION

Documentary sources exposed many differences between traditional Tsimshian education and Western-style schooling introduced by missionaries during the nineteenth century. First and foremost, formal schooling imposed a mandatory curriculum that required all children to demonstrate mastery of the same content between Grades 1 and 8, after which only the most academically endowed could continue their studies at residential or high school. Today, youngsters must still master a uniform curriculum until the age of at least sixteen, at which point they may drop out of school. Formal schooling differs significantly from traditional Tsimshian ways of learning, where the mastery of knowledge and skills depends on gender, age, and individual talent or inclination.[1]

Formal, Western-style schooling also segregated learners from their community in specially designated buildings for up to six or more hours a day. By contrast, within traditional Indigenous cultures, education was embedded within daily comings and goings of the community.[2] By learning skills such as hunting, fishing, weaving, and preserving food, children could see the immediate applications of the knowledge, abilities, and values that they were acquiring. This was not always the case with formal schooling, where children had to assume that the knowledge and skills they were learning would have a delayed, long-term application.

Traditional Tsimshian education also differed from formal schooling with respect to who delivered and oversaw the learning. In traditional Tsimshian society, youngsters' first "teachers" were usually family members: parents, aunts, uncles, and grandparents. Thus education hinged on relationships. Due to the bonds of caring and trust that developed between adult and child, First Nations elders were careful to avoid damaging the learner's self-esteem. As was the case among other First Nations, the Tsimshian did not consider "failure" to be a viable outcome of learning since parents and elders did not formally assess youngsters' learning.[3] Indeed, "self-evaluation" was expected of children as part of their learning processes.[4] Such was not the case at the day school, where students were regularly evaluated without regard for the consequences on their morale.

In formal school settings, both teacher and student transiency work against children's holistic development by blocking the establishment of tight relational bonds.[5] In her study of women who taught on American reserves in the early twentieth century, Patricia Carter notes that such employment represented one of the many ways that women of the time could expand their "cultural, social, and geographic horizons."[6] Nevertheless, teachers' aspirations for adventure ran head-on into the problems presented by a large bureaucracy attempting to oversee from afar hundreds of schools in mostly rural areas. Like many remote schools of the time, Port Essington Indian Day School shared many of these problems, including a high rate of teacher turnover, isolation, inadequate housing, poor salaries, and irregular pupil attendance. Yet, over its history, the day school employed fewer teachers, the total being fifteen, than did the public school, at twenty-two, indicating that transiency was not a challenge only for the Indian day schools.

This study indicates that teacher transiency at Port Essington Indian Day School had less to do with teachers' unwillingness to teach on rural reserves than with the negative effects of self-interested church officials, neglectful federal government authorities, and overly idealistic school inspectors. James R. Miller argues in *Shingwauk's Vision*, his seminal book on the history of Native residential schooling, that "three distinct interest groups" – the church, government officials, and Native communities – intersected in creating and maintaining these schools.[7] In the case of the day school at Port Essington, the three competing constituencies were government bureaucrats, church officials, and teachers. Whereas teachers continually advocated for adequate accommodation and fair treatment, church officials lobbied for a residential school and endured a high rate of teacher turnover in the hopes of securing male missionaries rather than women as teachers. These diverse agendas led to unstable relationships between the day school teachers and their students, highlighting a key difference between Indigenous and non-Indigenous education. Contemporary Indigenous educators continue to lament instructor turnover, as it prevents teachers from fully integrating into Indigenous communities.[8] Yet it would be wrong to suggest that factors such as turnover inhibited all students from succeeding academically. As early as 1935, Port Essington's Edward Bolton was the first Indigenous day school student to pass the province's high school entrance examination, and he took up his studies at Prince Rupert's King Edward High School in the fall of that year.

The role played by Methodist Church authorities in Port Essington provides an interesting counternarrative to that of the oppressive church officials who administered Canada's residential schools. Historian E. Brian Titley has noted that Canadian missionaries who laid claim to a specific Indigenous community tended to assume the rights of nominating and hiring teachers.[9] This was the case until the 1920s, when Port Essington's Methodist church was strong and could attract interested missionary teachers. By the late 1920s, however, the church's influence had weakened considerably. Government authorities increasingly assumed the roles once played by church officials – particularly with respect to interacting with teachers. Although the archival record does not explicitly indicate this, it is possible that government officials may also have increased their presence at Port Essington due to concerns about church officials' conduct. Examples of such behaviour include the Reverend Raley forgetting to instruct Fanny Noble to begin the school year in August 1913 and the church's decision to hire Roy Vannatter, who was not a certified teacher and had a criminal record.

Despite their forced involvement with hiring and/or dismissing teachers, authorities of the Department of Indian Affairs in Ottawa seemed to want as little interaction as possible with the school's daily dealings. This is hardly surprising given the classical liberal ideology that characterized the era. Indeed, officials' dealings reflected a view that each individual was capable of and should be left to make one's own way in life.[10] The arm's-length attitude that Ottawa's officials adopted regarding the school's dilemmas may also have been rooted in what several scholars have noted as the "prevailing belief" among Indian Affairs personnel "in the superiority of white civilization."[11] In the words of Carleton social work professor Hugh Shewell, many of the department's employees were "unabashed British imperialists, 'faithful and obedient' civil servants unswerving in their dedication to the task, which was to subjugate Indians and assimilate them into Canadian society."[12] As Brian Titley has also pointed out, appointment to the administrative echelons of Indian Affairs often had more to do with political patronage than with one's merit.[13]

Historians have suggested that teachers in Aboriginal schools were "with rare exceptions untrained."[14] Yet, despite poor salaries and living conditions, the teachers hired at Port Essington Indian Day School were generally well educated.[15] Beginning with Dorothy Deane in 1929, all of the teachers subsequently employed at the school – aside from Roy Vannatter – had at least a second-class teaching certificate and several years of experience, often in public schools. Were Port Essington teachers anomalous or were day school teachers in general better educated than their residential school counterparts? Vannatter's tenure at the school raises other important questions: How and why was Vannatter appointed when he had previous criminal convictions and no apparent teaching credentials? Were such hirings commonplace among the day schools? Only future day school research can provide answers to these questions.

The documentary evidence about education at Port Essington tells us little about how students experienced that education. However, the voices of the participants, gathered through oral interviews, illustrate the varied ways that traditional Tsimshian education and formal schooling were experienced by individuals over time. To a certain extent, the participants' broad – sometimes circuitous – recollections were prompted by the wide-ranging research questions framing this study: How has Tsimshian education changed over time and place? What has remained stable? What factors have prompted stability and change? How was education – both informal and formal – experienced by the children who were being educated? What impacts have their educational experiences had on their adult lives overall? Given the parameters set by these research questions, the participants' educational recollections also connected to "individual actions, emotions, and outcomes" that were, to some degree, "idiosyncratic or unique."[16]

Despite this fact, there are several themes that link the individual stories both within and across the generations.

THEMES FROM THE PRE-1950S GENERATION

Several themes emerge as noteworthy in the narratives of Mildred, Wally, Sam, Verna, Clifford, Harvey, and Charlotte. The first is a broad, multi-faceted view of education that reaches beyond the narrow notion of formal schooling. The second is how the geographic environment and a sense of place shaped the elders' notions of self. The third is the impact, both positive and negative, of formal schooling on Tsimshian culture and language. The fourth is the importance of building good relationships between students and teachers. The fifth is that, as numerous historians have argued, decisions and policies impacting the lives of Aboriginal peoples have not only been inconsistent over time but also oppressive, largely due to disinterest or lack of awareness among government officials and self-interested church organizations.[17] And the final theme is how the participants navigated through disruptive and discriminatory policies and came to resist oppression while developing a solid sense of agency that carried them through their adolescence and into the world of work. Each of these themes is discussed in the following paragraphs.

During their early childhood, the generation of learners who began their schooling at Port Essington Indian Day School prior to the 1950s walked in two distinct cultural spheres: on the one hand, the traditional hunter-gatherer lifestyle practised for millennia by their ancestors; on the other, the "white" world of the formal day school, where they were "Anglicized" through activities such as memorizing passages from *Dick and Jane* readers and singing "Silent Night." Although there has been a tendency among non-Indigenous scholars to equate education with formal schooling, the elders' experiences and perceptions reveal a broad, multi-faceted view of education encompassing both formal schooling and traditional Tsimshian learning. Their view of education as something far broader than schooling is in keeping with a worldwide Indigenous perspective that defines education as a "lifelong continuum of experience gleaned from interaction with one another, with all of nature (seen and unseen), as well as with all of the cosmos."[18] Furthermore, the elders in this study tell of forging adult identities that were rooted in traditional Tsimshian society, but they also adapted to mainstream Canadian culture. In short, this generation was essentially "bicultural."

Due to the forbidding physical environment surrounding Port Essington, traditional Tsimshian knowledge, skills, and values constituted formative aspects of the elders' educational experiences. Whether it was procuring and preserving food supplies or contributing respectfully to their communal life, the elders heeded their parents' warnings not to depend on the welfare of the Canadian government – perhaps none so well as Wally, who told the Indian Agent quite frankly that his services were neither necessary nor welcome. All seven of the elders credited their families' traditional teachings with being foundational to their development of self-reliance, respect, and a strong work ethic, qualities that served them well as they assumed adult roles in their communities and in the Canadian economic system. Indeed, the elders demonstrated outstanding levels of responsibility at very early ages, as illustrated, for example, by Verna's anecdote of cleaning house for a blind member of the community and Wally's story of cooking for the crew of his uncle's fishing vessel at age ten. Their stories support the contention of Emma LaRocque and others that "Native knowledge is informed by an ethical and spiritual basis which is intimately linked with Aboriginal people's relationships with each other and with the land and its resources."[19]

The role of the land as a formative aspect in the elders' lives cannot be overstated. As numerous Indigenous scholars have noted, "Indigenous people remain attached to an area of land over an extended period of time," and this connection is manifested through knowledge of sacred sites, uses of land-based resources, and songs and ceremonies, along with the language used to convey these.[20] One of the key themes to emerge from the day school generation's stories is the importance of the land to Tsimshian spiritual and physical survival. Verna, Mildred, and Clifford all mentioned the importance of Tsimshian spirituality in their recollections. Both Mildred and Verna also spoke extensively about the amount of time spent at camp procuring and preserving food and how this activity instilled in them a communal approach to living that meant respecting all of earth's creation and assisting others where needed. Mildred's story of Xbishuunt highlights the interrelationship between Indigenous peoples and all entities, both animate and inanimate in the ecosystem.[21] As Emma LaRocque, Margaret Kovach, and others have argued, it is the land upon which a particular tribe is grounded that gives birth to its epistemology.[22]

For Verna and Mildred, spirituality was framed both in terms of Indigenous epistemology as well as in religious terms, illustrating Susan Neylan's contention that early Christian missionary activity led not to a replacement of Tsimshian spiritual beliefs but to a melding of the two belief systems into a unique but robust manifestation of faith.[23] In a similar vein, Clifford referred to his grandmother's visionary capacity and observed that spiritual capabilities are not as widely practised among the Tsimshian today as they were in previous generations. His observation is borne out by the fact that the younger generation's stories failed to mention either Western religious practices or Tsimshian spirituality. It is not entirely surprising that Mildred and Verna equated spirituality with religion whereas Clifford spoke only of Tsimshian spirituality given that he was much younger than the other two. In addition, as the documentary evidence suggests, by the time Clifford was born, churches had already ceased to exercise much influence over Port Essington's population. By the 1950s neither religion nor spirituality were significant features of the community.

I cannot overstate the important roles played by the traditional Tsimshian skills and values transmitted to this generation by their families while out on the land. It is on the land that most of the members of this generation developed their sense of self, their work ethic, and their important cultural traditions. All seven of the participants from this generation had warm memories of Port Essington, with Wally arguing that it was one of the most beautiful places he had visited in his long career as a fisherman. Harvey, Wally, and Sam all talked of developing a love of the land and how it shaped their work ethic and values as they fished and logged. In this regard, the foundational aspects of Tsimshian education remained stable for this generation, as they inherited land-based traditions practised before them by their ancestors. In the words of Marie Battiste, "Indigenous knowledge is what directly links knowledge to place and to the relationships within that place."[24] The connection to the land was weaker for Clifford and Charlotte, who left Port Essington at an early age to attend residential school. Their experiences of physical distance and return to their Native land echo Indigenous researcher Neal McLeod's argument that when Indigenous peoples are removed from the land, they experience a form of spatial exile – a precursor to spiritual exile.[25] For Indigenous peoples, land is considered less "a thing in itself" than "a set of social relations" through which one travels and evolves as a person.[26]

Indigenous researchers have long stressed the importance of connection to land in the overall well-being of Indigenous individuals.[27] In *Protecting Indigenous Knowledge and Heritage,* Marie Battiste and James (Sa'ke'j) Youngblood Henderson have argued that within Indigenous worldviews, "knowledge is the expression of the vibrant relationships between the people, their ecosystems and other living beings and spirits that share their lands."[28] This interconnectedness is certainly evident in the narratives of the elders who were educated at Port Essington and walked confidently in two worlds: their traditional Tsimshian realm, which was tied to the land, and the colonial setting in which they were formally schooled. Yet, as Native Studies professor Andrea Bear Nicholas has rightly noted, "colonialism is not something that existed only at the time that Canada was a colony of either France or Great Britain ... It has continued into the present" in the form of school systems that narrowly define learning in terms of cognition that is separate from the kind of relational knowing described by Battiste and Henderson.[29]

Scholars of contemporary Indigenous education are increasingly advocating for more holistic approaches to learning in order to nourish each student's "learning spirit."[30] That is, educators must recognize that each learner is primarily motivated by a spirit that is inextricably linked to one's heart, mind, and body. Some researchers are actively promoting place-based education as a guiding construct for educational reform that seeks to decolonize mainstream education. For example, Michael Marker's research on the schooling experiences of Coast Salish youth during the 1960s and 1970s has convinced him that "present-day Indigenous decolonization movements are efforts to re-implant this place-based consciousness, [necessary for] reorienting and healing ... communities."[31]

Nevertheless, some Indigenous scholars argue that the physical connection to the land is less important than acknowledging that one's Aboriginality is "inherent and undiminished by distance from home."[32] They argue that what enhances one's inherent sense of indigeneity is not necessarily one's ties to territory but the kinship networks that sustain one's inner identity. These two opposing views open new lines for future inquiry about how Indigenous students can maintain elements of cultural identity while living at a distance from their communities.

Most of the elders interviewed for this study felt that their formal education experiences were less instrumental than their traditional Tsimshian learning in shaping their adult lives. The elders' stories also reveal the negative effects of the day school on Tsimshian culture and language. As Clifford's discussion of his grandmother's generation illustrates, overt ceremonial practices, such as the potlatch, had disappeared from the Port Essington area by the early 1900s. This is not surprising given that the federal government had forbidden it since 1884. It appears, however, that use of the Sm'algyax language declined most precipitously after the 1940s. Although five of the seven elders were raised using Sm'algyax, their children are not fluent speakers. The elders' decisions not to raise their children with Sm'algyax were precipitated by their own negative school experiences, such as Miss Lau's forcing Mildred to write "I must not speak Indian" up to 500 times. If, as Andrea Bear Nicholas has observed, "native languages have suffered the worse losses since the implementation of integration,"[33] then the postwar era of integrated schooling merits further scholarly inquiry.

Yet it would be wrong to conclude that the elders' school experiences had less impact on them than on their offspring. Clifford and Charlotte, the two participants who had completed high school, found their residential school experiences to be not only helpful but also superior to their day schooling at Port Essington. Clifford gained self-esteem by training as an expert marksman. The lapidary skills that he acquired from Ron Purvis provided a lucrative livelihood and recognition from the upper echelons of society. Charlotte's years at St. George's Residential School opened the door to postsecondary training that brought her a varied and interesting career, in the end enabling her to influence future generations of Tsimshian learners. Nevertheless, Clifford's own words remind us of what it takes to survive in a large boarding school setting.

> We had to learn how to survive [among roughly] 200 boys and 200 girls ... There had to be some rules. And you either chose to obey them or not obey them. And if you choose not to obey them, then you can live in hell. And I'd seen boys who chose not to obey them, and they lived in hell.

Charlotte's and Clifford's experiences offer interesting counternarratives to the dominant discourse characterizing residential schooling. It is important to acknowledge that the goal of Canada's residential school policy was to teach Indigenous children "Western ways" in order to enable them to assimilate eventually into mainstream society. This aim was premised on the assumption that the traditional lifestyles of Indigenous populations were disappearing under the pressures of a socially and economically modernizing nation. Yet, as various researchers have shown, the goal of the policy was not fully achieved. Rather than assimilating into Canadian society, young Indigenous people found themselves marginalized "both from the Canadian mainstream and from home environments."[34] Scholars have argued that a key aspect of the residential system that hindered Indigenous students' entry into mainstream Canadian society was the "half-day system." That is, students spent only half of their day involved in academic pursuits, with the remainder spent on work-related skill development like cooking and carpentry that assisted with the operation of

---

the school itself. In some cases, the entire "student body was out of class for long periods at critical times such as harvest."[35] As a result, Indigenous students found themselves academically far behind their non-Indigenous peers, making it difficult for residential students to transition to public high schools. Furthermore, long absences from family alienated students from their own cultures. But most devastating of all were the physical and psychological hardships that students experienced, ranging from strappings for minor infractions such as speaking their Native languages to enforced hunger, improperly diagnosed and often untreated illness, as well as sexual abuse.[36] The legacy of this segregated schooling continues to permeate Indigenous lives as entire communities struggle with the consequences of cultural disruption and family breakup.[37]

That Clifford and Charlotte preferred their residential school experiences to their schooling at Port Essington reminds us to resist the temptation to reduce all Indigenous experiences to generalized communal accounts.[38] Their narratives also align with the argument made by American researchers Clifford Trafzer, Jean Keller, and Lorene Sisquoc in *Boarding School Blues*. These authors have suggested that whereas many students were traumatized by their experiences, others thrived. Boarding schools, it has been argued, were complex places that ultimately "failed to destroy Indian identity," partly due to government neglect but mainly due to the agency exerted by Indigenous children and their families.[39]

Clifford's and Charlotte's successful perseverance in their studies partially reflected their abilities to establish good relationships with significant adults: in Clifford's case, with Ron Purvis; and in Charlotte's case, with the canon's wife. This raises another important theme pertaining to the education of the day school generation: the importance of teacher-student relationships. Establishing good teacher-pupil relations is much easier with low levels of either pupil or teacher transiency. Like rural schools in general, one of the greatest challenges faced by the Indian day schools was finding and attracting qualified teachers.[40] Over its history, Port Essington endured its share of teacher turnover, which seriously compromised the continuity of relations between teachers and pupils. This was less problematic at the residential schools, as illustrated by Clifford's and Charlotte's experiences. Again, accounts of the relationships that they struck with their teachers provide an interesting counternarrative to the prevailing literature on residential schools, which emphasizes their failure to educate students adequately due to the half-day system, as well as physical, emotional, and sexual abuse.[41]

Another important counternarrative to the residential school discourse can be found in the role played by the churches at Port Essington. Historians have illustrated that Canada's churches were an indispensible part of the "quest for souls and minds of Indian pupils" and that they had enormous influence not only on government policies and financial allocations but also on the actions of the civil service.[42] The interlocking relationship of church and state in the realm of residential schooling is well captured by sociologist David Nock, who has argued that "the missionary was not just an apostle of Christ, but a government-supported civil servant who directed or forced the ignoble savage into accepting the Anglo-Canadian civilization."[43]

Nevertheless, neither the documents reviewed nor the elders' narratives portray such a strong role for the churches at Port Essington. None of the elders' stories focused on denominational aspects of their schooling, although both Verna and Mildred mentioned the influence of the church on their lives more broadly. The documentary evidence presented in Chapter 3 illustrates that by the 1920s the Methodist Church no longer exerted much influence on the day school's affairs. In 1929 A.F. McKenzie, acting assistant deputy and secretary of Indian affairs, stepped in after Louise Fakeley's resignation and replaced her with Dorothy Deane.[44] It was District Inspector Gerald H. Barry, not church officials, who precipitated Elizabeth Pogson's resignation. Although Pogson was replaced by missionaries, their work was overseen by department inspectors, not church officials. Furthermore, when Roy Vannatter admitted to sexually abusing several of the day school children, it was Indian Affairs authorities, not church officials, who handled the matter. Although large-scale residential school studies have revealed the integral role played by Canada's churches, only future microlevel research can ascertain their influence over the operations of on-reserve day schools.

Stories from this generation also indicate the extent to which the participants felt the consequences of ill-conceived government legislation and policy. The negative impact of Canada's inclination to make Indian policies by "administrative fiat"[45] is clearly illustrated by Wally's story of how he was barred from attending the day school and required to move off the reserve. That he insisted on staying on the reserve with his uncle attests to the remarkable resistance that the Tsimshian manifested, even at very young ages. Indeed, the elders who told their stories could never be described as simply victims of circumstance. They actively resisted their oppressors in different ways. Irregular school attendance was one mechanism for

communicating to authorities that formal schooling was less valuable than
the education they received while fishing, hunting, and preparing food to
ensure their families' subsistence. Another example of active resistance can
be seen when Mildred held and broke the hickory stick with which Mrs.
Pogson attempted to beat her. Anishinaabeg researcher Leanne Simpson
has pointed out that resistance tends to be defined narrowly as "large-scale
political mobilization." This tendency has masked the important roles played
by individuals who have kept "languages, cultures, and systems of govern-
ance alive" in the face of policies and legislation that sought to eradicate
them.[46] Further historical inquiry into on-reserve Aboriginal schooling
has the potential to illuminate more profoundly the nature of Indigenous
children's resistance as well as their agency – that is, the "capacity to exercise
control over the nature and quality of one's life."[47]

Many of the forces acting upon the elders were overtly discriminatory,
as illustrated by Harvey's unending search for a classroom to settle in at
Booth Junior High School and his teacher's blunt message that regardless
of achievement, Harvey would fail his studies. In contrast, other forms of
discrimination were more covert. A good example of this is Charlotte's
invitation to the canon's home to learn important life skills, such as setting
a table. Not permitting Charlotte or her peers to dine with the family
subtly communicated the deep-rooted racism designating Indigenous
peoples as "lesser" than whites well into the mid-twentieth century.[48]
Interestingly, Charlotte remains thankful for the life skills she acquired
and either failed to – or chose not to – acknowledge the racist actions of
the canon's wife, illustrating what Marie Battiste refers to as cognitive
imperialism, or the "white-washing" of Indigenous minds to accept their
own status as inferior.[49]

Despite the discrimination to which these participants were exposed,
they remained resilient and transitioned successfully from their youth to
adulthood. All of the elders in this study entered the paid labour force at
an early age, and some maintained their place in the economy well beyond
the usual age of retirement. In this regard, their experiences provide important counternarratives to the notion that following the decline of the
fur trade, Aboriginal peoples became irrelevant to the Canadian economic
cycle.[50] Although this claim may accurately reflect situations in other parts
of Canada, it was not the case on the northwest coast of British Columbia.
Historian John Lutz has argued that during the nineteenth century, Aboriginal peoples in the province operated in several economies, including
capitalist, waged labour as well as noncapitalist, subsistence (or traditional)
work.[51] The elders' stories presented here suggest that these varied economic

modes continued among the Tsimshian well into the twentieth century until the death of Port Essington forced its inhabitants to relocate. However, as illustrated by the younger generation's stories in Chapter 5, Tsimshian involvement in dual economic modes weakened considerably after the 1950s.

What has been less well explored in the research literature are the reasons for Tsimshian participation in multimode economies. I argue that Tsimshian involvement in both the wage-labour and subsistence economies did not merely reflect personal choice but was also mandatory for survival. Indeed, the word "survival" appears repeatedly throughout this group's narratives, illustrating the extent to which policy decisions in one sphere of government can negatively impact the intentions of other government branches. The stories from this group of participants reflect historian John Leslie's comment that Indian Affairs suffered from a "splintered" vision, which hindered "adequate coordination and unity of action."[52] For instance, at the same time that government officials in the education branch funded Port Essington Indian Day School while lamenting poor attendance and allegedly unsatisfactory results, administrators in another branch vigorously encouraged Indians to be financially self-reliant, reflecting officials' almost obsessive fear of Indian dependency on the state.[53] Ironically, economic self-sufficiency dictated that school-aged Tsimshian children accompany their parents to traditional hunting and gathering sites to secure sustenance – which in turn precluded regular school attendance and therefore hampered satisfactory outcomes. "Splintered" – and at times arbitrary – policies clearly impeded the Indigenous children of Port Essington from achieving academically and pursuing professional careers that would have permitted them greater social mobility. In the words of John Lutz, "the 'state' was not a single entity, but rather, a hydra-headed being that pursued many different policies at once, some of which were at odds with others."[54] At the same time, government policies banning certain Indigenous traditions, combined with colonial schooling, prevented Tsimshian children from inheriting their cultural and linguistic birthright. Future research on the circumstances surrounding other Indian day schools and their communities may reveal the extent to which this has been the case elsewhere in Canada.

THEMES FROM THE POST-1950S GENERATION

The stories from the post-1950s generation in some ways overlap with but in other ways differ from those of the pre-1950s generation. Like their elders, the individuals who constituted the younger generation revealed both positive and negative experiences with schooling. However, unlike the elders, those of the younger generation framed their learning experiences almost exclusively within the Western notion of schooling rather than the broader Indigenous concept of education. Thus one of the most salient themes to arise in this group's narratives is that schooling was seen as synonymous with education. This finding is linked to the second important theme among the younger generation's stories: estrangement from their language, culture, environment, and spiritual roots. This alienation was caused, in part, by their physical distance and time spent away from their elders when the community members moved from Port Essington to Kitsumkalum. Related to this is a third important theme: the difficulty of establishing positive relationships between students and teachers. Fourth, although the stories from both groups of participants revealed elements of discrimination, the younger generation experienced more of it, likely due to their exposure to a larger and more diverse population of students and a lack of familiarity between teachers and the families of the children who attended Terrace schools. Fifth, those of the younger generation found their school experiences and transitions to adulthood framed by shifting government policies and theories about education that discouraged biculturalism and bilingualism as potential barriers to learning. Despite the hardships that the members of this generation faced, they too transitioned successfully to the world of work and parenthood, as did their elders. Each of these themes is analyzed below.

The most significant difference between the elders' recollections and those of the younger generation is the obvious cultural and linguistic rift that the younger participants experienced. None of the five who recounted their stories recalled learning the traditional Tsimshian language of Sm'algyax or overt cultural practices. Instead, they acknowledged their parents' decisions not to raise their families "in the Tsimshian way" due to their parents' own negative experiences both during school and within the broader society. By the time Steve was born in 1953, fewer families were taking their children "out to camp," where they hunted and fished for subsistence purposes. Provincial game and land laws were increasingly pushing Aboriginal people out of their subsistence economy,[55] which forced Tsimshian men to seek full-time (i.e., nonseasonal) paid employment in order to support their families. This left little time for traditional hunting, fishing, and food-preservation activities. The dual economies of subsistence and wage labour that developed during the nineteenth century had wound down for the Tsimshian by the mid-twentieth. Whereas Don, the eldest of this group, was taught as a child to fish and hunt by his father and uncles, others were not. As children, neither Carol, Richard, Steve, nor Jim benefited from their elders' knowledge and skills to the same extent that their ancestors had in prior generations. Without a connection to their ancestral land, the younger generation's stories fail to make reference to the spirituality that figured in the stories of Mildred, Verna, and Clifford. As a result, the very notion of Tsimshian education as lifelong learning gave way for this generation to a much narrower – more Westernized – concept of schooling.

The stories of the postwar generation are striking for their lack of discussion about the land and its impact during their formative years. The older generation's attachment to the land base at Port Essington does not seem to have been replicated at Kitsumkalum – among either generation. Lacking the opportunities to learn Tsimshian land-based traditions, participants from the younger generation focused their stories more narrowly on formal schooling than on the broader notion of education as a lifetime of experiential interactions with animate and inanimate beings as well as one's traditional lands and the broader cosmos.[56]

The relocation of the interviewees' families to Kitsumkalum played a role in severing the children from traditional Tsimshian learning. Since the reserve is approximately ten minutes by vehicle outside the town of Terrace, the children were required to board the school bus early in the morning and remained away from their homes and families for up to seven hours each day. This physical separation was very different from the setting in Port Essington, where children lived only two minutes by foot from their school. At lunch the proximity of their homes to the school allowed the children of Port Essington to walk home, where they would both eat and help to prepare traditional Tsimshian foods. As Mildred recounted, at least one member from within their large extended family would be on hand to walk with the children and oversee their comings and goings. Watching her children separated from the community in this way pained Mildred, but without a car, she and the children were at the mercy of the school bus. The profound effects of physical displacement on the conceptual understandings of the post-1950s generation lead me to support other scholars' advocacy for land-based approaches to learning as a means of regaining cultural and linguistic traditions.[57]

The most striking change in Tsimshian education revealed by this research is that the displacement of two generations of Tsimshian from one place, Port Essington, to another, Kitsumkalum, resulted in a significant loss of cultural and linguistic knowledge in a very short period of time:

one generation. This loss is deeply rooted in the younger generation's dislocation from their ancestral territories, which had enabled the older generation to develop Tsimshian knowledge, skills, and a sense of spirituality manifested in a deep attachment to the land. As Battiste and Henderson argue, "the core belief of Indigenous spirituality is that everything is alive, and Indigenous peoples seek spirituality through intimate communion with ecological biodiversity."[58]

The cultural and linguistic loss that characterized the upbringings of Steve, Richard, Jim, Carol, and – to a lesser extent – Don is unfortunate since research linking cultural affiliation with overall well-being has become plentiful in recent years. Studies indicate that healthy youth development is dependent upon the formation of cultural identity, defined as "recognition of one's attributes – beliefs, values, practices, norms, traditions, and heritage" – paired "with understanding how they are (and are not) reflected in one's self."[59] As early as 1972 the National Indian Brotherhood noted in its seminal policy piece *Indian Control of Indian Education* that "unless a child learns about the forces which shape him: the history of his people, their values and customs, their language, he will never really know himself or his potential as a human being."[60] Furthermore, culture and cognition are intertwined. According to Reuven Feuerstein, the foundation of all learning takes place when parents teach their children language and culture, thus enabling children to "learn how to learn." Parental "mediation" of those early learning encounters sets the pattern for future learning, including learning from teachers in formal settings.[61]

Although 60 percent of Indigenous children were enrolled in public schools in Canada by 1971, only 4 percent completed high school.[62] Not surprisingly, Steve, Richard, Jim, and Don all left school as soon as they could to undertake work in resource-based industries, which they viewed as being more relevant to life than their formal education. The physical separation between the schools at Terrace and the community at Kitsumkalum may have contributed to this view. For instance, one of Steve's fondest memories of schooling at Port Essington was class hikes with Mrs. McDougall, the teacher. Through such activities, Mrs. McDougall established relationships between the school and its social context. In this regard, she was ahead of her time since educational researchers today emphasize the importance of building such links.[63] Of course, Indigenous peoples have always espoused a holistic view of education as a communal social activity. In the words of Tewa researcher Gregory Cajete, what have "characterized and formed Indigenous education since time immemorial" are affective factors such as "subjective experience and observations," as well as "communal relationships," to name but a few key elements.[64] According to Battiste, today's "postcolonial quest for Indigenous peoples is to bring their knowledge and practices fully into their children's lives."[65] The task facing all educators and administrators is to "respectfully blend Indigenous epistemology and pedagogy with Euro-Canadian epistemology to create an innovative, ethical, trans-systemic Canadian educational system."[66]

The importance of teachers building good personal relations between themselves and First Nations children cannot be overemphasized.[67] Carol was the only one of the five interviewed from this generation who had graduated from high school in Terrace. Importantly, she attributed her success at school to two instrumental teachers who modelled respectful relations with their students. Like Charlotte and Clifford before her, Carol experienced strong teacher-student relationships that created a sense of place and belonging within an often alienating school structure. Carol insightfully observed that "in the first few years ... in school life, if you have really good teachers, you'll go all the way. But if you don't, oh, you're ... not gonna wanna go." This sentiment was echoed by Richard, who hated school himself but whose daughter found success within the warm, caring atmosphere of Parkside Alternative School. Nevertheless, developing close personal relations is much easier in alternative schools due to the small student population and low teacher-student ratios. In large, impersonal settings, discriminatory acts – both overt and covert – are much more easily perpetrated.[68] This dilemma is well illustrated by Jim's school experiences. Despite his good academic standing, his high school counsellor clearly expected him to pursue a life of fishing and hunting – not academics. Unfortunately, even after years of crosscultural education, teachers' negative prejudgment of Aboriginal children's abilities still forms a major barrier to academic success. To quote Lorna Williams, a specialist on Indigenous education, "Teachers have to believe that the students are capable of learning demanding and abstract ideas. Without that belief, teachers are likely to give up on the students too quickly."[69]

Throughout the 1960s and 1970s, the federal government increasingly promoted the integration of Indigenous children into provincial public schools. With more children forced to travel to attend school, the separation of Indian children from familial influences intensified, oftentimes with negative results.[70] Indeed, social scientists of the day believed that minority children would benefit from immersion in the mainstream language and culture due to what was perceived to be negative interference from the children's home language and culture.[71] Although such views later gave way to notions that favoured bilingualism, the damage was done.

Indigenous lawyer and social critic Harold Cardinal pointed out as early as 1977 that integration often benefited schools to a greater extent than the Indigenous children who attended them. Through the establishment of master tuition agreements, which transferred Canadian government funding to provincial coffers, federal authorities pursued a goal of "dumping the responsibility for Indian education, with its mounting costs, on provincial shoulders."[72] During the 1971 school year alone, the federal government allocated $9 million for capital costs to enable the expansion of British Columbian schools in order to accommodate increasing numbers of Indigenous children.[73] Not surprisingly, provincial officials welcomed the much-needed dollars.

Despite the hardships that the younger generation of participants faced, they too adapted well to adult life, although they had to work harder to maintain their places in British Columbia's changing wage economy, which was increasingly shaped by global economic shifts.[74] More importantly, however, their own experiences with physical displacement and with dispossession of their land and culture propelled them to begin reclaiming their heritage and to instil a desire for it in their children. For example, Jim expressed happiness that his daughters are learning to speak Haida and to make button blankets at their school in Haida Gwaii. As well, the participants of this generation recognized that global developments had altered local economies, and they had encouraged their own children to stay in school. Richard had gone to great lengths to ensure that his children were placed in schools that best met their needs. This helped his children to develop aspirations for higher education: "The older one, she wants to go through early childhood development, open up her own daycare. And then the youngest one, she either wants to be a vet or a fishery officer."

According to Marie Battiste, Indigenous peoples across Canada "recognize that they are in between stories ... The old story is one of destruction and pain, while the emerging one is that of the ongoing vitality of Aboriginal people from whose experience we can learn."[75] The stories of the generation schooled during the 1950s, 1960s, and into the 1970s illustrate their liminal or "in-between" status. As a bridge between two eras, their lives – despite illustrating more cultural and linguistic loss than the lives of their parents – have sowed the seeds of rebirth and revitalization that the Tsimshian are experiencing today.

SHIFTING IDEAS ACROSS TIME AND PLACE

Although there is a tendency for researchers to present Indigenous societies as monolithic and static, in reality all societies change over time.[76] The two generations of Tsimshian participants in this study had differing experiences, partially due to varying government policies enacted during the diverse social contexts in which they were schooled.

The "older" generation was schooled during the 1930s and 1940s, when classical liberal ideas dominated Canadian policy agendas and conceptions of citizenship. Classical liberal ideology posits that "each individual ought to be free both to join cooperatively with others and to compete with others to satisfy his or her wants and preferences."[77] These ideas sit alongside the broader view that "all individuals ... have an equal opportunity to compete for material prosperity and individual self-realization."[78] Such perspectives bestow a weak role upon the state. That is, a government operating within a classical liberal framework recognizes society's inherent inequality and refrains from intervening in the alleged free market of life. Within such a context, Indian Affairs officials involved themselves in the daily workings of Port Essington Indian Day School only under extraordinary circumstances.[79] Such circumstances included assistance with hiring teachers when church officials were desperate, as well as investigating Roy Vannatter on allegation of sexual abuse at the day school. Prior to the 1950s, Indian Affairs authorities were content to have Indigenous peoples live and work in their communities, where various religious denominations managed day schools paid for by the federal government. This arm's-length policy enabled the pre-1950s generation to be educated mainly in one place – Port Essington – where students also learned their language and cultural traditions from ancestors who had ties to the land surrounding them.

By the end of the Second World War, Canadian liberalism had shifted from a focus on political and economic matters to allegedly more ethical concerns.[80] During the war, the nation's social welfare system took root with the creation of various foundational federal programs such as Unemployment Insurance and Family Allowance.[81] Historians have argued that this era was marked by more concerted efforts on the part of government to support Indigenous youth in their efforts to integrate into Canada's social and economic fabric.[82] The emphasis on citizenship through integration was manifested in various policies, including integrated schooling, which government increasingly pursued during the postwar era.[83] Yet as the stories of the postwar generation illustrate, integration also meant being schooled far from homes and families. This precipitated

greater loss of Tsimshian language and culture among the younger generation than it did among the older. Unfortunately, shifting government
policy not only resulted in physical displacement and the loss of language
and culture but also exposed the children to levels of discrimination that
dampened their schooling aspirations.[84] Indeed, four out of the five interviewed dropped out of school and joined the workforce as soon as legally
possible.

The shift to postwar integrated schooling also occurred within a context
of financial austerity that had plagued Indian Affairs for almost a century.
In the words of historian Jim Miller, integration was the "latest nostrum
of a bureaucracy that had been without an effective policy for Native
education since the early years of the twentieth century."[85] During this
era, no official efforts were made to prepare teachers or students for integration.[86] Consequently, the narratives of this study's participants support
various critics' views that the integration policy meant that federal authorities simply offloaded the responsibility and attendant costs of educating
Indian children onto the provinces. Ironically, the federal government's
willingness to provide financial support to schools, while offloading matters of administration and pedagogy onto the provinces, perpetuated its
practice, begun in the late 1800s, of paying the bills for educational projects
undertaken "on the ground" by religious denominations across the country.
This raises an important issue pertaining to how the federal government
has fulfilled – or rather failed to fulfil – its responsibility to educate
Indigenous children in Canada. I agree with scholars such as Marie Battiste
who argue that the Canadian government has not maintained its obliga-
tion to ensure the adequate education of Indigenous peoples, as outlined
in the 1867 British North America Act and the 1876 Indian Act.[87]

MOVING FORWARD

Although the narratives presented in this study reflect events far away in
time and space, they provide rich guides for both educators and policy
makers charting the futures of Indigenous learners. The stories from
the participants in this study highlight the importance to Indigenous
peoples of conceiving of education as a broad, holistic undertaking that
builds students' cognitive, emotional, spiritual, and relational well-being.[88]
Consequently, schooling practices that focus solely on developing students' cognition will fall short of meeting the needs and desires of Indigenous children and their families. Schools that take a holistic view of

learning and incorporate traditional language and cultural components into their programs of study will help to maintain Indigenous well-being. Where possible, land-based teachings should be promoted as appropriate vehicles for fostering the growth of children's traditional languages and cultures.[89] Acquiring traditional linguistic and cultural skills helps children to take responsibility for their own learning journeys and to develop their sense of agency. However, none of these critical educational components can be achieved without first ensuring good relationships between students and teachers. Such relationships can flourish only in settings where teachers have high expectations of their Indigenous students and do not hold discriminatory views based on language or cultural biases.[90] In turn, the onus is on government officials to ensure that teacher-preparation programs, educational policies, and school-based regulations foster good pupil-teacher relationships in inclusive settings that operate using equitable school practices.

EDUCATION HAD MANY manifestations among the Tsimshian at Port Essington and Kitsumkalum over time. Members of the older generation were exposed to and retained more of their Tsimshian language and traditions than did those of the younger generation. Furthermore, in their recollections of their experiences, the elders maintained a broad view of education, which they saw as encompassing more than just formal schooling. That those of the younger generation framed their recollections within the parameters of Western-style schooling indicates the rapidity with which the Tsimshian experienced educational change from the 1940s to the 1970s.

The recollections of the two generations reveal several themes that characterized the experiences of both generations. These included cultural and language loss, the significance of place in Indigenous learning, the importance of teacher-pupil relationships, and the impact of disruptive government policies on multiple aspects of both generations' lives. These themes can animate a way forward for educators working with Indigenous children today.

MY JOURNEY TO EXPLORE Tsimshian education began in 2006 with the discovery of an archived 1947 class list announcing the closure of the Port Essington Indian Day School and the integration of its pupils into Port Essington Elementary School. Over the years, my search to more fully understand education among the Tsimshian has taken many more twists and turns than I anticipated. Nevertheless, the class list was a gift that united participants from Tsimshian communities in the northern reaches of the province with southern, non-Indigenous, urban researchers navigating a longer path to decolonize our minds, hearts, and souls.

Learning to work collaboratively with Indigenous communities is not a linear process; nor is it free of challenges. My research assistants and I found much help in the literature about best practices for working with and for Indigenous communities. But the terrain was bumpier than expected. Much of this kind of learning inevitably takes place at the moment when the researcher and the participant encounter one another. Such encounters are sometimes emotional; but they are never straightforward and always call for humility and judicious decision making. My hope is that, over time, more non-Indigenous researchers will share their own stories of both successes and challenges encountered while working to build respectful research relationships with Indigenous communities.

Epilogue

THE STORIES OF THESE two distinctive generations not only answer predetermined questions but also raise issues for future consideration. In particular, the extent of cultural and linguistic loss experienced by the Tsimshian raises questions pertaining to residential schooling and Canada's ongoing efforts at reparation and reconciliation.

The vast majority of historical literature on Indigenous education has focused almost exclusively on residential schools and their devastating legacy. Being removed from one's home at the age of six and, in some cases, not returning until age sixteen had monumental effects both on children individually and on communities collectively – not to mention the physical and emotional abuses meted out by various teachers and administrators.

Problems inherent in the system came to light as early as 1907, when Dr. Peter Bryce, the Department of Indian Affairs' chief medical officer, revealed the high mortality rates among students in Manitoba and the Northwest. Almost 100 years would pass before the Canadian government acknowledged the devastating effects of the ill-conceived residential schools policy. In 2005 Canada agreed to allocate $2 billion in reparations to residential school survivors. Three years later, the federal government issued an official apology to former residential school pupils for the schools' negative effects on Aboriginal culture, heritage, and language. Yet as Tsimshian reflections illustrate, not all students had negative experiences at residential school. Both Charlotte and Clifford credited their experiences at St. George's Residential School in Lytton with affording them opportunities that they would never have had at home in Port Essington.

According to Deena Rymhs, a professor of English at UBC, national reconciliation initiatives may function less as a way for nations to "re-imagine and perform" themselves than as a means of replacing one master narrative with another.[1] Rymhs has observed that whereas government attention and media coverage have left mainstream Canadians reeling in the shameful and tragic legacy of residential schooling, Indigenous scholars have used their writing to move forward. Works such as Basil Johnston's *Indian School Days* focus less on the tragedies and losses sustained by students than on their resilience and resistance to the authority of both church and state.[2]

Indeed, various scholars have recorded the multiple ways that residential students resisted their oppressors, from ridicule and nicknaming of teachers to failure to cooperate in class. Jim Miller recounts a story from Elkhorn School during the 1940s about several boys who secured themselves a healthy snack when they sprayed one of the school's pigs with water, causing it to freeze. When school officials decided to incinerate the pig, whose cause of death eluded them, the boys offered their assistance to dispose of the animal and roasted it for a snack instead.[3] In a case study of All Hallows School near Yale, British Columbia, which boarded both white and Indigenous girls, Jean Barman has noted that because education was not mandatory until the 1920s, people had "to decide themselves if they wanted a formal education."[4] In some cases, Indigenous peoples chose residential school for the skills it offered, such as reading and writing. In other instances, the school was a last resort due to parental illness, death, or dislocation. For example, one little girl was left on the school's doorstep with a note from her dying mother asking that her daughter be taken into the care of the All Hallows nuns. Barman also indicates that despite the challenges of transitioning to the school's foreign environment, former students tended to make good use of their education, with some graduates transitioning to domestic service and others becoming teachers in British Columbia's mission day schools.[5]

As is the case with residential school survivors, the educational journeys of Tsimshian students varied greatly across time and place. Their narratives remind us that "each person has a unique and personal journey that will yield to their learning."[6] Yet both the day schools prior to the Second World War and the public schools afterward also played important roles in eroding traditional Tsimshian learning and livelihood. Whether they were attending residential schools, day schools, or integrated public schools, Tsimshian students experienced the negative effects of ill-conceived government policies pertaining not only to schooling but also to the fabric of their individual and communal lives.

Their stories and experiences expose discrimination, linguistic and cultural dispossession, and estrangement from the land, whether it be Wally's experiences of being barred from Port Essington Indian Day School and the reserve upon which he lived because his mother lost her Native status or Jim's experience with a school counsellor directing him to take up fishing or hunting – despite his lack of interest and expertise. Nevertheless, it would be wrong to suggest that their stories are simply narratives about Indigenous victimization vis-à-vis Canadian society. Like many of their counterparts in residential settings, Tsimshian students not only survived but also thrived despite the challenges they faced as they manoeuvred through culturally foreign institutions called schools. The parallels among residential schooling, day schools, and postwar integrated schooling for Indigenous populations raise the thorny matter of national atonement for past transgressions.

Although the Canadian government and various religious organizations have issued apologies and reparations to the survivors of residential schooling, no such reparations or apologies have been issued to the children who grew up on reserves but whose culture, families, and languages were disrupted by oppressive government policies and decisions that circumscribed their daily lives in schools and beyond in the varied ways outlined in this study. These facts prompt an important question: is it the residential school system or the broader social policies and decisions of the Canadian government – in many domains, not just education – that are responsible for cultural disruption among Canada's First Nations peoples? In responding to this question, I and members of the Tsimshian nation agree with Stó:lō educator William Julius Mussell, who argues that the residential school system was just one plank in a larger colonization strategy that, by the mid-twentieth century, had devastated "all aspects of First Nations life – social, intellectual, spiritual, and physical."[7]

I also argue that government apologies and attempts at reparation with residential school survivors constitute necessary steps on a longer path to eventual reconciliation – or the re-establishment of negotiated, consultative relations. But they do not go far enough. In the words of Jim Miller, residential schools "were merely one important cog in a machine of cultural oppression and coercive change."[8] It is long past the time for Canadians to acknowledge the many debilitating policies and legislative acts that have not promoted "liberty or equality for First Nations people" but rather have

Port Essington shoreline today. With remnants of the boardwalk *(foreground)*, a boat *(middle)*, and dock pylons *(background)*. *Courtesy of Don Roberts Junior.*

negatively influenced "virtually every aspect of their lives from their economic strategies and adaptations, to their spirituality ... to their familial relationships" and beyond.[9]

Furthermore, I maintain that critical evaluations of the federal government's historical role in educating Indigenous peoples in multiple broad historical settings have been hampered by historians' almost singular focus on residential schooling. This is not to say that studies of residential school have not been critical to our understanding of Indigenous peoples in Canada. Nevertheless, scholars' and policy makers' main focus on the negative legacy of residential schooling has resulted in the distorted view that most Indigenous children were educated in such institutions until 1951, when revisions to the Indian Act legalized their entry into provincial schools. As Ken Coates has noted, more Indigenous children in Canada attended on-reserve day schools than boarding schools.[10] In British Columbia, for example, calculations indicate that day schools educated roughly 58 percent of Indigenous students, whereas residential schools accounted for roughly 42 percent.[11] In addition, chronic underfunding and culturally unwelcoming classrooms resulted in many Native children not attending school at all. In British Columbia, in 1945–46, of the 6,227 students aged seven to seventeen, only 3,478 (56 percent) attended school.[12]

Michael Marker has argued that scholars' focus on residential schooling has generated a "conflated" educational narrative that is problematic for another reason.[13] According to Marker, the postwar integration policy aggressively pursued by both American and Canadian government officials has been as destructive to Indigenous students' well-being as residential schools given that schools today continue to require children to "shake off the darkness" of their home cultures and adopt the liberal lifeways of their colonizers.[14] It seems that colonialism is alive and well in today's schools.[15] For these reasons, I invite historians to look beyond the shadow of the residential school and to explore broader notions of Indigenous education – across time and place – in order to create a more comprehensive historical portrait of Indigenous education.

Finally, the resilience that Tsimshian students showed as they transitioned from childhood into the adult world of work and parenthood is a testament to their strength. That they continue to "enable the autumn seed" by revitalizing dormant traditions, languages, spirituality, and values[16] bodes well for future reconciliation.

Notes

Chapter 1: A Class List and a Puzzle

1 Verna Inkster, interview by author, Kitsumkalum, British Columbia, January 30, 2010.

2 Emma LaRocque, *When the Other Is Me: Native Resistance Discourse, 1850–1990* (Winnipeg: University of Manitoba Press, 2010), 127.

3 Jean Barman, "Schooled for Inequality: The Education of British Columbia Aboriginal Children," in *Children, Teachers, and Schools in the History of British Columbia*, ed. Jean Barman, Neil Sutherland, and J. Donald Wilson (Calgary: Detselig, 1995), 57.

4 Ken Coates, "A Very Imperfect Means of Education: Indian Day Schools in the Yukon Territory," in *Indian Education in Canada*, vol. 1, *The Legacy*, ed. Jean Barman, Yvonne Hébert, and Don McCaskill (Vancouver: UBC Press, 1986), 147.

5 Between the 1930s and the 1970s, Canadians experienced economic devastation during the Depression; material rations and personal losses during the Second World War; the postwar development of the welfare state, followed by unbounded economic prosperity during the late 1950s and the 1960s, which came to an abrupt halt with runaway inflation and the oil embargo in the early 1970s. See Jean Barman, *The West beyond the West: A History of British Columbia* (Toronto: University of Toronto Press, 1991).

6 K. Tsianina Lomawaima and Teresa L. McCarty, *"To Remain an Indian": Lessons in Democracy from a Century of Native American Education* (New York: Teachers College Press, 2006), 20, emphasis in original.

7 Brenda Tsioniaon LaFrance, "Culturally Negotiated Education in First Nations Communities," in *Aboriginal Education: Fulfilling the Promise*, ed. Marlene Brant Castellano, Lynne Davis, and Louise Lahache (Vancouver: UBC Press, 2000), 101.

8 See, for example, the special thematic issue of *History of Education Quarterly* 54, 3 (2014).

9 John Tosh, *The Pursuit of History: Aims, Methods and New Directions in the Study of Modern History*, 3rd ed. (London: Longman, 1999), 37.

10 For more on the notion of surveillance, see Keith D. Smith, *Liberalism, Surveillance, and Resistance: Indigenous Communities in Western Canada, 1877–1927* (Edmonton: Athabasca University Press, 2009).

11 For information on Tsimshian social structure, see Viola E. Garfield, "Tsimshian Clan and Society," *University of Washington Publications in Anthropology* 7, 3 (1939): 167–340.

12 James A. McDonald, *People of the Robin: The Tsimshian of Kitsumkalum* (Edmonton: CCI Press and Alberta ACADRE Network, 2003), 8.

13 Wilson Duff, *The Indian History of British Columbia*, vol. 1, *The Impact of the White Man* (Victoria: Department of Recreation and Conservation, Province of British Columbia, 1964), 39; Examination of Indian Agent C.C. Perry of the Naas Agency at Victoria, *Royal Commission on Indian Affairs for the Province of British Columbia, 1913–1916*, December 16, 1915, 188, http://www.ubcic.bc.ca/Resources/ourhomesare/Testimonies2/index.html.

14 Richard G. Large, *The Skeena: River of Destiny* (Vancouver: Mitchell, 1957), 34–39; Ernest A. Harris, *Spokeshute: Skeena River Memory* (Vancouver: Orca, 1990), 23. Born in Ireland in 1837, Cunningham had joined the Church Missionary Society and was an assistant to William Duncan at Metlakatla for two years before accepting work with the Hudson's Bay Company. See also Robert M. Galois, "Colonial Encounters: The Worlds of Arthur Wellington Clah, 1855–1881," *BC Studies*, 115–16 (1997–98): 105–47.

15 The Skeena region reserves had been allotted, surveyed, and confirmed by 1892. Daniel Clayton, "Geographies of the Lower Skeena," *BC Studies*, 94 (1992): 51. Despite the willingness of some Tsimshian to take up Cunningham's "offer" of land, many resisted what they considered to be the appropriation of their land and in 1884 blocked land surveyors, forcing the Canadian government to send a gunboat to assist Indian Affairs officials. James A. McDonald, "Images of the Nineteenth-Century Economy of the Tsimshian," in *The Tsimshian: Images of the Past, Views for the Present*, ed. Margaret Seguin (Vancouver: UBC Press, 1984), 51. See also *Methodist Missionary Society Reports, 1884–85*, xxii, Bob Stewart Archives (BSA).

16 Kenneth Campbell, *Persistence and Change: A History of the Tsimsyen Nation* (Prince Rupert, BC: Tsimshian Nation and School District 52, 2005), 182–83; Jay Miller, "Feasting with the Southern Tsimshian," in *The Tsimshian: Images of the Past, Views for the Present*, ed. Margaret Seguin (Vancouver: UBC Press, 1984), 33.

17 Large, *Skeena*, 34–39; Ron Greene, "Robert Cunningham and Son of Skeena (Port Essington)," *British Columbia History* 42, 3 (2009): 24–27. The Indians from Kitsumkalum and Kitselas generally supplied fish for Cunningham's cannery. Minutes of the Port Essington meeting, September 25, 1915, *Royal Commission on Indian Affairs for the Province of British Columbia, 1913–1916*, 18, http://www.ubcic.bc.ca/Resources/ourhomesare/Testimonies2/index.html.

18 Walter Wicks, *Memories of the Skeena* (Seattle: Hancock House, 1976), 47–48; Sandra McHarg and Maureen Cassidy, *Early Days on the Skeena River* (Hazelton, BC: Northwest Community College, 1983), 24.

19 Nancy Robertson, "Port Essington: Only a Dream," *Canadian West*, 10 (1987): 158. By 1936 the permanent population included 165 Indians, 145 Japanese, and 55 "whites." "A Cruise among Historic Missions in Northern British Columbia," *Western Recorder* 37, 11 (1936): 4, BSA.

20 Information from a street map of Port Essington, registered at Victoria, October 17, 1893, Land Registry Office, courtesy of the Prince Rupert City and Regional Archives.

21 The origins of Port Essington Elementary School are unclear. Evidence suggests that it was established in the late 1890s.
22 Clayton, "Geographies of the Lower Skeena," 48.
23 Eileen Sutherland, "My Skeena Childhood," *BC Historical News* 36, 2 (2003): 7. The town even boasted the establishment of four newspapers.
24 Robertson, "Port Essington," 162; Walter Wicks Interview, July 20, 1961, 48, 48a, 49, T1194:0004, British Columbia Archives (BCA).
25 Large, *Skeena*, 43.
26 Wicks, *Memories of the Skeena*, 48. Despite significant Tsimshian opposition to land appropriation for laying the track, there is no evidence to suggest that Port Essington residents protested placing the terminus at Prince Rupert. James A. McDonald, "Bleeding Day and Night: The Construction of the Grand Trunk Pacific Railway across Tsimshian Reserve Lands," *Canadian Journal of Native Studies* 10, 1 (1990): 33–69; Frank Leonard, *A Thousand Blunders: The Grand Trunk Pacific Railway and Northern British Columbia* (Vancouver: UBC Press, 1996), 165–88.
27 Phylis Bowman, *Klondike of the Skeena* (Chilliwack, BC: Sunrise, 1982), 64.
28 Charles R. Menzies and Caroline F. Butler, "The Indigenous Foundation of the Resource Economy of BC's North Coast," *Labour/Le Travail* 61 (2008): 146; Dianne Newell, *Tangled Webs of History: Indians and the Law in Canada's Pacific Coast Fisheries* (Toronto: University of Toronto Press, 1993), 122.
29 Harris, *Spokeshute*, 200–2. *Minutes*, September 4, 1947, Prince Rupert School District (PRSD).
30 Peter Ward, "British Columbia and the Japanese Evacuation," *Canadian Historical Review* 57, 3 (1976): 289–308; Patricia Roy, "BC's Fear of Asians," in *A History of British Columbia: Selected Readings*, ed. Patricia Roy, 285–99 (Toronto: Copp Clark Pitman, 1989); Thomas Berger, "The Banished Japanese Canadians," in *Ethnic Canada*, ed. Leo Driedger, 374–94 (Toronto: Copp Clark Pitman, 1987); H.K. Hutchinson, "Dimensions of Ethnic Education: The Japanese in British Columbia, 1880–1940" (MA thesis, University of Victoria, 1972).
31 Bowman, *Klondike of the Skeena*, 68; British Columbia Department of Education, *Annual Report of the Public Schools of the Province of British Columbia (ARPS)*, 1940 and 1942.
32 Harris, *Spokeshute*, 229–34.
33 For details of the fires that destroyed Port Essington, see ibid., 230.
34 "Only Smoke Still Marks Site of Fishing Village," *Vancouver Sun*, July 6, 1961, Prince Rupert City and Regional Archives (PRCRA). See also, "The Ghosts Walk in This B.C. Town," *Vancouver Province*, May 3, 1958, PRCRA.
35 Norma V. Bennett, *Pioneer Legacy: Chronicles of the Lower Skeena River*, vol. 1 (Terrace, BC: Dr. R.E.M. Lee Hospital Foundation, 1997), 77.
36 Kate Rousmaniere, "Sixteen Years in a Classroom," in *Silences and Images: The Social History of the Classroom*, ed. Ian Grosvenor, Martin Lawn, and Kate Rousmaniere (New York: Peter Lang, 1999), 239.
37 LaRocque, *When the Other Is Me*, 142; Leslie Brown and Susan Strega, eds., *Research as Resistance: Critical Indigenous and Anti-oppressive Approaches* (Toronto: Canadian Scholars' Press, 2005), 11.
38 Philip Gardner, "Oral History in Education: Teacher's Memory and Teachers' History," *History of Education* 32, 2 (2003): 187.
39 Gillian Weiss, ed., with Pearl McKenzie, Pauline Coulthard, Charlene Tree, Bernie Sound, Valerie Bourne, and Brandi McLeod, *Trying to Get It Back: Indigenous Women, Education and Culture* (Waterloo, ON: Wilfrid Laurier University Press, 2000), 48.

40 Sarah Carter and Patricia McCormack, eds., *Recollecting: Lives of Aboriginal Women of the Canadian Northwest and Borderlands* (Edmonton: Athabasca University Press, 2011), 17. See also Donald A. Ritchie, *Doing Oral History: A Practical Guide* (Oxford: Oxford University Press, 2003), 19; and Bruce L. Berg and Howard Lune, *Qualitative Research Methods for the Social Sciences,* 8th ed. (Boston: Pearson, 2012), 318.

41 Angela Zusman, *Story Bridges: A Guide for Conducting Intergenerational Oral History Projects* (Walnut Creek, CA: Left Coast, 2010), 13.

42 For a critical discussion about the need for settlers to decolonize and heal ourselves, see Paulette Regan, *Unsettling the Settler Within: Indian Residential Schools, Truth Telling, and Reconciliation in Canada* (Vancouver: UBC Press, 2010).

43 Shawn Wilson, "Progressing towards an Indigenous Research Paradigm in Canada and Australia," *Canadian Journal of Native Education* 27, 2 (2003): 164; Brown and Strega, eds., *Research as Resistance,* 11.

44 See Judith C. Lapadat and Harold Janzen, "Collaborative Research in Northern Communities: Possibilities and Pitfalls," *BC Studies,* 104 (1994): 76.

45 Donald L. Fixico, *The American Indian Mind in a Linear World* (New York: Routledge, 2003), 8.

46 James A. McDonald, "The Tsimshian Protocols: Locating and Empowering Community-based Research," *Canadian Journal of Native Education* 28, 1–2 (2008): 82; Sandra Styres et al., "Walking in Two Worlds: Engaging the Space between Indigenous Community and Academia," *Canadian Journal of Education* 33, 3 (2010): 639–41.

47 K.P. Binda and Sharilyn Calliou, "Introduction: Situating the Puppet Masters," in *Aboriginal Education in Canada: A Study in Decolonization,* ed. K.P. Binda and Sharilyn Calliou (Mississauga, ON: Canadian Educators' Press, 2001), 2.

48 Leslie A. Robertson, with the Kwagu'l Gixsam Clan, *Standing Up with Ga'axsta'las: Jane Constance Cook and the Politics of Memory, Church, and Custom* (Vancouver: UBC Press, 2012), 26.

49 Ibid., 27. On the difficult relationship between researcher and research participants, see also Aaron Glass, "The Intention of Tradition: Contemporary Contexts and Contests of the Kwakwaka'wakw Hamat'sa Dance" (MA thesis, University of British Columbia, 1994), 2–18.

50 Shawn Wilson, "What Is an Indigenist Research Paradigm?" *Canadian Journal of Native Education* 30, 2 (2007): 193–95; Shawn Wilson, *Research Is Ceremony: Indigenous Research Methods* (Blackpoint, NS: Fernwood, 2008).

51 Julie Cruikshank, with Angela Sidney, Kitty Smith, and Annie Ned, *Life Lived Like a Story: Life Stories of Three Yukon Native Elders* (Vancouver: UBC Press, 1990), 14. See also Margaret Kovach, *Indigenous Methodologies: Characteristics, Conversations, and Contexts* (Toronto: University of Toronto Press, 2009), 145.

52 Cora Weber-Pillwax, "What Is Indigenous Research?" *Canadian Journal of Native Education* 25, 2 (2001): 170.

53 Augie Fleras, "Researching Together Differently: Bridging the Research Paradigm Gap," *Native Studies Review* 15, 2 (2004): 126.

54 Ibid., 127.

55 Cruikshank, *Life Lived Like a Story,* 15.

56 Fleras, "Researching Together Differently," 127.

57 The full account of resources consulted can be found in Chapter 3, which contrasts Tsimshian education from "time immemorial" with Western-style schooling at the Port Essington Indian Day School.

58 Fleras, "Researching Together Differently," 127.
59 Kovach, *Indigenous Methodologies*, 145.
60 Helen Raptis, "Exploring the Factors Prompting British Columbia's First Integration Initiative: The Case of Port Essington Indian Day School," *History of Education Quarterly* 51, 4 (2011): 519–43; Helen Raptis and Sam Bowker, "Maintaining the Illusion of Democracy: Policy-Making and Aboriginal Education in Canada," *Canadian Journal of Educational Administration and Policy,* 102 (2010): 1–21.
61 Barman, "Schooled for Inequality," 57.
62 Coates, "Very Imperfect Means," 147. See also Martha E. Walls, "'The Teacher That Cannot Understand Their Language Should Not Be Allowed': Colonialism, Resistance, and Female Mi'kmaw Teachers of New Brunswick Day Schools, 1900–1923," *Journal of the Canadian Historical Association* 22, 1 (2011): 39.
63 Regan, *Unsettling the Settler Within*, 16, 196–97.
64 James (Sa'ke'j) Youngblood Henderson, "The Context of the State of Nature," in *Reclaiming Indigenous Voice and Vision,* ed. Marie Battiste, 11–38 (Vancouver: UBC Press, 2000).
65 Wilson, "What Is an Indigenist?"
66 Kovach, *Indigenous Methodologies*, 110.
67 Kathy Absolon and Cam Willett, "Putting Ourselves Forward: Location in Aboriginal Research," in *Research as Resistance: Critical Indigenous and Anti-oppressive Approaches,* ed. Leslie Brown and Susan Strega (Toronto: Canadian Scholars' Press, 2005), 109.
68 As is commonly the case with immigrant families, my parents ran a family business that my father could not leave. My siblings and I grew accustomed to spending summer vacations without him.
69 Apparently, my eight-year-old brother was the spitting image of my grandfather John.
70 Cruikshank, *Life Lived Like a Story,* 15.
71 McDonald, "Tsimshian Protocols," 89. On the importance of community events in establishing "significant relationships," see Cora Weber-Pillwax, "Indigenous Researchers and Indigenous Research Methods: Cultural Influences or Cultural Determinants of Research Methods," *Pimatisiwin: A Journal of Aboriginal and Indigenous Community Health* 2, 1 (2004): 87.
72 At the heart of the matter was the question of whose needs were to guide the research. If the project was truly intended to benefit the former students of Port Essington, then the needs of my family had to come second. When we place the question of whose interests are served at the core of scholarly inquiry, we disrupt traditional hierarchies of "dominance and subordination." Brown and Strega, eds., *Research as Resistance,* 10. My husband arranged for his parents to care for our children while he convalesced in hospital for a few days. The difficulty was that they had tickets to depart for France on August 1. Ironically, this was the day of my husband's discharge. Unable to walk and heavily sedated with morphine, he would be left to care for our children for approximately twenty-four hours until my return from Terrace.
73 Neal McLeod, *Cree Narrative Memory: From Treaties to Contemporary Times* (Saskatoon: Purich, 2007), 19.
74 National Indian Brotherhood, *Indian Control of Indian Education* (Ottawa: National Indian Brotherhood, 1972), 9.
75 See Jay Miller, *Tsimshian Culture: A Light through the Ages* (Lincoln: University of Nebraska Press, 1997), 9.
76 In February 2010 I returned to Kitsumkalum and attended the Band Council meeting to present a proposal, oral and written, for the research project. After some discussion, council

members provided their written consent on a jointly agreed upon project protocol and permitted me to begin formal interviews.

77 Kovach, *Indigenous Methodologies*, 85.

78 Ibid., 125.

79 Ibid., 172.

80 Ibid., 99. The connection that a researcher makes to people "is not to people in general or to a collectivity, but to specific individuals, with real faces, personalities, histories, and identities, and no matter how we collectivize them, the connections are unique and individualized with each person." Weber-Pillwax, "Indigenous Researchers," 89.

81 Harry Robinson, *Living by Stories: A Journey of Landscape and Memory,* ed. Wendy Wickwire (Vancouver: Talonbooks, 2005), 21.

82 LaRocque, *When the Other Is Me,* 155, 12. Similarly, the typical academic practice of ensuring anonymity of participants "can obscure community authority and voice." See Mike Evans, "Ethics, Anonymity, and Authorship in Community Centred Research, or Anonymity and the Island Cache," *Pimatisiwin: A Journal of Aboriginal and Indigenous Community Health* 2, 1 (2004): 72. See also Jo-ann Archibald, "Researching with Mutual Respect," *Canadian Journal of Native Education* 20, 2 (1993): 191; and Jo-ann Archibald, ed., *Giving Voice to Our Ancestors,* special issue of *Canadian Journal of Native Education* 19, 2 (1992).

83 Absolon and Willett, "Putting Ourselves Forward," 110.

84 Kovach, *Indigenous Methodologies*, 100.

85 Steven High, "Sharing Authority: An Introduction," *Journal of Canadian Studies/Revue d'Études Canadiennes* 43, 1 (2009): 21.

86 Kovach, *Indigenous Methodologies*, 100.

87 Qwul'sih'yah'maht (Robina Anne Thomas), "Honouring the Oral Traditions of My Ancestors through Storytelling," in *Research as Resistance: Critical Indigenous and Anti-oppressive Approaches,* ed. Leslie Brown and Susan Strega (Toronto: Canadian Scholars' Press, 2005), 248.

CHAPTER 2: INDIGENOUS SCHOOLING AS EDUCATION

1 James R. Miller, *Shingwauk's Vision: A History of Native Residential Schools* (Toronto: University of Toronto Press, 1996), 62. See also Agnes Grant, *No End of Grief: Indian Residential Schools in Canada* (Winnipeg: Pemmican, 1996), 56.

2 Marie Battiste, "Micmac Literacy and Cognitive Assimilation," in *Indian Education in Canada,* vol. 1, *The Legacy,* ed. Jean Barman, Yvonne Hébert, and Don McCaskill (Vancouver: UBC Press, 1986), 23.

3 E. Brian Titley, *A Narrow Vision: Duncan Campbell Scott and the Administration of Indian Affairs in Canada* (Vancouver: UBC Press, 1986), 15; E. Brian Titley, "Indian Industrial Schools in Western Canada," in *Schools in the West: Essays in Canadian Educational History,* ed. Nancy M. Sheehan, J. Donald Wilson, and David C. Jones (Calgary: Detselig, 1986), 134.

4 See Edward Ahenakew, "Little Pine: An Indian Day School," ed. Ruth Matheson Buck, *Saskatchewan History* 18, 2 (1965): 55–62; Susan Elaine Gray, "Methodist Indian Day Schools and Indian Communities in Northern Manitoba, 1890–1925," *Manitoba History,* 30 (1995): http://www.mhs.mb.ca/docs/mb_history/30/methodistdayschools.shtml; and W.D. Hamilton, *The Federal Indian Day Schools of the Maritimes* (Fredericton: University of New Brunswick Press, 1986). For American works on day schools, see Thomas G. Andrews, "Turning the Tables on Assimilation: Oglala Lakotas and the Pine Ridge Day Schools,

1889–1920s," *Western Historical Quarterly* 33, 4 (2002): 407–30; Katherine Jensen, "Teachers and Progressives: The Navajo Day-School Experiment, 1935–1945," *Arizona and the West* 25, 1 (1983): 49–62; and Laura Woodworth-Ney, "The Diaries of a Day-School Teacher: Daily Realities on the Pine Ridge Indian Reservation, 1932–1942," *South Dakota History* 24, 3–4 (1994): 194–211.

5 Hope MacLean, "A Positive Experiment in Aboriginal Education: The Methodist Ojibwa Day Schools in Upper Canada, 1824–1833," *Canadian Journal of Native Studies* 22, 1 (2002): 23–63.

6 Andrews, "Turning the Tables"; Edwin Dexter, *History of Education in the United States* (New York: Burt Franklin, 1906); Thomas Fleming, Lisa Smith, and Helen Raptis, "An Accidental Teacher: Anthony Walsh and the Aboriginal Day Schools at Six Mile Creek and Inkameep, British Columbia, 1929–1942," *Historical Studies in Education* 19, 1 (2007): 1–24; Noel Dyck, *What Is the Indian 'Problem': Tutelage and Resistance in Canadian Indian Administration* (St. John's, NL: Institute of Social and Economic Research, 1991), 50.

7 Coates, "Very Imperfect Means," 138–40; Titley, *Narrow Vision*, 89.

8 For rural BC experiences, see Alastair Glegg, "Anatomy of a Tragedy: The Assisted Schools of British Columbia and the Death of Mabel Jones," *Historical Studies in Education* 17, 1 (2005): 145–64; Robert S. Patterson, "Voices from the Past: The Personal and Professional Struggle of Rural School Teachers," in *Schools in the West: Essays in Canadian Educational History*, ed. Nancy Sheehan, J. Donald Wilson, and David C. Jones, 99–112 (Calgary: Detselig, 1986); Paul J. Stortz and J. Donald Wilson, "Education on the Frontier: Schools, Teachers and Community Influence in North-Central British Columbia," *Histoire Sociale/Social History* 26 (1993): 265–90; J. Donald Wilson and Paul J. Stortz, "May the Lord Have Mercy on You: The Rural School Problem in British Columbia in the 1920s," *BC Studies*, 79 (1988): 24–57.

9 Barman, "Schooled for Inequality," 65; Fleming, Smith, and Raptis, "Accidental Teacher," 5; John W. Friesen and Virginia Lyons Friesen, *Aboriginal Education in Canada: A Plea for Integration* (Calgary: Detselig, 2002), 110; Jerry P. White and Julie Peters, "A Short History of Aboriginal Education in Canada," in *Aboriginal Education: Current Crisis and Future Alternatives*, ed. Jerry P. White et al. (Toronto: Thompson Educational, 2009), 18; Walls, "Teacher That Cannot Understand," 41.

10 Hamilton, *Federal Indian Day Schools*, 14.

11 Coates, "Very Imperfect Means," 134; E. Brian Titley, "Duncan Campbell Scott and Indian Educational Policy," in *An Imperfect Past: Education and Society in Canadian History*, ed. J. Donald Wilson (Vancouver: Canadian History in Education Association, 1984), 143. See also John Leslie, "The Bagot Commission: Developing Corporate Memory for the Indian Department," *Historical Papers of the Canadian Historical Association* 17, 1 (1982): 40; and Reverend Thompson Ferrier, *Our Indians and Their Training for Citizenship* (Toronto: Young People's Forward Movement, n.d.).

12 Brian Rice and Anna Snyder, "Reconciliation in the Context of a Settler Society: Healing the Legacy of Colonialism in Canada," in *From Truth to Reconciliation: Transforming the Legacy of Residential Schools*, ed. Marlene Brant Castellano, Linda Archibald, and Mike DeGagné (Ottawa: Aboriginal Healing Foundation, 2008), 52.

13 Edgar Dewdney, quoted in James (Sa'ke'j) Youngblood Henderson, "Treaties and Indian Education," in *First Nations Education in Canada: The Circle Unfolds*, ed. Marie Battiste and Jean Barman (Vancouver: UBC Press, 1995), 252–53.

14 D.J. Hall, *Clifford Sifton*, vol. 1, *The Young Napoleon, 1861–1900* (Vancouver: UBC Press, 1981), 270; Titley, *Narrow Vision*, 77.

15 Titley, *Narrow Vision*, 83; Titley, "Duncan Campbell Scott," 145. See also Miller, *Shingwauk's Vision*, 103.

16 Titley, "Duncan Campbell Scott," 147.

17 Miller, *Shingwauk's Vision*, 418–19.

18 E. Brian Titley, "Red Deer Indian Industrial School: A Case Study in the History of Native Education," in *Exploring Our Educational Past*, ed. Nick Kach and Kas Mazurek (Calgary: Detselig, 1992), 57.

19 Barman, "Schooled for Inequality," 64.

20 Grant, *No End of Grief*, 247.

21 Ibid., 35.

22 Theodore Fontaine, *Broken Circle: The Dark Legacy of Indian Residential Schools* (Vancouver: Heritage House, 2010); McLeod, *Cree Narrative Memory*, 55–58.

23 Grant, *No End of Grief*, 226.

24 John S. Milloy, *A National Crime: The Canadian Government and the Residential School System, 1879 to 1986* (Winnipeg: University of Manitoba Press, 1999), 295–96.

25 Richard A. Enns, "'But What Is the Object of Educating These Children, If It Costs Their Lives to Educate Them?' Federal Indian Education Policy in Western Canada in the Late 1800s," *Journal of Canadian Studies* 43, 3 (2009): 119.

26 P.H. Bryce, *The Story of a National Crime: Being an Appeal for Justice to the Indians of Canada* (Ottawa: James Hope and Sons, 1922), 14.

27 Barman, "Schooled for Inequality."

28 Department of Indian Affairs (DIA), *Annual Report, 1951;* Coates, "Very Imperfect Means," 146–47. Calculations from DIA *Annual Reports* for 1891 to 1951 indicate that day schools educated roughly 58 percent of British Columbia's Aboriginal students, whereas the residential schools accounted for 42 percent.

29 Dominion of Canada, DIA, *Annual Report for the Year Ended 31st December, 1914*, 245.

30 Ibid.

31 Two Arrow Lake Band children attended public school at Burton and several others in New Westminster. One Aboriginal student, Harry Harris, was enrolled in Armstrong High School's matriculation class and was expected to succeed at his exam that summer. DIA, *Annual Report, 1915*, 207.

32 The increased figure may reflect the late-1920 amendment to the Indian Act that compelled children between the ages of seven and fifteen to attend school. The highest figure ($6,717.80) for tuition fees was paid to Quebec in 1915. The second highest was paid to Ontario at $1,362.57. DIA, *Annual Report, 1915*, 123.

33 Eve Chapple and Helen Raptis, "From Integration to Segregation: Government Education Policy and the School at Telegraph Creek, British Columbia, 1906–1951," *Journal of the Canadian Historical Association* 24, 1 (2013): 139.

34 "Indians Must Quit School," *Victoria Times*, November 15, 1928.

35 Ernest A. Harris recalls that "during the 1930's the federal government withdrew its support of church mission schools, and the assimilation of the Native children into the provincial education system provided enough pupils for a two-room school for several years." Harris, *Spokeshute*, 123.

36 DIA, *Annual Report, 1934–35*.

37 Chief Sittingstone, "An Indian Speaks! ... An Appeal from Northwestern Indians –
    Northwest Angle Treaty No. 3 – to the Canadian Government (1944)," *Indian Missionary
    Record,* January 1946, 15–16; "War Has Helped Indians in Comeback," *Indian Missionary
    Record,* January 1946, 4. Aboriginal people gained the right to vote in British Columbia
    in 1949 and in Canada in 1960.
38 Miller, *Shingwauk's Vision,* 296; Special Joint Committee of the Senate and the House of
    Commons Appointed to Examine and Consider the Indian Act, *Minutes of the Proceedings
    and Evidence, No. 5* (Ottawa: Edmond Cloutier, 1946), 165; George Manuel and Michael
    Posluns, *The Fourth World: An Indian Reality* (New York: Free Press, 1974), 64. Formation
    of the committee was prompted by a brief submitted to Canada by the Okanagan Society
    for the Revival of Indian Arts and Crafts requesting an examination of the Indian Act.
    Andrea N. Walsh, *Nk'Mip Chronicles: Art from the Inkameep Day School* (Osoyoos, BC:
    Osoyoos Indian Band, 2005), 14.
39 Indian Act, 1951, sec. 113 (b).
40 Trefor Smith, "John Freemont Smith and Indian Administration in the Kamloops Agency,
    1912–1923," *Native Studies Review* 10, 2 (1995): 1–2.
41 Miller, *Shingwauk's Vision,* 382.
42 Milloy, *National Crime,* 192. For other historical references that refer to the 1951 federal
    integration policy, see Sonia Brookes, "An Analysis of Indian Education Policy, 1960–1989"
    (MA thesis, University of Calgary, 1990); Sonia Brookes, "The Persistence of Native
    Education Policy in Canada," in *The Cultural Maze: Complex Questions on Native Destiny
    in Western Canada,* ed. John Friesen, 163–80 (Calgary: Detselig, 1991); Titley, "Duncan
    Campbell Scott"; and Indian and Northern Affairs, *The Historical Development of the Indian
    Act* (Ottawa: Indian and Northern Affairs, 1978). For a particularly British Columbian
    perspective on nineteenth-century government policies pertaining to Aboriginal education,
    see Jean Barman, "Families versus Schools: Children of Aboriginal Descent in British Col-
    umbia Classrooms of the Late Nineteenth Century," in *Family Matters: Papers in Post-
    Confederation Canadian Family History,* ed. Edgar-André Montigny and Lori Chambers,
    73–89 (Toronto: Canadian Scholars' Press, 1998).
43 Michael Marker, "'It Was Two Different Times of the Day, but in the Same Place': Coast
    Salish High School Experience in the 1970s," *BC Studies,* 144 (2004–05): 95; Michael
    Marker, "After the Makah Whale Hunt: Indigenous Knowledge and Limits to Multicultural
    Discourse," *Urban Education* 41, 5 (2006): 495.
44 *United States v. Washington,* 384 F. Supp. 312 (W.D. Wash. 1974).
45 Marker, "'It Was Two,'" 96.
46 Diane Persson, "The Changing Experience of Indian Residential Schooling: Blue Quills,
    1931–1970," in *Indian Education in Canada,* vol. 1, *The Legacy,* ed. Jean Barman, Yvonne
    Hébert, and Don McCaskill (Vancouver: UBC Press, 1986), 160.
47 Ibid., 162.

CHAPTER 3: TSIMSHIAN EDUCATION VERSUS WESTERN-STYLE SCHOOLING

 1 Thom Henley, *River of Mist, Journey of Dreams* (Victoria, BC: Rediscovery International
    Foundation, 2009), 42; McDonald, *People of the Robin,* 8.
 2 Marjorie M. Halpin and Margaret Seguin, "Tsimshian Peoples: Southern Tsimshian, Coast
    Tsimshian, Nishga, and Gitksan," in *Handbook of North American Indians,* vol. 7, *Northwest
    Coast,* ed. Wayne Suttles (Washington, DC: Smithsonian Institution, 1990), 267.

3   Kenneth B. Harris, with Frances M.P. Robinson, *Visitors Who Never Left: The Origin of the People of Damelahamid* (Vancouver: UBC Press, 1974), xi–xii; Richard I. Inglis and George MacDonald, *Skeena River Prehistory* (Ottawa: National Museums of Canada, 1979), 2. The name "Tsimshian" literally means "inside the Skeena River" and was used by both Coastal and Southern Tsimshian groups. Halpin and Seguin, "Tsimshian Peoples," 282.

4   Barman, *West beyond the West*, 15.

5   Campbell, *Persistence and Change*, 33.

6   Margaret Seguin Anderson and Tammy Anderson Blumhagen, "Memories and Moments: Conversations and Recollections," *BC Studies*, 104 (1994–95): 89.

7   Miller, *Tsimshian Culture*, 77–78.

8   See McDonald, *People of the Robin*, 74–75; Harris, with Robinson, *Visitors Who Never Left*, xii; Halpin and Seguin, "Tsimshian Peoples," 276;

9   Garfield, "Tsimshian Clan and Society," 178.

10 Philip Drucker, *Cultures of the North Pacific Coast* (San Francisco, CA: Chandler, 1965), 55–65.

11 Campbell, *Persistence and Change*, 35–36; Halpin and Seguin, "Tsimshian Peoples," 276.

12 Seguin Anderson and Anderson Blumhagen, "Memories and Moments," 97.

13 Marie Battiste and James (Sa'ke'j) Youngblood Henderson, *Protecting Indigenous Knowledge and Heritage* (Saskatoon: Purich, 2000), 49.

14 Ibid., 279. See also Christopher F. Roth, *Becoming Tsimshian: The Social Life of Names* (Seattle: University of Washington Press, 2008), 62–68.

15 Roth, *Becoming Tsimshian*, 4.

16 Ibid., 14.

17 Ibid., 32–33.

18 It is not unusual for individuals to have more than one name during their lifetime. Campbell, *Persistence and Change*, 42.

19 Christopher F. Roth, "'The Names Spread in All Directions': Hereditary Titles in Tsimshian Social and Political Life," *BC Studies*, 130 (2001): 76.

20 Jean Barman, *British Columbia: Spirit of the People* (Madeira Park, BC: Harbour, 2009), 87; Miller, *Tsimshian Culture*, 21; Campbell, *Persistence and Change*, 39.

21 William H. Pierce, *From Potlatch to Pulpit, Being the Autobiography of the Reverend William Henry Pierce* (Vancouver: Vancouver Bindery, 1933), 18.

22 Henley, *River of Mist*, 111.

23 Miller, *Tsimshian Culture*, 23.

24 Anthropologists Marjorie Halpin and Margaret Seguin suggest that the story of Raven is an example of a generally shared story/myth. Raven is a heroic character who delivered light, fire, and conscious thought – among other things – to the Tsimshian world. Halpin and Seguin, "Tsimshian Peoples," 280.

25 Ibid., 280.

26 Harris, with Robinson, *Visitors Who Never Left*, xvi. An example of such a saying is "You think you are as handsome as the sun's (moon's) child," which was used to point out someone who was vain or self-absorbed. For other proverbs and sayings, see Campbell, *Persistence and Change*, 67–68.

27 Susan Marsden, Margaret Seguin Anderson, and Deanna Nyce, "Aboriginals: Tsimshian," in *Encyclopedia of Canada's Peoples*, ed. Paul Robert Magocsi (Toronto: University of Toronto Press, 1999), 104.

28 Battiste and Henderson, *Protecting Indigenous Knowledge*, 42.

29 Anderson and Blumhagen, "Memories and Moments," 93.

30 Campbell, *Persistence and Change*, 185.

31 Jonathan Anuik, Marie Battiste, and Priscilla (Nignwakwe) George, "Learning from Promising Programs and Applications in Nourishing the Learning Spirit," *Canadian Journal of Native Education* 33, 1 (2010): 81.

32 Campbell, *Persistence and Change*, 66–74.

33 This view of human disease is not unlike that of contemporary Western practitioners who see a link between psychological or emotional stressors and physical disease.

34 Halpin and Seguin, "Tsimshian Peoples," 279; Marsden, Anderson, and Nyce, "Aboriginals," 104.

35 LaFrance, "Culturally Negotiated Education," 108.

36 Interestingly, this notion is not unlike Lev Vygotsky's notion of mediation, which posits that children can reach a higher plane in their "zone of proximal development" with the assistance of skilled individuals. C.D. Lee and P. Smagorinsky, eds., *Vygotskian Perspectives on Literacy Research: Constructing Meaning through Collaborative Inquiry* (New York: Cambridge University Press, 2000).

37 Robin Fisher, *Contact and Conflict: Indian-European Relations in British Columbia, 1774–1890* (Vancouver: UBC Press, 1977), 129.

38 Duff, *Indian History*, 97.

39 Ibid., 98.

40 Pierce, *From Potlatch to Pulpit*, 18. Methodists had arrived from eastern Canada in the 1860s, beginning their missionary work in Nanaimo. Duff, *Indian History*, 96–98. By 1873 Methodists had 108 Indian members at Victoria, Nanaimo, New Westminster, and Chilliwack. By 1907 the church counted 3,224 mission houses, 12 schools, 4 hospitals, and some 7,000 Indian followers across Canada. Thomas Crosby, *Among the An-Ko-me-nums or Flathead Tribes of Indians of the Pacific Coast* (Edmonton: Universal Bindery, 1907), 241–42.

41 Ernest A. Harris, notes for *Spokeshute*, Accession No. 1997.006, Harris Family Fonds, Prince Rupert City and Regional Archives (PRCRA).

42 William Henry Pierce File, Bob Stewart Archives (BSA).

43 Coates, "Very Imperfect Means," 138. See also Barman, "Schooled for Inequality," 65; Friesen and Lyons Friesen, *Aboriginal Education in Canada*, 110; and White and Peters, "Short History," 18.

44 Duff, *Indian History*, 62.

45 Titley, *Narrow Vision*, 13.

46 Ibid., 89.

47 Tranter also taught at Port Simpson and Bella Bella. She died in Victoria on May 7, 1939. "Catherine Tranter," *Western Recorder*, August 16, 1939, 13, BSA.

48 *Annual Report of the Department of Indian Affairs for the Year Ended June 30, 1906*, 282, Department of Indian Affairs, RG-10, Library and Archives Canada (LAC).

49 J.D. McLean to C.C. Perry, May 3, 1911; and A.E. Green to Charles Clifton Perry, May 17 1911, Department of Indian Affairs, RG-10, vol. 6407, file 836–1, LAC.

50 Charles Clifton Perry to J.D. McLean, 17 May 1912, Department of Indian Affairs, RG-10, vol. 6407, file 836–1, LAC.

51 Charles Clifton Perry to J.D. McLean, October 24, 1912; and J.D. McLean to Charles Clifton Perry, November 5, 1912, Department of Indian Affairs, RG-10, vol. 6407, file 836–1, LAC.

52 Ernest A. Harris, Spokeshute file, Acession No. 1997.006, Harris Family Fonds, PRCRA. Fanny's father, Alex, was a net-man for a cannery and also dabbled in real estate. The family "went below" during the Depression and moved to Vancouver after Fanny's marriage to Alex MacKenzie. Harris, *Spokeshute,* 300.

53 Charles Clifton Perry, Agent's Report, 121237–7, April 1914; and A.M. Tyson, Agent's Report, 427021–61, October 10, 1915, Department of Indian Affairs, RG-10, vol. 6407, file 836–1, LAC.

54 Charles Clifton Perry to J.D. McLean, September 1, 1913; and Charles Clifton Perry to J.D. McLean, September 19, 1913, Department of Indian Affairs, RG-10, vol. 6407, file 836–1, LAC.

55 W.H. Pierce to Duncan Campbell Scott, October 12, 1916, Department of Indian Affairs, RG-10, vol. 6407, file 836–1, LAC.

56 Fanny J. Noble to C.C. Perry, December 30, 1916, Department of Indian Affairs, RG-10, vol. 6407, file 836–1, LAC.

57 J.D. McLean to C.C. Perry, January 11, 1917, Department of Indian Affairs, RG-10, vol. 6407, file 836–1, LAC.

58 Department of Indian Affairs (DIA), *Annual Report,* March 31, 1919, 33, LAC.

59 Gray, "Methodist Indian Day Schools," 11.

60 British Columbia Department of Education, *Annual Report of the Public Schools of the Province of British Columbia (ARPS),* 1919–20.

61 Illegible to Mr. Scott, February 6, 1920; and Fanny J. Noble to Reverend T. Ferrier, March 7, 1920, Department of Indian Affairs, RG-10, vol. 6407, file 836–1, LAC.

62 Teachers' Salaries, Invoice, March 31, 1925, Department of Indian Affairs, RG-10, vol. 6407, file 836–1, LAC.

63 J.D. McLean to W.E. Collison, July 13, 1927, Department of Indian Affairs, RG-10, vol. 6407, file 836–1, LAC.

64 Louise Fakeley to Mr. Barner, September 18, 1929; and W.E. Collison to A.F. MacKenzie, October 9, 1929, Department of Indian Affairs, RG-10, vol. 6407, file 836–1, LAC.

65 Indian Agent to Mrs. L. Fakeley, September 25, 1929, Kitsumkalum Social History Project. Many thanks to Dr. James McDonald for sharing the letter and the artwork. It appears that the exhibition was an ongoing affair, as works from the following year were submitted by Fakeley's successor, Mrs. Elizabeth Pogson.

66 A.F. MacKenzie to W.E. Collison, November 26, 1929, Department of Indian Affairs, RG-10, vol. 6407, file 836–1, LAC.

67 A.F. MacKenzie to W.E. Collison, January 20, 1930, Department of Indian Affairs, RG-10, vol. 6407, file 836–1, LAC.

68 A.F. MacKenzie to W.E. Collison, January 20, 1930; A.F. MacKenzie to R.B. Cochrane, January 20, 1930; R.B. Cochrane to A.F. MacKenzie, January 21, 1930; and W.C. Hartley to Whom It May Concern, n.d., Department of Indian Affairs, RG-10, vol. 6407, file 836–1, LAC. Mr. Pogson apparently had crippled feet from his involvement in the First World War.

69 Bowman, *Klondike of the Skeena,* 65. Edward was the father of Charlotte Guno, an elder who participated in this study. See Charlotte's story in Chapter 4.

70 Elizabeth Pogson to A.F. MacKenzie, April 14, 1930, Department of Indian Affairs, RG-10, vol. 6407, file 836–1, LAC.

71 A.F. MacKenzie to Elizabeth Pogson, May 7, 1930, Department of Indian Affairs, RG-10, vol. 6407, file 836–1, LAC.

72 Inspector's Report on Port Essington Indian Day School, May 1, 1936, and May 14, 1936; A.F. MacKenzie to W.E. Collison, May 29, 1936, and June 19, 1936; and W.E. Collison to A.F. MacKenzie, June 11, 1936, Department of Indian Affairs, RG-10, vol. 6407, file 836–1, LAC.

73 "Regulations and Courses of Study for Provincial Normal Schools, 1928–1929," http://www.mala.bc.ca/homeroom/content/topics/programs/Curriclm/nschool.htm. See also Robert S. Patterson, "Society and Education during the Wars and Their Interlude, 1914–1945," in *Canadian Education: A History*, ed. J. Donald Wilson, Robert Stamp, and Louis-Philippe Audet, 360–84 (Scarborough, ON: Prentice-Hall, 1970); Neil Sutherland, *Children in English Canadian Society: Framing the Twentieth Century Consensus* (Toronto: University of Toronto Press, 1976), 182–201; and George Tomkins, *A Common Countenance: Stability and Change in the Canadian Curriculum* (Scarborough, ON: Prentice-Hall, 1986), 242–47.

74 R.A. Hoey to George Dorey, August 13, 1937; George Dorey to R.A. Hoey, August 19, 1937; R.A. Hoey to W.E. Collison, August 31, 1937; and G. Stillwell to the Home Board of Missions, June 5, 1937, Department of Indian Affairs, RG-10, vol. 6407, file 836–1, LAC.

75 Inspector's Report on Port Essington Indian Day School, October 29, 1937, Department of Indian Affairs, RG-10, vol. 6407, file 836–1, LAC.

76 Philip Phelan to Representative of the Treasury, July 14, 1938, Department of Indian Affairs, RG-10, vol. 6407, file 836–1, LAC.

77 G. Dorey to R.A. Hoey, July 7, 1938, Department of Indian Affairs, RG-10, vol. 6407, file 836–1, LAC.

78 Inspector's Report on Port Essington Indian Day School, May 4, 1939, and May 8, 1940, Department of Indian Affairs, RG-10, vol. 6407, file 836–1, LAC.

79 Smith, *Liberalism, Surveillance, and Resistance*, 55.

80 Gerald H. Barry to Major D.M. MacKay, May 6, 1939, Department of Indian Affairs, RG-10, vol. 6407, file 836–1, LAC.

81 A. Rutherford to Major D.M. MacKay, September, 1940; and G. Dorey to R.A Hoey, September 18, 1940, Department of Indian Affairs, RG-10, vol. 6407, file 836–1, LAC.

82 F.W. Chilton to Department of Indian Affairs, December 1, 1940, Department of Indian Affairs, RG-10, vol. 6407, file 836–1, LAC.

83 G. Dorey to R.A. Hoey, January 9, 1941; R.A. Hoey to Major D.M. MacKay, January 14, 1941; and J. Gillett to the Secretary, Indian Affairs, March 14, 1941, Department of Indian Affairs, RG-10, vol. 6407, file 836–1, LAC.

84 James Coleman to the Secretary, Indian Affairs, July 25, 1941, Department of Indian Affairs, RG-10, vol. 6407, file 836–1, LAC.

85 J. Gillett to Major D.M. MacKay, May 26, 1942, Department of Indian Affairs, RG-10, vol. 6407, file 836–1, LAC.

86 Ibid. No record could be found indicating on what basis he was charged.

87 *United Church of Canada Yearbook, 1940*, 123, BSA. In 1925 the Methodist Church joined with the Congregational Union of Canada, the Union of Western Churches of Canada, and two-thirds of the Presbyterian Church in Canada to form the United Church of Canada.

88 *United Church of Canada Yearbook, 1943*, 130, BSA.

89 *United Church of Canada Yearbook, 1947*, 532–33, BSA.

90 R.B. Cochrane to R.A. Hoey, August 29, 1942, Department of Indian Affairs, RG-10, vol. 6407, file 836–1, LAC.

91 Harry B. Hawthorn, Cyril S. Belshaw, and Stuart M. Jamieson, *The Indians of British Columbia* (Berkeley: University of California Press, 1960), 291; *Annual Report 1951,* Indian Advisory Committee, GR-1071, box 1, file 8, British Columbia Archives (BCA).

92 Inspector's Report, December 13, 1943, Department of Indian Affairs, RG-10, vol. 6407, file 8, 836–1, LAC.

93 R.A. Hoey to Major D.M. MacKay, September 7, 1943, Department of Indian Affairs, RG-10, vol. 6407, file 8, 836–1, LAC.

94 Inspector's Report on Port Essington Indian Day School, November 3, 1944; and Port Essington Indian Day School, Quarterly Return, March 1944, Department of Indian Affairs, RG-10, vol. 6407, file 8, 836–1, LAC.

95 J. Gillett to Major D.M. MacKay, January 23, 1945, Department of Indian Affairs, RG-10, vol. 6407, file 8, 836–1, LAC; *Prince Rupert Presbytery: Minutes,* August 23, 1944, 60, BSA.

96 British Columbia, Division of Vital Statistics, vol. 012A, reel B13214, Province of British Columbia, Registration of Death, 52–09–012390, BCA.

97 Quarterly School Return, June 30, 1947, Department of Indian Affairs, RG-10, vol. 6407, file 836–2, BCA.

98 Bowman, *Klondike of the Skeena,* 68; British Columbia Department of Education, *ARPS,* 1940 and 1942.

99 *Minutes,* August 6, 1947, Prince Rupert School District (PRSD).

100 Bernard F. Neary to Major D.M. MacKay, August 21, 1947; Bernard F. Neary to F. Earl Anfield, August 28, 1947; F. Earl Anfield to Major D.M. MacKay, September 1, 1947; and Barnard F. Neary to Major D.M. MacKay, 10 September 1947, Department of Indian Affairs, RG-10, vol. 6407, file 836–1, LAC.

101 Harris, *Spokeshute,* 113–14.

102 Calculations are generated from British Columbia Department of Education, *ARPS,* 1895 to 1963.

103 Harris, *Spokeshute,* 117–21.

104 R.F. Davey to W.S. Arneil, April 16, 1948, Department of Indian Affairs, RG-10, vol. 6407, file 836–1, LAC.

105 British Columbia Department of Education, *Report of Inspection,* June 18, 1948, School Inspector Reports, GR-0122, BCA.

106 "Pass List," Port Essington Indian Day School, Class Register, n.d., PRCRA.

107 Myrtle M. Roper to F.E. Anfield, August 15, 1949; Bernard F. Neary to W.S. Arneil, October 28, 1949; and F. Earl Anfield to W.S. Arneil, December 19, 1949, Department of Indian Affairs, RG-10, vol. 6407, file 836–1, LAC. It is unclear why the federal government paid for 60 percent of the capital costs when only eighteen of the thirty-eight children were status Indians.

108 "Government Widens Plan to Recruit More Teachers: Stopgap Methods May Assist Rural Schools to Combat Shortage," *Vancouver Sun,* August 28, 1942, 17.

109 "Teaching of Indians," *Prince Rupert Daily News,* April 4, 1946, 3.

110 By 1950 six provincial districts had negotiated such cost-sharing agreements. Hazelton integrated in 1948; Ashcroft in 1949; Telegraph Creek, Campbell River, and Terrace in 1950; and Alberni, Nanaimo, and Alert Bay in 1951. Helen Raptis, "Implementing Integrated Education Policy for On-Reserve Aboriginal Children in British Columbia, 1951–1981," *Historical Studies in Education* 20, 1 (2008): 119–20.

111 E. Brian Titley, "Unsteady Debut: J.A.N. Provencher and the Beginnings of Indian Administration in Manitoba," *Prairie Forum* 22, 1 (1997): 21–46.

112 Bowman, *Klondike of the Skeena,* 70; James A. McDonald, "Trying to Make a Life: The Historical Political Economy of Kitsumkalum" (PhD diss., University of British Columbia, 1985), 401.
113 Unfortunately, Coast Mountain School District did not reply to requests for access to archival documents for the Terrace schools.
114 Celia Haig-Brown et al., eds., *Making the Spirit Dance Within: Joe Duquette High School and an Aboriginal Community* (Toronto: James Lorimer, 1997), 21.
115 These are sometimes referred to as individuals' gifts. Anuik, Battiste, and George, "Learning from Promising Programs," 73–75.
116 It has been argued further that First Nations groups valued mistakes as "opportunities to grow." Lorenzo Cherubini, Julian Kitchen, and Lyn Trudeau, "Having the Spirit within to Vision: New Aboriginal Teachers' Commitment to Reclaiming Space," *Canadian Journal of Native Education* 32, 2 (2009): 38–51.
117 See, for example, Sheila Watt-Cloutier, "Honouring Our Past, Creating Our Future: Education in Northern and Remote Communities," in *Aboriginal Education: Fulfilling the Promise,* ed. Marlene Brant Castellano, Lynne Davis, and Louise Lahache (Vancouver: UBC Press, 2000), 118.
118 Lomawaima and McCarty, *"To Remain an Indian,"* 20–21.
119 Gerald L. Gutek, *Historical and Philosophical Foundations of Education,* 5th ed. (Boston: Pearson, 2011), 39.

CHAPTER 4: WALKING ON TWO PATHS

1 Educational historians continue to focus their research mainly on formal schooling, despite historian Bernard Bailyn's admonition in 1960 that education is "the entire process by which a culture transmits itself across the generations." Bernard Bailyn, *Education in the Forming of American Society* (New York: Vintage, 1960), 15.
2 LaFrance, "Culturally Negotiated Education," 101. According to Gregory Cajete, all "Indians of the Americas share common metaphors of Indigenous knowledge and education." Gregory Cajete, *Look to the Mountain: An Ecology of Indigenous Education* (Durango, CO: Kivaki, 1994), 35.
3 A hospital that operated during the summer months was established at Port Essington in 1895. Unless otherwise indicated, information about Mildred comes from interviews undertaken January 29, 2010, May 2, 2011, and July 3, 2011.
4 See Miller, *Tsimshian Culture,* 20–24.
5 See also Campbell, *Persistence and Change,* 60.
6 Susan Neylan, *The Heavens Are Changing: Nineteenth-Century Protestant Missions and Tsimshian Christianity* (Montreal and Kingston: McGill-Queen's University Press, 2003), 249; Maureen L. Atkinson, "The 'Accomplished' Odille Quintal Morison: Tsimshian Cultural Intermediary of Metlakatla, British Columbia," in *Recollecting: Lives of Aboriginal Women of the Canadian Northwest and Borderlands,* ed. Sarah Carter and Patricia McCormack (Edmonton: Athabasca University Press, 2011), 142.
7 Scientists have carbon-dated the occurrences of earthquakes and tsunamis in the Pacific Northwest that have been memorialized in First Nations stories, art, and ceremonies for millenia. See, for example, Ruth S. Ludwin et al., "Dating the 1700 Cascadia Earthquake: Great Coastal Earthquakes in Native Stories," *Seismological Research Letters* 76, 2 (2005): 140–48.

8 See Harris, with Robinson, *Visitors Who Never Left.*

9 For more information about the Tsimshian concept of naxnox, see Neylan, *Heavens Are Changing,* 31; and Roth, *Becoming Tsimshian.*

10 Mildred's father, James Bolton, did not value education, having completed only Grade 5. Her mother, Selina Gosnell, attended public school in Terrace, completing Grade 6. Yet her father's brother Edward went to high school and completed Grade 10. Her paternal grandmother, Rebecca Bolton (née Anderson), had attended the Crosby Home for Girls in Port Simpson, although she allegedly seldom spoke about her experiences. For more about the Crosby school, see Jan Hare and Jean Barman, *Good Intentions Gone Awry: Emma Crosby and the Methodist Mission on the Northwest Coast* (Vancouver: UBC Press, 2006).

11 Cecelia and Josie were the sisters of Mildred's mother, Selina Gosnell. They were educated at public school in Terrace.

12 See John Lutz, "After the Fur Trade: The Aboriginal Labouring Class of British Columbia, 1849–1890," *Journal of the Canadian Historical Association* 3, 1 (1992): 84.

13 When refrigerators were developed, canneries no longer needed to be near the fish runs. Fewer, larger canneries concentrated production closer to urban areas in the province's southern region. Menzies and Butler, "Indigenous Foundation"; Newell, *Tangled Webs of History.*

14 See photograph on page 71, "The Happy Gang." In addition to playing music, the group sang and performed comedy skits. It took the name the "Happy Gang" from a group of musical entertainers that aired on CBC Radio from 1937 to 1959 over weekday lunch hours. "The Happy Gang," http://www.thecanadianencyclopedia.ca/en/article/the-happy -gang-emc.

15 The tradition of performing for the community dates from prior to Mildred's birth. Ernest A. Harris recounts a salient performance that he attended as a boy in the 1920s that focused on the skills of the traditional Tsimshian medicine man. Harris, *Spokeshute,* 177–78.

16 Elizabeth Pogson to A.F. MacKenzie, April 14, 1930; and Bernard F. Neary to Major D.M. MacKay, August 21, 1947, Department of Indian Affairs, RG-10, vol. 6407, file 836–1, Library and Archives Canada (LAC).

17 Mr. Severson taught from 1937 to 1938. R.A. Hoey to George Dorey, August 13, 1937; George Dorey to R.A. Hoey, August 19, 1937; R.A. Hoey to W.E. Collison, August 31, 1937; and G. Stillwell to the Home Board of Missions, June 5, 1937, Department of Indian Affairs, RG-10, vol. 6407, file 836–1, LAC.

18 Mr. Chilton taught in 1940. F.W. Chilton to Department of Indian Affairs, December 1, 1940, Department of Indian Affairs, RG-10, vol. 6407, file 836–1, LAC.

19 G. Dorey to R.A. Hoey, January 9, 1941; R.A. Hoey to Major D.M. MacKay, January 14, 1941; and J. Gillett to the Secretary, Indian Affairs, March 14, 1941, Department of Indian Affairs, RG-10, vol. 6407, file 836–1, LAC.

20 J. Gillett to Major D.M. MacKay, May 26, 1942, Department of Indian Affairs, RG-10, vol. 6407, file 836–1, LAC.

21 James R. Miller, *Skyscrapers Hide the Heavens: A History of Indian-White Relations in Canada,* 3rd ed. (Toronto: University of Toronto Press, 2000), 65. See also Diamond Jenness, *The Indians of Canada,* 3rd ed. (Ottawa: National Museum of Canada, 1955), 152. By the mid-twentieth century, corporal punishment was commonplace in Indigenous homes; nevertheless, oral testimony by chiefs and elders indicates that the practice contravenes traditional Aboriginal principles of childrearing. Jo-Anne Fiske and Betty Patrick, *Cis Dideen Kat (When the Plumes Rise): The Way of the Lake Babine Nation* (Vancouver: UBC Press, 2000), 144.

22 For information about Port Essington's Japanese population, see Harris, *Spokeshute,* 70–73, 127.

23 Mildred is referring to the Enfranchisement Act. During the Second World War, able-bodied men had to serve in the Canadian services at Prince Rupert or on the dry docks at Port Essington. As a result, they lost their Indian status and did not regain it until the passage of Bill C-31 in 1985.

24 See McDonald, "Trying to Make a Life."

25 Bowman, *Klondike of the Skeena,* 70.

26 Unless otherwise indicated, all information about Wally has been taken from interviews conducted at Kitsumkalum, August 16, 2010, and July 4, 2011.

27 Gillnetting required fishermen to drag a net between a larger and a smaller vessel in order to collect fish. For seining, a skiff anchored one end of an open net, while the seiner encircled the fish and then quickly "pursed up" the bottom to enclose the fish. A "dip-net" was then lowered from the seiner into the pile of fish, which were scooped onto the deck.

28 The day school teacher at the time was Mrs. Elizabeth Pogson.

29 See Brenda McLeod, "First Nations Women and Sustainability on the Canadian Prairies," in *First Voices: An Aboriginal Women's Reader,* ed. Patricia A. Monture and Patricia D. McGuire (Toronto: Inanna, 2009), 159–60.

30 Henley, *River of Mist,* 111.

31 The Donaldsons owned a hotel in Prince Rupert, which was managed by Mr. Donaldson.

32 The Happy Gang got its start in the 1940s when Bill (Willy) Spalding initiated door-to-door Christmas carolling among the children on the reserve. See the story of Mildred Roberts.

33 Wally was referring to Big Lake, which sits roughly three miles away in the hills behind Port Essington. Harris, *Spokeshute,* 167.

34 Fishermen's hands were distinguishable due to chapping from exposure to wind and sea salt. Gladys Young Blyth, *Salmon Canneries: British Columbia North Coast* (Victoria, BC: Trafford, 2006), 11.

35 Beginning in 1919, the province began supplying correspondence programs to families in settlements too small to furnish the ten school-aged children necessary for the establishment of a school. For many rural learners, correspondence was the only option for high school graduation, as rural regions seldom offered secondary schooling. Tara S. Toutant, "Equality by Mail: Correspondence Education in British Columbia, 1919–1969" (MA thesis, University of Victoria, 2003).

36 Unless otherwise indicated, all information about Sam has been taken from interviews held August 17, 2010, and July 3, 2011.

37 See Campbell, *Persistence and Change,* 43; and Roth, *Becoming Tsimshian,* 84–85.

38 "Old Tom" was a type of "one-base baseball" where one player would hit the ball with a bat and then run to the end of the field and home again while trying to avoid being hit by the ball, thrown by fielders. In 1925 a ballpark complete with backstop and bleachers was built on the south end of the reserve.

39 The Port Essington Concert Band also played at Dominion Day celebrations, weddings, funerals, and sports events such as baseball games. During the 1930s members included John Wesley (president), Mark Bolton (honorary president), Louis Starr (vice-president and secretary), and David Spalding (conductor). Information courtesy of the North Pacific Cannery Museum, Port Edward, BC. For more about brass bands among First Nations communities in the province, see Susan Neylan and Melissa Meyer, ""Here Comes The

Band!": Cultural Collaboration, Connective Traditions and Aboriginal Brass Bands on British Columbia's North Coast, 1875–1964," *BC Studies*, 152 (2006–07): 35–66.

40 Regarding the loss of land among the Tsimshian of Kitsumkalum, see McDonald, "Bleeding Day and Night."

41 In 1939 Jimmy Donaldson took over the mill after the death in 1914 of James A. Brown, who had married Jimmy's widowed mother, Janet. Harris, *Spokeshute*, 52.

42 In 1915 the British-American Cannery, Skeena River Commercial Cannery, and Cunningham's Cannery combined to establish the Port Essington Water Company. They constructed a three-mile pipeline that transported spring water from up in the mountains down to the town, except during the winter, when the water froze over. Harris, *Spokeshute*, 34. During the winter months, residents who could afford to paid Ging, a resident of Chinese origin, to fill the water barrel at the side of their home. Residents paid twenty-five cents per bucket, which Ging carried two at a time "Chinese fashion" – that is, hooked over each end of a pole slung across his shoulders. Interview of Mrs. A.G. (Agnes) Harris, February 8, 1962, T1212:0001, British Columbia Archives (BCA).

43 Gladys Blyth, *History of Port Edward, 1907–1970* (Port Edward, BC: n.p., 1970), 30; K. Mack Campbell, *Cannery Village – Company Town: A History of British Columbia's Outlying Salmon Canneries* (Victoria, BC: Trafford, 2004).

44 Lutz, *After the Fur Trade*, 88–89. For a discussion of the negative elements of the potlatch, see Roberston, with the Kwaqu'l Gixsam Clan, *Standing Up with Ga'axsta'las*.

45 Unless otherwise indicated, information about Verna comes from interviews conducted at Kitsumkalum, January 30, 2010, August 18, 2010, and July 2, 2011.

46 Gregory Cajete, a Tewa educator and artist from Santa Clara Pueblo, explains that traditional Indian education "unfolded through mutual, reciprocal relationships between one's social group and the natural world." Cajete, *Look to the Mountain*, 26.

47 In 1944 the federal government made receiving Family Allowance payments dependent upon children's school attendance. Persson, "Changing Experience," 157.

48 By the time Verna was seven, the vitality of the United Church had diminished. No baptisms, marriages, or burials were performed that year. *United Church of Canada Yearbook, 1940*, 123; and *United Church of Canada Yearbook, 1947*, 532–33, Bob Stewart Archives (BSA). Apparently, the Salvation Army held open-air services from spring to fall. Members would march in uniform from the hall at the south end of the reserve and up along Kitselas Street to midway along Dufferin. A band consisting of trumpets, trombones, tambourines, and drums would play. Services were conducted partly in Tsimshian and partly in English. Harris, *Spokeshute*, 130–31.

49 Until 1985 Canada's Indian Act forced Indian women who married non-Indian men to lose their Indian status. Status could also be lost through "enfranchisement," which required Native peoples to denounce their Indian heritage, move off reserves, and fully accept Canadian legal rights. In 1985 Bill C-31 ended loss of status through marriage and enfranchisement. Native Women's Association of Canada, "Aboriginal Women and Bill C-31," paper presented at the National Aboriginal Women's Summit, June 20–22, 2007, Corner Brook, Newfoundland. See also Sharon D. McIvor, "Aboriginal Women's Rights as 'Existing Rights,'" in *First Voices: An Aboriginal Women's Reader*, ed. Patricia A. Monture and Patricia D. McGuire, 374–81 (Toronto: Inanna, 2009); and the story of Wally Miller.

50 See Clayton, "Geographies of the Lower Skeena."

51 Dr. Richard Geddes Large, the son of pioneer Methodist missionary Dr. Richard Whitefield Large, was born in Bella Bella in 1901. Following in his father's footsteps, he obtained a

medical degree from the University of Toronto in 1923. In 1926 he took over the super-
intendency at the hospital in Port Simpson. During the summer months, he operated
clinics at Port Essington's hospital and at several of the canneries along the Skeena River.
Large, *Skeena*.

52 Unless otherwise indicated, information about Clifford is taken from interviews conducted
August 16 and 18, 2010, at Zimacord, British Columbia, just west of Terrace.

53 For an analysis of social change among the Tsimshian, see James A. McDonald, "Social
Change and the Creation of Underdevelopment: A Northwest Coast Case," *American
Ethnologist* 21, 1 (1994): 152–75.

54 Cajete, *Look to the Mountain*, 170.

55 The main goal of the Crosby boarding home was to Anglicize Tsimshian girls by teaching
them limited literacy skills as well as the practical arts of cooking, cleaning, and service.
Hare and Barman, *Good Intentions Gone Awry*.

56 Starting in the early 1900s, townspeople would signal "fire" by ringing the bell on the
Anglican church on Dufferin Street. All able-bodied adults would swing into action to
help fight the blaze. See Harris, *Spokeshute*, 60.

57 Anthropologist Jay Miller has discovered that some Tsimshian today prefer not to acknowledge certain aspects of their spirituality because knowledge of how to treat powers
and objects with respect has been lost. "There is always the danger that these powers, once
summoned, might inadvertently hurt, maim, or kill all those involved." See Miller, *Tsimshian Culture*, 99–100.

58 Clifford's failure to pass Grade 1 is curious. Although school records indicate that Clifford
attended school only about 65 percent of the time, Mrs. Pogson recorded his academic
progress as "good" and awarded him an "A" for his conduct. Port Essington Indian Day
School, Quarterly School Return, March 31, 1947, Department of Indian Affairs, RG-10,
vol. 6407, file 836–2, part 1, LAC.

59 For more about the National Rifle Association and the Bisley competitions, see http://
www.nra.org.uk.

60 "Terrace Man Makes Jade 'Talk,'" *Queen Charlotte Islands News Advertiser*, August 1, 1978,
2–3.

61 Ibid. See also "Indian dancing, totem poles, carvings displayed at Salmon Festival," *Prince
Rupert Daily News*, June 14, 1971, 2.

62 The First Citizens Fund was established in 1969 to promote cultural, educational, and
economic development among First Nations peoples. See http://www.gov.bc.ca/arr/
economic/fcf. One of the catalysts prompting First Nations across the country to collaborate for cultural revitalization was the White Paper introduced by the federal government
in 1967, which recommended eliminating Indian status and special rights. John Lutz,
Makúk: A New History of Aboriginal-White Relations (Vancouver: UBC Press, 2008), 289.

63 Unless otherwise indicated, information about Harvey Wing comes from interviews held
August 16, 2010, and July 5, 2011.

64 Lily Chow, *Chasing Their Dreams* (Prince George, BC: Caitlin, 2000), 36. Lee Wing opened
the café in 1921. Harris, *Spokeshute*, 130.

65 According to Harvey, Lee closed down the café but the store with the pool room was taken
over by Bill and Anne Ingram.

66 Charlotte Jang, quoted in Chow, *Chasing Their Dreams*, 35.

67 See Raptis and Bowker, "Maintaining the Illusion."

68 Lorna Williams, "Urban Aboriginal Education: The Vancouver Experience," in *Aboriginal Education: Fulfilling the Promise*, ed. Marlene Brant Castellano, Lynne Davis, and Louise Lahache (Vancouver: UBC Press, 2000), 139.

69 Miller, *Skyscrapers Hide the Heavens*, 121; Barman, *West beyond the West*, 134–35.

70 After immigrating from Norway in 1909, the Nelson family established several canneries around British Columbia and then moved to Port Edward in 1943. Blyth, *History of Port Edward*, 30; Campbell, *Cannery Village*.

71 Unless otherwise indicated, information about Charlotte has been derived from an interview conducted July 5, 2011.

72 Bowman, *Klondike of the Skeena*, 64; Harris, *Spokeshute*, 200–2; *Minutes*, September 4, 1946, Prince Rupert School District (PRSD).

73 Edward Bolton, the "first native scholar in BC to have been successful in passing his [high school] entrance examination from an Indian Reserve day school," had enrolled at King Edward High School in Prince Rupert in 1935. Bowman, *Klondike of the Skeena*, 65. Edward later served as chief of the reserve and was among the last to leave Port Essington after fires decimated the town during the 1960s. Harris, *Spokeshute*, 231.

74 St. George's was originally opened by Anglican missionaries as the Indian Boys Day School in 1867. See http://www.anglican.ca/relationships/histories/st-georges-school-lytton.

75 Mrs. McDougall's June 1951 "Pass List for Port Essington School" noted that Charlotte was a "good pupil" who had "almost completed all subjects except Language." Port Essington Indian Day School, Class Register, June 1957, Prince Rupert City and Regional Archives (PRCRA).

76 Lydia Miljan, *Public Policy in Canada: An Introduction*, 5th ed. (Don Mills, ON: Oxford University Press, 2008), 260.

77 Vancouver Vocational Institute was established in 1949. In 1965 it amalgamated with Vancouver City College, Vancouver School of Art, the Vancouver School District's night school program, and the King Edward Senior Matriculation and Continuing Education Centre to form Vancouver Community College.

78 Minister of Public Works and Government Services Canada, "Students Thrive at Kitsumkalum Adult Learning Centre," in *Community Stories: Aboriginal Successes in British Columbia*, 29–30 (Vancouver: Indian and Northern Affairs Canada, 2009), https://www.aadnc-aandc.gc.ca/eng/1100100021663/1100100021726.

79 Indigenous high school completion rates in the district run about 46 percent, compared with a provincial average for non-Aboriginal learners of roughly 81 percent. Coast Mountains Board of Education, School District 82, *2011–2012 Achievement Contract*, http://www.bced.gov.bc.ca/schools/sdinfo/acc_contracts/2012/82.pdf.

80 LaFrance, "Culturally Negotiated Education," 101.

81 See, for example, Barman, "Schooled for Inequality," 62–63; and Miller, *Shingwauk's Vision*, 268.

82 Marie Battiste, *Decolonizing Education: Nourishing the Learning Spirit* (Saskatoon: Purich, 2013), 26.

83 Jerry Paquette, *Aboriginal Self-government and Education in Canada* (Kingston: Institute of Intergovernmental Relations, 1986), 35. See also Noel Dyck, *Differing Visions: Administering Indian Residential Schooling in Prince Albert, 1867–1995* (Halifax: Fernwood, 1997), 61.

84 Barman, "Schooled for Inequality," 63–65; Miller, *Shingwauk's Vision*, 390–92.

CHAPTER 5: BURIED SEEDS TAKING ROOT

1 Marie Battiste, "Enabling the Autumn Seed: Toward a Decolonized Approach to Aboriginal Knowledge, Language, and Education," *Canadian Journal of Native Education* 22, 1 (1998): 25.

2 "Roberts Returns as Kitsumkalum Chief Councillor," *Terrace Standard,* March 1, 2011, http://www.terracestandard.com/news/117198778.html. Unless otherwise indicated, information about Don Roberts Junior has been taken from interviews held July 29, 2009, and February 17, 2012.

3 "Old Tom" was a type of "one-base baseball" where one player would hit the ball with a bat and then run to the end of the field and home again while trying to avoid being hit by the ball, thrown by fielders. See also the stories of Mildred and Sam in Chapter 4.

4 For information on the controversies surrounding government regulation of Tsimshian resources, see McDonald, "Social Change"; and Charles R. Menzies and Caroline F. Butler, "Working in the Woods," *American Indian Quarterly* 25, 3 (2001): 409–30.

5 It is important to note that land is not merely linked to economic matters for First Nations peoples. It also has political and spiritual importance. First Nations Education Standing Committee (FNESC), BC Teachers' Federation (BCTF), and Tripartite Public Education Committee (TPEC), *Understanding the BC Treaty Process: An Opportunity for Dialogue,* 2nd ed. (Vancouver: FNESC, BCTF, and TPEC, 1998), 24, http://www.fns.bc.ca/pdf/uttp -pages1-8.pdf. In the words of Emma LaRocque, "forced spatial displacement and subjugation ravage the human spirit." LaRocque, *When the Other Is Me,* 88. See also Paul Tennant, *Aboriginal Peoples and Politics: The Indian Land Question in British Columbia, 1849–1989* (Vancouver: UBC Press, 1990).

6 Marker, "Indigenous Resistance and Racist Schooling," 760; Battiste and Henderson, *Protecting Indigenous Knowledge,* 42.

7 Unless otherwise noted, information about Steve is drawn from interviews conducted August 18, 2010, and July 6, 2011.

8 During this period, the town's water flume was no longer operational.

9 Helena was apparently a fisherwoman, a rare occupation for women of the time. Jo-Anne Fiske, "Fishing Is Women's Business: Changing Economic Roles of Carrier Women and Men," in *Native People, Native Lands: Canadian Indians, Inuit, and Metis,* ed. Bruce Alden Cox, 186–98 (Montreal and Kingston: McGill-Queen's University Press, 2002).

10 This approach whereby more able pupils assisted younger ones gained popularity in the nineteenth century when it was formalized as the "monitorial system" by British educators Andrew Bell and Joseph Lancaster. Ronald Rayman, "Joseph Lancaster's Monitorial System of Instruction and American Indian Education, 1815–1838," *History of Education Quarterly* 21, 4 (1981): 395–409.

11 British Columbia Department of Education, *Annual Report of the Public Schools of the Province of British Columbia (ARPS),* 1963, xliii.

12 Although the school had space for roughly forty children, it enrolled sixty-one pupils at its high point in 1906–07. Harris, *Spokeshute,* 114; British Columbia Department of Education, *ARPS,* 1906–07.

13 See Toutant, "Equality by Mail."

14 Information about Richard is from interviews undertaken August 16, 2010, and August 17, 2011.

15 Richard is father to Diana, Kyle, Sheena, Monica, and Laurie-Dawn. His grandchildren are Thallen, Peyton, and Cali.

16 Andrea Bear Nicholas, "Canada's Colonial Mission: The Great White Bird," in *Aboriginal Education in Canada: A Study in Decolonization,* ed. K.P. Binda and Sharilyn Calliou (Mississauga, ON: Canadian Educators' Press, 2001), 10.

17 Peggy Wilson, "Trauma of Sioux Indian High School Students," *Anthropology and Education Quarterly* 22, 4 (1991): 380. See also Judith Kleinfeld, *A Long Way from Home* (Fairbanks, AK: Center for Northern and Educational Research and Institute for Social, Economic and Government Research, 1973).

18 Regarding the pseudoscientific claims that helped to entrench racism in North America, see Stephen J. Gould, *The Mismeasure of Man* (New York: Norton, 1981).

19 Duff, *Indian History,* 86.

20 Unless otherwise indicated, information about Carol is taken from interviews held August 18, 2010, and August 4, 2011.

21 See Robert Lado, *Linguistics across Cultures: Applied Linguistics for Language Teachers* (Ann Arbor: University of Michigan Press, 1957); and H.H. Stern, *Fundamental Concepts of Language Teaching* (Oxford: Oxford University Press, 1986), 330–31.

22 Apparently, the trip up the Ecstall River to Brown's Mill is "a scenic one with high vertical mountains on either side of the river, and silvery threads of cataracts spilling down the sheer rock faces." Harris, *Spokeshute,* 95.

23 Carol's children are Christina, Jolene, Troy, Andrea, Tracy, and Jenna. Her grandchildren are Ethan, Noah, Sophie, Gabriella, Soraya, Victoria, Hannah, Kayleen, and Lauren.

24 Unless otherwise indicated, information about Jim is taken from an interview conducted July 5, 2011.

25 Paul Axelrod, "Banning the Strap: The End of Corporal Punishment in Canadian Schools," *Canadian Historical Review* 91, 2 (2010): 261–85.

26 Williams, "Urban Aboriginal Education," 139.

27 Jim's two daughters live with him at Kitsumkalum during the summers and with his former wife in Haida Gwaii during the school year. His son lives with him year round.

28 Lutz, *Makúk,* 269.

29 LaFrance, "Culturally Negotiated Education," 101.

30 See Jan Hare and Michelle Pidgeon, "The Way of the Warrior," *Canadian Journal of Education* 34, 2 (2011): 102–3.

31 See, for example, Lisa Wexler, "The Importance of Identity, History, and Culture in the Wellbeing of Indigenous Youth," *Journal of the History of Childhood and Youth* 2, 2 (2009): 267–76.

32 Battiste, "Enabling the Autumn Seed," 25.

Chapter 6: Stability and Change

1 Campbell, *Persistence and Change,* 66–74.

2 LaFrance, "Culturally Negotiated Education," 101.

3 Rita Irwin and J. Karen Reynolds, "Creativity in a Cultural Context," *Canadian Journal of Native Education* 19, 1 (1992): 93; LaFrance, "Culturally Negotiated Education," 108. See also Ellen White and Jo-ann Archibald, "Kwulasulwut S yuth (Ellen White's Teachings)," *Canadian Journal of Native Education* 19, 2 (1992): 150–64.

4 Irwin and Reynolds, "Creativity in a Cultural Context," 93.

5 Williams, "Urban Aboriginal Education," 140–41.

6 Patricia A. Carter, "'Completely Discouraged': Women Teachers' Resistance in the Bureau of Indian Affairs Schools, 1900–1910," *Frontiers* 15, 3 (1995): 53.

7 Miller, *Shingwauk's Vision*, 413.

8 John Taylor, "Non-Native Teachers Teaching in Native Communities," *First Nations Education in Canada: The Circle Unfolds*, ed. Marie Battiste and Jean Barman, 224–42 (Vancouver: UBC Press, 1995).

9 Titley, *Narrow Vision*, 89.

10 Ronald Manzer, *Public Schools and Political Ideas: Canadian Educational Policy in Historical Perspective* (Toronto: University of Toronto Press, 1994), 13.

11 Hugh Shewell, *'Enough to Keep Them Alive': Indian Welfare in Canada, 1873–1965* (Toronto: University of Toronto Press, 2004), 14.

12 Ibid.

13 E. Brian Titley, *The Indian Commissioners: Agents of the State and Indian Policy in Canada's Prairie West, 1873–1932* (Edmonton: University of Alberta Press, 2009), 211.

14 Barman, "Schooled for Inequality," 65.

15 Statistics indicate that, despite their credentials, teachers at Port Essington Indian Day School were paid approximately two-thirds of the rate of British Columbia's teachers with similar credentials and experience. British Columbia Department of Education, *Annual Reports of the Public Schools of the Province of British Columbia (ARPS)*, 1890–1947.

16 Joan W. Scott, "Storytelling," *History and Theory* 50, 2 (2011): 205.

17 Paquette, *Aboriginal Self-government*, 35. See also Dyck, *Differing Visions*, 61.

18 LaFrance, "Culturally Negotiated Education," 101.

19 Emma LaRocque, "From the Land to the Classroom: Broadening Epistemology," in *Pushing the Margins: Native and Northern Studies*, ed. Jill Oakes et al. (Winnipeg: University of Manitoba Press, 2001), 67.

20 McLeod, *Cree Narrative Memory*, 19. See also Michael Marker, "Sacred Mountains and Ivory Towers: Indigenous Pedagogies of Place and Invasions from Modernity," in *Indigenous Philosophies and Critical Education: A Reader*, ed. George J. Sefa Dei, 197–211 (New York: Peter Lang, 2011).

21 Battiste and Henderson, *Protecting Indigenous Knowledge*.

22 LaRocque, "From the Land"; Margaret Kovach, "Emerging from the Margins: Indigenous Methodologies," in *Research as Resistance: Critical Indigenous and Anti-oppressive Approaches*, ed. Leslie Brown and Susan Strega (Toronto: Canadian Scholars' Press, 2005), 28.

23 Neylan, *Heavens Are Changing*, 249.

24 Battiste, *Decolonizing Education*, 151.

25 McLeod, *Cree Narrative Memory*, 55–58. See also Larissa Behrendt, "Home: The Importance of Place to the Dispossessed," *South Atlantic Quarterly* 108, 1 (2009): 71–85.

26 Sophie McCall, *First Person Plural: Aboriginal Storytelling and the Ethics of Collaborative Authorship* (Vancouver: UBC Press, 2011), 168.

27 See, for example, David A. Gruenewald, "The Best of Both Worlds: A Critical Pedagogy of Place," *Educational Researcher* 32, 4 (2003): 3–12.

28 Battiste and Henderson, *Protecting Indigenous Knowledge*, 42.

29 Bear Nicholas, "Canada's Colonial Mission," 10.

30 Anuik, Battiste, and George, "Learning from Promising Programs," 65; Battiste, *Decolonizing Education*, 183.

31 Michael Marker, "Indigenous Resistance and Racist Schooling on the Borders of Empires: Coast Salish Cultural Survival," *Paedagogica Historica* 45, 6 (2009): 758.

32 See Robinson, *Living by Stories*, 29; and LaRocque, *When the Other Is Me*, 127.

33 Bear Nicholas, "Canada's Colonial Mission," 14.

34 Barman, "Schooled for Inequality," 57. From the early twentieth century to 1996, 130 residential schools housed a total of 150,000 Aboriginal, Métis, and Inuit children.

35 Miller, *Shingwauk's Vision*, 418–19.

36 The most comprehensive study of the residential schools is Miller, *Shingwauk's Vision*. See also Celia Haig-Brown, *Resistance and Renewal: Surviving the Indian Residential School* (Vancouver: Arsenal Pulp, 1988); and Milloy, *National Crime*.

37 Milloy, *National Crime*, 73.

38 For a more positive account of boarding school experiences in the United States, see also David Wallace Adams, "Beyond Bleakness: The Brighter Side of Indian Boarding Schools, 1870–1940," in *Boarding School Blues: Revisiting American Indian Educational Experiences*, ed. Clifford E. Trafzer, Jean A. Keller, and Lorene Sisquoc (Lincoln: University of Nebraska Press, 2006), 36. In the Canadian context, see works that contrast negative and positive experiences, such as Grant, *No End of Grief*, 226; and Haig-Brown, *Resistance and Renewal*.

39 Clyde Ellis, "'We Had a Lot of Fun, but of Course, That Wasn't the School Part': Life at the Rainy Mountain Boarding School, 1893–1920," in *Boarding School Blues: Revisiting American Indian Educational Experiences*, ed. Clifford E. Trafzer, Jean A. Keller, and Lorene Sisquoc (Lincoln: University of Nebraska Press, 2006), 67.

40 Coates, "Very Imperfect Means," 138–40; Titley, *Narrow Vision*, 89.

41 See, for example, Miller, *Shingwauk's Vision;* and Milloy, *National Crime*.

42 Milloy, *National Crime*, 57–58.

43 David A. Nock, *A Victorian Missionary and Canadian Indian Policy* (Waterloo, ON: Wilfrid Laurier University Press, 1988), 70. That religious denominations – particularly the Catholic Church – retained their power in Canada long after church-state separation in other Western nations has been attributed to the English defeat of the French on the Plains of Abraham in 1759. This historical event led to "a tacit agreement between the church, the politicians ... and the economic leaders of St. James and Bay Streets," enabling the church to continue overseeing people's spiritual and educational development but not their political or economic affairs. John Webster Grant, *The Church in the Canadian Era* (Burlington, ON: Welch, 1988), 15.

44 A.F. MacKenzie to W.E. Collison, November 26, 1929, Department of Indian Affairs, RG-10, vol. 6407, file 836–1, Library and Archives Canada (LAC).

45 For a discussion of government's heavy-handed approach to policy making, see Paquette, *Aboriginal Self-government*, 35. See also Dyck, *Differing Visions*, 61; and Miljan, *Public Policy in Canada*, 260.

46 Leanne Simpson, *Dancing on our Turtle's Back: Stories of Nishnaabeg Re-creation, Resurgence and a New Emergence* (Winnipeg: Arbeiter Ring, 2011), 16.

47 Albert Bandura, "Social Cognitive Theory: An Agentic Perspective," *Annual Review of Psychology* 52, 1 (2001): 1.

48 Miller, *Skyscrapers Hide the Heavens*, 121.

49 Battiste, *Decolonizing Education*, 26.

50 Fisher, *Contact and Conflict*, 109. Miller, *Skyscrapers Hide the Heavens*, 118; Jean Barman, Yvonne Hébert, and Don McCaskill, "The Legacy of the Past: An Overview," in *Indian Education in Canada*, vol. 1, *The Legacy*, ed. Jean Barman, Neil Sutherland, and J. Donald Wilson (Vancouver: UBC Press, 1986), 4.

51 Lutz, *Makúk*, 23.

52 Leslie, "Bagot Commission," 52.

53 Titley, *Narrow Vision*, 15. See also Shewell, *'Enough to Keep Them Alive,'* 29.

54 Lutz, *Makúk*, 287.

55 Ibid., 269.

56 See LaFrance, "Culturally Negotiated Education," 101.

57 See, for example, ibid., 101–13; and Battiste and Henderson, *Protecting Indigenous Knowledge*, 100.

58 Battiste and Henderson, *Protecting Indigenous Knowledge*, 100.

59 Wexler, "Importance of Identity," 269; Jessica Ball, "As If Indigenous Knowledge and Communities Mattered: Transformative Education in First Nations Communities in Canada," *American Indian Quarterly* 28, 3–4 (2004): 455.

60 National Indian Brotherhood, *Indian Control*, 16.

61 Feuerstein's learning theories have shaped successful programs for Aboriginal students in the Vancouver School District. Williams, "Urban Aboriginal Education."

62 Verna J. Kirkness, "Aboriginal Education in Canada: A Retrospective and a Prospective," *Journal of American Indian Education* 39, 1 (1999): 19–20.

63 Helen Raptis and Thomas Fleming, *Reframing Education: How to Create Effective Schools* (Toronto: C.D. Howe Institute, 2003).

64 Cajete, *Look to the Mountain*, 20.

65 Battiste, *Decolonizing Education*, 163.

66 Ibid., 168.

67 See, for example, Wexler, "Importance of Identity."

68 See Hare and Pidgeon, "Way of the Warrior," 102–3.

69 Williams, "Urban Aboriginal Education," 139.

70 Wilson, "Trauma"; Kleinfeld, *Long Way from Home*.

71 On language interference, see Lado, *Linguistics across Cultures;* and Stern, *Fundamental Concepts*, 330–31. For views on cultural interference, see Harry B. Hawthorn, ed., *A Survey of Contemporary Indians of Canada: Economic, Political, Educational Needs and Policies* (Ottawa: Indian Affairs Branch, 1967), 109–17.

72 Harold Cardinal, *The Rebirth of Canada's Indians* (Edmonton: Hurtig, 1977), 195. See also Raptis, "Implementing Integrated Education Policy."

73 Department of Indian Affairs, *Annual Report, 1970–71* (Ottawa: Government of Canada, 1972), 10.

74 John Lutz has argued that "Aboriginal Peoples in British Columbia hit bottom around 1970," due in large part to economic shifts. Lutz, *Makúk*, 289.

75 Marie Battiste, "Foreword," in *Aboriginal Education: Fulfilling the Promise*, ed. Marlene Brant Castellano, Lynne Davis, and Louise Lahache (Vancouver: UBC Press, 2008), viii.

76 LaRoque, *When the Other Is Me*, 127; Battiste and Henderson, *Protecting Indigenous Knowledge*, 29.

77 Manzer, *Public Schools*, 13.

78 Ibid.

79 For analyses of the "self-aggrandizement and inertia" that characterized the Department of Indian Affairs, see Titley, *Indian Commissioners*; and Titley, *Narrow Vision*.

80 Manzer, *Public Schools*, 46.

81 J.L. Granatstein, *Canada's War: The Politics of the Mackenzie King Government, 1939–1945*, 2nd ed. (Toronto: University of Toronto Press, 1990), 272–78.

82 Shewell, *'Enough to Keep Them Alive,'* 171–73.

83 In addition to a policy of integrating Indian children into public school systems, by the mid-1960s Indian Affairs had embarked on an extensive agenda of community development that sought to employ human and material resources from Indigenous reserves.

Anticipated outcomes included increasing the amount of decision making and administrative work allocated to reserve residents with a consequent decrease in administrative control by Indian Affairs officials. See Robert Craig Cunningham, "Community Development at the Department of Indian Affairs in the 1960s: Much Ado about Nothing" (MA thesis, University of Saskatchewan, 1997).

84 For an interesting perspective on the roots and persistence of systemic racism, see Verna St. Denis, "Rethinking Culture Theory in Aboriginal Education," in *Canadian Perspectives on the Sociology of Education*, ed. Cynthia Levine-Rasky, 163–82 (Don Mills, ON: Oxford University Press, 2009).
85 Miller, *Shingwauk's Vision*, 382–83; Cardinal, *Rebirth of Canada's Indians*, 195.
86 Raptis, "Implementing Integrated Education Policy," 137.
87 Battiste, *Decolonizing Education*, 24. See also Miller, *Shingwauk's Vision*, 62–63.
88 LaFrance, "Culturally Negotiated Education," 101; McLeod, *Cree Narrative Memory*, 19: Anuik, Battiste, and George, "Learning from Promising Programs," 65; Battiste, *Decolonizing Education*, 183.
89 Battiste and Henderson, *Protecting Indigenous Knowledge*, 42; Marker, "Indigenous Resistance," 758.
90 Williams, "Urban Aboriginal Education," 139.

EPILOGUE

1 Deena Rymhs, "Appropriating Guilt: Reconciliation in an Aboriginal Canadian Context," *English Studies in Canada* 32, 1 (2006): 105.
2 Basil H. Johnston, *Indian School Days* (Toronto: Key Porter, 1988).
3 Miller, *Singwauk's Vision*, 361.
4 Jean Barman, "Separate and Unequal: Indian and White Girls at All Hallows School, 1884–1920," in *Indian Education in Canada*, vol. 1, *The Legacy*, ed. Jean Barman, Yvonne Hébert, and Don McCaskill, 110–27 (Vancouver: UBC Press, 1986).
5 Ibid., 124.
6 Battiste, *Decolonizing Education*, 183.
7 William Julius Mussell, "Decolonizing Education: A Building Block for Reconciliation," in *From Truth to Reconciliation: Transforming the Legacy of Residential Schools*, ed. Marlene Brant Castellano, Linda Archibald, and Mike DeGagné (Ottawa: Aboriginal Healing Foundation, 2008), 323.
8 Miller, *Shingwauk's Vision*, 427.
9 Smith, *Liberalism, Surveillance, and Resistance*, 233.
10 Coates, "Very Imperfect Means," 147.
11 Raptis, "Exploring the Factors," 525.
12 Raptis and Bowker, "Maintaining the Illusion," 3.
13 Marker, "Indigenous Resistance," 771.
14 Ibid., 759.
15 Bear Nicholas, "Canada's Colonial Mission," 10.
16 Battiste, "Enabling the Autumn Seed," 26.

Bibliography

ARCHIVAL COLLECTIONS

British Columbia Archives, Victoria, BC (BCA)

Department of Indian Affairs, RG-10
Indian Advisory Committee, GR-1071
Mrs. A.G. (Agnes) Harris Interview, T1212:0001
School Inspector Reports, GR-0122
Walter Wicks Interview, T1194:0004

Bob Stewart Archives (BSA)

Methodist Missionary Society Reports, 1884–85
United Church of Canada Yearbooks
William Henry Pierce File

Library and Archives Canada, Ottawa (LAC)

Department of Indian Affairs, RG-10

North Pacific Cannery Museum, Port Edward, BC

Port Essington Display and Reserve Minute Book

Prince Rupert City and Regional Archives (PRCRA)

Harris Family Fonds, Acc. 1997.006
Port Essington Indian Day School, Class Registers
Port Essington Street Map

PRINCE RUPERT SCHOOL DISTRICT (PRSD)

Minutes of Meetings of Board of Trustees, 1947

INTERVIEWS

Clifford Bolton, August 16 and 18, 2010
Charlotte Guno, July 5, 2011
Verna Inkster, January 30, 2010, August 18, 2010, and July 2, 2011
Sam Lockerby, August 17, 2010, and July 3, 2011
Wally Miller, August 16, 2010, and July 4, 2011
Don Roberts Junior, July 29, 2009, and February 17, 2012
Jim Roberts, July 5, 2011
Mildred Roberts, January 29, 2010, May 2, 2011, and July 3, 2011
Richard Roberts, August 16, 2010, and August 17, 2011
Steve Roberts, August 18, 2010, and July 6, 2011
Carol Sam, August 18, 2010, and August 4, 2011
Harvey Wing, August 16, 2010, and July 5, 2011

OTHER SOURCES

Absolon, Kathy, and Cam Willett. "Putting Ourselves Forward: Location in Aboriginal Research." In *Research as Resistance: Critical Indigenous and Anti-oppressive Approaches*, ed. Leslie Brown and Susan Strega, 97–126. Toronto: Canadian Scholars' Press, 2005.

Adams, David Wallace. "Beyond Bleakness: The Brighter Side of Indian Boarding Schools, 1870–1940." In *Boarding School Blues: Revisiting American Indian Educational Experiences*, ed. Clifford E. Trafzer, Jean A. Keller, and Lorene Sisquoc, 35–64. Lincoln: University of Nebraska Press, 2006.

Ahenakew, Edward. "Little Pine: An Indian Day School." Ed. Ruth Matheson Buck. *Saskatchewan History* 18, 2 (1965): 55–62.

Anderson, Margaret Seguin, and Tammy Anderson Blumhagen. "Memories and Moments: Conversations and Recollections." *BC Studies*, 104 (1994–95): 85–102.

Andrews, Thomas G. "Turning the Tables on Assimilation: Oglala Lakotas and the Pine Ridge Day Schools, 1889–1920s." *Western Historical Quarterly* 33, 4 (2002): 407–30. http://dx.doi.org/10.2307/4144766.

Anuik, Jonathan, Marie Battiste, and Priscilla (Nignwakwe) George. "Learning from Promising Programs and Applications in Nourishing the Learning Spirit." *Canadian Journal of Native Education* 33, 1 (2010): 63–82.

Archibald, Jo-ann. "Researching with Mutual Respect." *Canadian Journal of Native Education* 20, 2 (1993): 189–92.

–, ed. *Giving Voice to Our Ancestors*. Special issue of *Canadian Journal of Native Education* 19, 2 (1992).

Atkinson, Maureen L. "The 'Accomplished' Odille Quintal Morrison: Tsimshian Cultural Intermediary of Metlakatla, British Columbia." In *Recollecting: Lives of Aboriginal Women of the Canadian Northwest and Borderlands*, ed. Sarah Carter and Patricia McCormack, 135–56. Edmonton: Athabasca University Press, 2011.

Axelrod, Paul. "Banning the Strap: The End of Corporal Punishment in Canadian Schools."
    Canadian Historical Review 91, 2 (2010): 261–85.
Bailyn, Bernard. *Education in the Forming of American Society*. New York: Vintage, 1960.
Ball, Jessica. "As If Indigenous Knowledge and Communities Mattered: Transformative
    Education in First Nations Communities in Canada." *American Indian Quarterly* 28,
    3–4 (2004): 454–79. http://dx.doi.org/10.1353/aiq.2004.0090.
Bandura, Albert. "Social Cognitive Theory: An Agentic Perspective." *Annual Review of
    Psychology* 52, 1 (2001): 1–26. http://dx.doi.org/10.1146/annurev.psych.52.1.1.
Barman, Jean. *British Columbia: Spirit of the People*. Madeira Park, BC: Harbour, 2009.
–. "Families versus Schools: Children of Aboriginal Descent in British Columbia Classrooms
    of the Late Nineteenth Century." In *Family Matters: Papers in Post-Confederation
    Canadian Family History*, ed. Edgar-André Montigny and Lori Chambers, 73–89.
    Toronto: Canadian Scholars' Press, 1998.
–. "Schooled for Inequality: The Education of British Columbia Aboriginal Children." In
    Children, Teachers, and Schools in the History of British Columbia, ed. Jean Barman, Neil
    Sutherland, and J. Donald Wilson, 57–80. Calgary: Detselig, 1995.
–. "Separate and Unequal: Indian and White Girls at All Hallows School, 1884–1920." In
    Indian Education in Canada, vol. 1, *The Legacy*, ed. Jean Barman, Yvonne Hébert, and
    Don McCaskill, 110–31. Vancouver: UBC Press, 1986.
–. *The West beyond the West: A History of British Columbia*. Toronto: University of Toronto
    Press, 1991.
Barman, Jean, Yvonne Hébert, and Don McCaskill. "The Legacy of the Past: An Overview."
    In *Indian Education in Canada*, vol. 1, *The Legacy*, ed. Jean Barman, Yvonne Hébert,
    and Don McCaskill, 1–22. Vancouver: UBC Press, 1986.
–, eds. *Indian Education in Canada*. Vol. 1, *The Legacy*. Vancouver: UBC Press, 1986.
Battiste, Marie. *Decolonizing Education: Nourishing the Learning Spirit*. Saskatoon: Purich,
    2013.
–. "Enabling the Autumn Seed: Toward a Decolonized Approach to Aboriginal Knowledge,
    Language, and Education." *Canadian Journal of Native Education* 22, 1 (1998): 16–27.
–. "Foreword." In *Aboriginal Education: Fulfilling the Promise*, ed. Marlene Brant Castellano,
    Lynne Davis, and Louise Lahache, vii–ix. Vancouver: UBC Press, 2008.
–. "Micmac Literacy and Cognitive Assimilation." In *Indian Education in Canada*, vol. 1,
    The Legacy, ed. Jean Barman, Yvonne Hébert, and Don McCaskill, 23–44. Vancouver:
    UBC Press, 1986.
Battiste, Marie, and James (Sa'ke'j) Youngblood Henderson. *Protecting Indigenous Know-
    ledge and Heritage*. Saskatoon: Purich, 2000.
Bear Nicholas, Andrea "Canada's Colonial Mission: The Great White Bird." In *Aboriginal
    Education in Canada: A Study in Decolonization*, ed. K.P. Binda and Sharilyn Calliou,
    9–24. Mississauga, ON: Canadian Educators' Press, 2001.
Behrendt, Larissa. "Home: The Importance of Place to the Dispossessed." *South Atlantic
    Quarterly* 108, 1 (2009): 71–85. http://dx.doi.org/10.1215/00382876-2008-023.
Bennett, Norma V. *Pioneer Legacy: Chronicles of the Lower Skeena River*. Vol. 1. Terrace,
    BC: Dr. R.E.M. Lee Hospital Foundation, 1997.
Berg, Bruce L., and Howard Lune. *Qualitative Research Methods for the Social Sciences*. 8th
    ed. Boston: Pearson, 2012.
Berger, Thomas. "The Banished Japanese Canadians." In *Ethnic Canada*, ed. Leo Driedger,
    374–94. Toronto: Copp Clark Pitman, 1987.

Binda, K.P., and Sharilyn Calliou. "Introduction: Situating the Puppet Masters." In *Aboriginal Education in Canada: A Study in Decolonization,* ed. K.P. Binda and Sharilyn Calliou, 1–7. Mississauga, ON: Canadian Educators' Press, 2001.

Blyth, Gladys. *History of Port Edward, 1907–1970.* Port Edward, BC: n.p., 1970.

–. *Salmon Canneries: British Columbia North Coast.* Victoria, BC: Trafford, 2006.

Bowman, Phylis. *Klondike of the Skeena.* Chilliwack, BC: Sunrise, 1982.

Brant Castellano, Marlene, Linda Archibald, and Mike DeGagné, eds. *From Truth to Reconciliation: Transforming the Legacy of the Residential Schools.* Ottawa: Aboriginal Healing Foundation, 2008.

Brookes, Sonia. "An Analysis of Indian Education Policy, 1960–1989." MA thesis, University of Calgary, 1990.

–. "The Persistence of Native Education Policy in Canada." In *The Cultural Maze: Complex Questions on Native Destiny in Western Canada,* ed. John Friesen, 163–80. Calgary: Detselig, 1991.

Brown, Leslie, and Susan Strega, eds. *Research as Resistance: Critical Indigenous and Anti-oppressive Approaches.* Toronto: Canadian Scholars' Press, 2005.

Bryce, P.H. *The Story of a National Crime: Being an Appeal for Justice to the Indians of Canada.* Ottawa: James Hope and Sons, 1922.

Cajete, Gregory. *Look to the Mountain: An Ecology of Indigenous Education.* Durango, CO: Kivaki, 1994.

Campbell, K. Mack. *Cannery Village – Company Town: A History of British Columbia's Outlying Salmon Canneries.* Victoria, BC: Trafford, 2004.

Campbell, Kenneth. *Persistence and Change: A History of the Tsimsyen Nation.* Prince Rupert, BC: Tsimshian Nation and School District 52, 2005.

Cardinal, Harold. *The Rebirth of Canada's Indians.* Edmonton: Hurtig, 1977.

Carter, Patricia A. "'Completely Discouraged': Women Teachers' Resistance in the Bureau of Indian Affairs Schools, 1900–1910." *Frontiers* 15, 3 (1995): 53–86. http://dx.doi.org/10.2307/3346785.

Carter, Sarah, and Patricia McCormack, eds. *Recollecting: Lives of Aboriginal Women of the Canadian Northwest and Borderlands.* Edmonton: Athabasca University Press, 2011.

Chapple, Eve, and Helen Raptis. "From Integration to Segregation: Government Education Policy and the School at Telegraph Creek, British Columbia, 1906–1951." *Journal of the Canadian Historical Association* 24, 1 (2013): 131–62. http://dx.doi.org/10.7202/1024999ar.

Cherubini, Lorenzo, Julian Kitchen, and Lyn Trudeau. "Having the Spirit within to Vision: New Aboriginal Teachers' Commitment to Reclaiming Space." *Canadian Journal of Native Education* 32, 2 (2009): 38–51.

Chow, Lily. *Chasing Their Dreams.* Prince George, BC: Caitlin, 2000.

Clayton, Daniel. "Geographies of the Lower Skeena." *BC Studies,* 94 (1992): 29–58.

Coates, Ken. "A Very Imperfect Means of Education: Indian Day Schools in the Yukon Territory." In *Indian Education in Canada,* vol. 1, *The Legacy,* ed. Jean Barman, Yvonne Hébert, and Don McCaskill, 133–49. Vancouver: UBC Press, 1986.

Crosby, Thomas. *Among the An-Ko-me-nums or Flathead Tribes of Indians of the Pacific Coast.* Edmonton: Universal Bindery, 1907.

Cruikshank, Julie, with Angela Sidney, Kitty Smith, and Annie Ned. *Life Lived Like a Story: Life Stories of Three Yukon Native Elders.* Vancouver: UBC Press, 1990.

Cunningham, Robert Craig. "Community Development at the Department of Indian Affairs in the 1960s: Much Ado about Nothing." MA thesis, University of Saskatchewan, 1997.

Dexter, Edwin. *History of Education in the United States*. New York: Burt Franklin, 1906.

Drucker, Philip. *Cultures of the North Pacific Coast*. San Francisco, CA: Chandler, 1965.

Duff, Wilson. *The Indian History of British Columbia*. Vol. 1, *The Impact of the White Man*. Victoria: Department of Recreation and Conservation, Province of British Columbia, 1964.

Dyck, Noel. *Differing Visions: Administering Indian Residential Schooling in Prince Albert, 1867–1995*. Halifax: Fernwood, 1997.

–. *What Is the Indian 'Problem': Tutelage and Resistance in Canadian Indian Administration*. St. John's, NL: Institute of Social and Economic Research, 1991.

Ellis, Clyde. "'We Had a Lot of Fun, but of Course, That Wasn't the School Part': Life at the Rainy Mountain Boarding School, 1893–1920." In *Boarding School Blues: Revisiting American Indian Educational Experiences*, ed. Clifford E. Trafzer, Jean A. Keller, and Lorene Sisquoc, 69–72. Lincoln: University of Nebraska Press, 2006.

Enns, Richard A. "'But What Is the Object of Educating These Children, If It Costs Their Lives to Educate Them?': Federal Indian Education Policy in Western Canada in the Late 1800s." *Journal of Canadian Studies/Revue d'Études Canadiennes* 43, 3 (2009): 101–23.

Evans, Mike. "Ethics, Anonymity, and Authorship in Community Centred Research, or Anonymity and the Island Cache." *Pimatisiwin: A Journal of Aboriginal and Indigenous Community Health* 2, 1 (2004): 59–76.

Ferrier, Reverend Thompson. *Our Indians and Their Training for Citizenship*. Toronto: Young People's Forward Movement, n.d.

First Nations Education Standing Committee (FNESC), BC Teachers' Federation (BCTF), and Tripartite Public Education Committee (TPEC). *Understanding the BC Treaty Process: An Opportunity for Dialogue*, 2nd ed. Vancouver: FNESC, BCTF, and TPEC, 1998. http://www.fns.bc.ca/pdf/uttp-pages1-8.pdf.

Fisher, Robin. *Contact and Conflict: Indian-European Relations in British Columbia, 1774–1890*. Vancouver: UBC Press, 1977.

Fiske, Jo-Anne. "Fishing Is Women's Business: Changing Economic Roles of Carrier Women and Men." In *Native People, Native Lands: Canadian Indians, Inuit, and Metis*, ed. Bruce Alden Cox, 186–98. Montreal and Kingston: McGill-Queen's University Press, 2002.

Fiske, Jo-Anne, and Betty Patrick. *Cis Dideen Kat (When the Plumes Rise): The Way of the Lake Babine Nation*. Vancouver: UBC Press, 2000.

Fixico, Donald L. *The American Indian Mind in a Linear World*. New York: Routledge, 2003.

Fleming, Thomas, Lisa Smith, and Helen Raptis. "An Accidental Teacher: Anthony Walsh and the Aboriginal Day Schools at Six Mile Creek and Inkameep, British Columbia, 1929–1942." *Historical Studies in Education* 19, 1 (2007): 1–24.

Fleras, Augie. "Researching Together Differently: Bridging the Research Paradigm Gap." *Native Studies Review* 15, 2 (2004): 117–29.

Fontaine, Theodore. *Broken Circle: The Dark Legacy of Indian Residential Schools*. Vancouver: Heritage House, 2010.

Friesen, John W., and Virginia Lyons Friesen. *Aboriginal Education in Canada: A Plea for Integration*. Calgary: Detselig, 2002.

Galois, Robert M. "Colonial Encounters: The Worlds of Arthur Wellington Clah, 1855–1881." *BC Studies*, 115–16 (1997–98): 105–47.

Gardner, Philip. "Oral History in Education: Teacher's Memory and Teachers' History." *History of Education* 32, 2 (2003): 175–88. http://dx.doi.org/10.1080/00467600304159.

Garfield, Viola E. "Tsimshian Clan and Society." *University of Washington Publications in Anthropology* 7, 3 (1939): 167–340.

Glass, Aaron. "The Intention of Tradition: Contemporary Contexts and Contests of the Kwakwaka'wakw Hamat'sa Dance." MA thesis, University of British Columbia, 1994.

Glegg, Alastair. "Anatomy of a Tragedy: The Assisted Schools of British Columbia and the Death of Mabel Jones." *Historical Studies in Education* 17, 1 (2005): 145–64.

Gould, Stephen J. *The Mismeasure of Man.* New York: Norton, 1981.

Granatstein, J.L. *Canada's War: The Politics of the Mackenzie King Government, 1939–1945.* 2nd ed. Toronto: University of Toronto Press, 1990.

Grant, Agnes. *No End of Grief: Indian Residential Schools in Canada.* Winnipeg: Pemmican, 1996.

Grant, John Webster. *The Church in the Canadian Era.* Burlington, ON: Welch, 1988.

Gray, Susan Elaine. "Methodist Indian Day Schools and Indian Communities in Northern Manitoba, 1890–1925." *Manitoba History,* 30 (1995): http://www.mhs.mb.ca/docs/mb_history/30/methodistdayschools.shtml.

Greene, Ron. "Robert Cunningham and Son of Skeena (Port Essington)." *British Columbia History* 42, 3 (2009): 24–27.

Gruenewald, David A. "The Best of Both Worlds: A Critical Pedagogy of Place." *Educational Researcher* 32, 4 (2003): 3–12. http://dx.doi.org/10.3102/0013189X032004003.

Gutek, Gerald L. *Historical and Philosophical Foundations of Education.* 5th ed. Boston: Pearson, 2011.

Haig-Brown, Celia. *Resistance and Renewal: Surviving the Indian Residential School.* Vancouver: Arsenal Pulp, 1988.

Haig-Brown, Celia, Kathy L. Hodgson-Smith, Robert Regnier, and Jo-ann Archibald, eds. *Making the Spirit Dance Within: Joe Duquette High School and an Aboriginal Community.* Toronto: James Lorimer, 1997.

Hall, D.J. *Clifford Sifton.* Vol. 1, *The Young Napoleon, 1861–1900.* Vancouver: UBC Press, 1981.

Halpin, Marjorie M., and Margaret Seguin. "Tsimshian Peoples: Southern Tsimshian, Coast Tsimshian, Nishga, and Gitksan." In *Handbook of North American Indians,* vol. 7, *Northwest Coast,* ed. Wayne Suttles, 267–84. Washington, DC: Smithsonian Institution, 1990.

Hamilton, W.D. *The Federal Indian Day Schools of the Maritimes.* Fredericton: University of New Brunswick Press, 1986.

Hare, Jan, and Jean Barman. *Good Intentions Gone Awry: Emma Crosby and the Methodist Mission on the Northwest Coast.* Vancouver: UBC Press, 2006.

Hare, Jan, and Michelle Pidgeon. "The Way of the Warrior." *Canadian Journal of Education* 34, 2 (2011): 93–111.

Harris, Ernest A. *Spokeshute: Skeena River Memory.* Vancouver: Orca, 1990.

Harris, Kenneth B., with Frances M.P. Robinson. *Visitors Who Never Left: The Origin of the People of Damelahamid.* Vancouver: UBC Press, 1974.

Hawthorn, Harry B., ed. *A Survey of Contemporary Indians of Canada: Economic, Political, Educational Needs and Policies.* Ottawa: Indian Affairs Branch, 1967.

Hawthorn, Harry B., Cyril S. Belshaw, and Stuart M. Jamieson. *The Indians of British Columbia.* Berkeley: University of California Press, 1960.

Henderson, James (sákéj) Youngblood. "The Context of the State of Nature," in *Reclaiming Indigenous Voice and Vision,* ed. Marie Battiste, 11–38. Vancouver, BC: UBC Press, 2000.

–. "Treaties and Indian Education." In *First Nations Education in Canada: The Circle Unfolds,* ed. Marie Battiste and Jean Barman, 245–61. Vancouver: UBC Press, 1995.

Henley, Thom. *River of Mist, Journey of Dreams.* Victoria, BC: Rediscovery International Foundation, 2009.

High, Steven. "Sharing Authority: An Introduction." *Journal of Canadian Studies/Revue d'Études Canadiennes* 43, 1 (2009): 12–34.

Hutchinson, H.K. "Dimensions of Ethnic Education: The Japanese in British Columbia, 1880–1940." MA thesis, University of Victoria, 1972.

Indian and Northern Affairs. *The Historical Development of the Indian Act.* Ottawa: Indian and Northern Affairs, 1978.

Inglis, Richard I., and George MacDonald. *Skeena River Prehistory.* Ottawa: National Museums of Canada, 1979.

Irwin, Rita, and J. Karen Reynolds. "Creativity in a Cultural Context." *Canadian Journal of Native Education* 19, 1 (1992): 90–95.

Jenness, Diamond. *The Indians of Canada.* 3rd ed. Ottawa: National Museum of Canada, 1955.

Jensen, Katherine. "Teachers and Progressives: The Navajo Day-School Experiment, 1935–1945." *Arizona and the West* 25, 1 (1983): 49–62.

Johnston, Basil H. *Indian School Days.* Toronto: Key Porter, 1988.

Kirkness, Verna J. "Aboriginal Education in Canada: A Retrospective and a Prospective." *Journal of American Indian Education* 39, 1 (1999): 14–30.

Kleinfeld, Judith. *A Long Way from Home.* Fairbanks, AK: Center for Northern and Educational Research and Institute for Social, Economic and Government Research, 1973.

Kovach, Margaret. "Emerging from the Margins: Indigenous Methodologies." In *Research as Resistance: Critical, Indigenous, and Anti-oppressive Approaches,* ed. Leslie Brown and Susan Strega, 19–36. Toronto: Canadian Scholars' Press, 2005.

–. *Indigenous Methodologies: Characteristics, Conversations, and Contexts.* Toronto: University of Toronto Press, 2009.

Lado, Robert. *Linguistics across Cultures: Applied Linguistics for Language Teachers.* Ann Arbor: University of Michigan Press, 1957.

LaFrance, Brenda Tsioniaon. "Culturally Negotiated Education in First Nations Communities: Empowering Ourselves for Future Generations." In *Aboriginal Education: Fulfilling the Promise,* ed. Marlene Brant Castellano, Lynne Davis, and Louise Lahache, 101–13. Vancouver: UBC Press, 2000.

Lapadat, Judith C., and Harold Janzen. "Collaborative Research in Northern Communities: Possibilities and Pitfalls." *BC Studies,* 104 (1994): 69–83.

Large, Richard G. *The Skeena: River of Destiny.* Vancouver: Mitchell, 1957.

LaRocque, Emma. "From the Land to the Classroom: Broadening Epistemology." In *Pushing the Margins: Native and Northern Studies,* ed. Jill Oakes, Rick Riewe, Marilyn Bennet, and Brenda Chisholm, 62–83. Winnipeg: University of Manitoba Press, 2001.

–. *When the Other Is Me: Native Resistance Discourse, 1850–1990.* Winnipeg: University of Manitoba Press, 2010.

Lawrence, Adrea, KuuNUx TeeRIt Kroupa, and Donald Warren. "Introduction." *History of Education Quarterly* 54, 3 (2014): 253–54. http://dx.doi.org/10.1111/hoeq.12066.

Lee, C.D., and P. Smagorinsky, eds. *Vygotskian Perspectives on Literacy Research: Constructing Meaning through Collaborative Inquiry.* New York: Cambridge University Press, 2000.

Leonard, Frank. *A Thousand Blunders: The Grand Trunk Pacific Railway and Northern British Columbia.* Vancouver: UBC Press, 1996.

Leslie, John. "The Bagot Commission: Developing Corporate Memory for the Indian Department." *Historical Papers of the Canadian Historical Association* 17, 1 (1982): 31–52. http://dx.doi.org/10.7202/030883ar.

Lomawaima, K. Tsianina, and Teresa McCarty. *"To Remain An Indian": Lessons in Democracy from a Century of Native American Education.* New York: Teachers College Press, 2006.

Ludwin, Ruth S., Robert Dennis, Deborah Carver, Alan D. McMillan, Robert Losey, John Clague, Chris Jonientz-Trisler, Janine Bowechop, Jacilee Wray, and Karen James. "Dating the 1700 Cascadia Earthquake: Great Coastal Earthquakes in Native Stories." *Seismological Research Letters* 76, 2 (2005): 140–48. http://dx.doi.org/10.1785/gssrl.76. 2.140.

Lutz, John. "After the Fur Trade: The Aboriginal Labouring Class of British Columbia, 1849–1890." *Journal of the Canadian Historical Association* 3, 1 (1992): 69–93. http:// dx.doi.org/10.7202/031045ar.

–. *Makúk: A New History of Aboriginal-White Relations.* Vancouver: UBC Press, 2008.

MacLean, Hope. "A Positive Experiment in Aboriginal Education: The Methodist Ojibwa Day Schools in Upper Canada, 1824–1833." *Canadian Journal of Native Studies* 22, 1 (2002): 23–63.

Manuel, George, and Michael Posluns. *The Fourth World: An Indian Reality.* New York: Free Press, 1974.

Manzer, Ronald. *Public Schools and Political Ideas: Canadian Educational Policy in Historical Perspective.* Toronto: University of Toronto Press, 1994.

Marker, Michael. "After the Makah Whale Hunt: Indigenous Knowledge and Limits to Multicultural Discourse." *Urban Education* 41, 5 (2006): 482–505. http://dx.doi.org/10. 1177/0042085906291923.

–. "Indigenous Resistance and Racist Schooling on the Borders of Empires: Coast Salish Cultural Survival." *Paedagogica Historica* 45, 6 (2009): 757–72. http://dx.doi.org/10.1080/ 00309230903335678.

–. "'It Was Two Different Times of the Day, but in the Same Place': Coast Salish High School Experience in the 1970s." *BC Studies,* 144 (2004–05): 91–113.

–. "Sacred Mountains and Ivory Towers: Indigenous Pedagogies of Place and Invasions from Modernity." In *Indigenous Philosophies and Critical Education: A Reader,* ed. George J. Sefa Dei, 197–211. New York: Peter Lang, 2011.

Marsden, Susan, Margaret Seguin Anderson, and Deanna Nyce. "Aboriginals: Tsimshian." In *Encyclopedia of Canada's Peoples,* ed. Paul Robert Magocsi, 98–108. Toronto: University of Toronto Press, 1999.

McCall, Sophie. *First Person Plural: Aboriginal Storytelling and the Ethics of Collaborative Authorship.* Vancouver: UBC Press, 2011.

McDonald, James A. "Bleeding Day and Night: The Construction of the Grand Trunk Pacific Railway across Tsimshian Reserve Lands." *Canadian Journal of Native Studies* 10, 1 (1990): 33–69.

–. "Images of the Nineteenth-Century Economy of the Tsimshian." In *The Tsimshian: Images of the Past, Views for the Present,* ed. Margaret Seguin, 40–54. Vancouver: UBC Press, 1984.

–. *People of the Robin: The Tsimshian of Kitsumkalum.* Edmonton: CCI Press and Alberta ACADRE Network, 2003.

–. "Social Change and the Creation of Underdevelopment: A Northwest Coast Case." *American Ethnologist* 21, 1 (1994): 152–75. http://dx.doi.org/10.1525/ae.1994.21.1.02a00080.

–. "Trying to Make a Life: The Historical Political Economy of Kitsumkalum." PhD diss., University of British Columbia, 1985.

–. "The Tsimshian Protocols: Locating and Empowering Community-based Research." *Canadian Journal of Native Education* 28, 1–2 (2008): 80–91.

McHarg, Sandra, and Maureen Cassidy. *Early Days on the Skeena River.* Hazelton, BC: Northwest Community College, 1983.

McIvor, Sharon D. "Aboriginal Women's Rights as 'Existing Rights.'" In *First Voices: An Aboriginal Women's Reader,* ed. Patricia A. Monture and Patricia D. McGuire, 374–81. Toronto: Inanna, 2009.

McKay, Ian. "The Liberal Order Framework: A Prospectus for a Reconnaissance of Canadian History." *Canadian Historical Review* 81, 4 (2000): 617–51. http://dx.doi.org/10.3138/chr.81.4.616.

McLeod, Brenda. "First Nations Women and Sustainability on the Canadian Prairies." In *First Voices: An Aboriginal Women's Reader,* ed. Patricia A. Monture and Patricia D. McGuire, 154–68. Toronto: Inanna, 2009.

McLeod, Neal. *Cree Narrative Memory: From Treaties to Contemporary Times.* Saskatoon: Purich, 2007.

Menzies, Charles R., and Caroline F. Butler. "The Indigenous Foundation of the Resource Economy of BC's North Coast." *Labour/Le Travail* 61 (2008): 131–49.

–. "Working in the Woods." *American Indian Quarterly* 25, 3 (2001): 409–30. http://dx.doi.org/10.1353/aiq.2001.0051.

Miljan, Lydia. *Public Policy in Canada: An Introduction.* 5th ed. Don Mills, ON: Oxford University Press, 2008.

Miller, James R. *Shingwauk's Vision: A Hisory of Native Residential Schools.* Toronto: University of Toronto Press, 1996.

–. *Skyscrapers Hide the Heavens: A History of Indian-White Relations in Canada.* 3rd ed. Toronto: University of Toronto Press, 2000.

Miller, Jay. "Feasting with the Southern Tsimshian." In *The Tsimshian: Images of the Past, Views for the Present,* ed. Margaret Seguin, 27–39. Vancouver: UBC Press, 1984.

–. *Tsimshian Culture: A Light through the Ages.* Lincoln: University of Nebraska Press, 1997.

Milloy, John Sheridan. *A National Crime: The Canadian Government and the Residential School System, 1879 to 1986.* Winnipeg: University of Manitoba Press, 1999.

Minister of Public Works and Government Services Canada. "Students Thrive at Kitsumkalum Adult Learning Centre." In *Community Stories: Aboriginal Successes in British Columbia,* 29–30. Vancouver: Indian and Northern Affairs Canada, 2009. https://www.aadnc-aandc.gc.ca/eng/1100100021663/1100100021726.

Mussell, William Julius. "Decolonizing Education: A Building Block for Reconciliation." In *From Truth to Reconciliation: Transforming the Legacy of Residential Schools,* ed. Marlene Brant Castellano, Linda Archibald, and Mike DeGagné, 321–40. Ottawa: Aboriginal Healing Foundation, 2008.

National Indian Brotherhood. *Indian Control of Indian Education.* Ottawa: National Indian Brotherhood, 1972.

Native Women's Association of Canada. "Aboriginal Women and Bill C-31." Paper presented at the National Aboriginal Women's Summit, June 20–22, 2007, Corner Brook, Newfoundland.

Newell, Dianne. *Tangled Webs of History: Indians and the Law in Canada's Pacific Coast Fisheries*. Toronto: University of Toronto Press, 1993.

Neylan, Susan. *The Heavens Are Changing: Nineteenth-Century Protestant Missions and Tsimshian Christianity*. Montreal and Kingston: McGill-Queen's University Press, 2003.

Neylan, Susan, and Melissa Meyer. "'Here Comes the Band!': Cultural Collaboration, Connective Traditions and Aboriginal Brass Bands on British Columbia's North Coast, 1875–1964." *BC Studies*, 152 (2006–07): 35–66.

Nock, David A. *A Victorian Missionary and Canadian Indian Policy*. Waterloo, ON: Wilfrid Laurier University Press, 1988.

Paquette, Jerry. *Aboriginal Self-Government and Education in Canada*. Kingston: Institute of Intergovernmental Relations, 1986.

Patterson, Robert S. "Society and Education during the Wars and Their Interlude, 1914–1945." In *Canadian Education: A History*, ed. J. Donald Wilson, Robert Stamp, and Louis-Philippe Audet, 360–84. Scarborough, ON: Prentice-Hall, 1970.

–. "Voices from the Past: The Personal and Professional Struggle of Rural School Teachers." In *Schools in the West: Essays in Canadian Educational History*, ed. Nancy Sheehan, J. Donald Wilson, and David C. Jones, 99–112. Calgary: Detselig, 1986.

Persson, Diane. "The Changing Experience of Indian Residential Schooling: Blue Quills, 1931–1970." In *Indian Education in Canada*, vol. 1, *The Legacy*, ed. Jean Barman, Yvonne Hébert, and Don McCaskill, 150–68. Vancouver: UBC Press, 1986.

Pierce, William H. *From Potlatch to Pulpit, Being the Autobiography of the Reverend William Henry Pierce*. Vancouver: Vancouver Bindery, 1933.

Qwul'sih'yah'maht (Robina Anne Thomas). "Honouring the Oral Traditions of My Ancestors through Storytelling." In *Research as Resistance: Critical Indigenous and Anti-oppressive Approaches*, ed. Leslie Brown and Susan Strega, 237–54. Toronto: Canadian Scholars' Press, 2005.

Raptis, Helen. "Exploring the Factors Prompting British Columbia's First Integration Initiative: The Case of Port Essington Indian Day School." *History of Education Quarterly* 51, 4 (2011): 519–43. http://dx.doi.org/10.1111/j.1748-5959.2011.00356.x.

–. "Implementing Integrated Education Policy for On-Reserve Aboriginal Children in British Columbia, 1951–1981." *Historical Studies in Education* 20, 1 (2008): 118–46.

Raptis, Helen, and Sam Bowker. "Maintaining the Illusion of Democracy: Policy-Making and Aboriginal Education in Canada." *Canadian Journal of Educational Administration and Policy*, 102 (2010): 1–21.

Raptis, Helen, and Thomas Fleming. *Reframing Education: How to Create Effective Schools*. Toronto: C.D. Howe Insitute, 2003.

Rayman, Ronald. "Joseph Lancaster's Monitorial System of Instruction and American Indian Education, 1815–1838." *History of Education Quarterly* 21, 4 (1981): 395–409. http://dx.doi.org/10.2307/367922.

Regan, Paulette. *Unsettling the Settler Within: Indian Residential Schools, Truth Telling, and Reconciliation in Canada*. Vancouver: UBC Press, 2010.

Rice, Brian, and Anna Snyder. "Reconciliation in the Context of a Settler Society: Healing the Legacy of Colonialism in Canada." In *From Truth to Reconciliation: Transforming the Legacy of Residential Schools*, ed. Marlene Brant Castellano, Linda Archibald, and Mike DeGagné, 45–61. Ottawa: Aboriginal Healing Foundation, 2008.

Ritchie, Donald A. *Doing Oral History: A Practical Guide.* Oxford: Oxford University Press, 2003.

Robertson, Leslie A., with the Kwagu'l Gixsam Clan. *Standing Up with Ga'axsta'las: Jane Constance Cook and the Politics of Memory, Church, and Custom.* Vancouver: UBC Press, 2012.

Robertson, Nancy. "Port Essington: Only a Dream." *Canadian West,* 10 (1987): 156–64.

Robinson, Harry. *Living by Stories: A Journey of Landscape and Memory.* Ed. Wendy Wickwire. Vancouver: Talonbooks, 2005.

Roth, Christopher F. "The Names Spread in All Directions: Hereditary Titles in Tsimshian Social and Political Life." *BC Studies,* 130 (2001): 69–92.

–. *Becoming Tsimshian: The Social Life of Names.* Seattle: University of Washington Press, 2008.

Rousmaniere, Kate. "Sixteen Years in a Classroom." In *Silences and Images: The Social History of the Classroom,* ed. Ian Grosvenor, Martin Lawn, and Kate Rousmaniere, 235–55. New York: Peter Lang, 1999.

Roy, Patricia. "BC's Fear of Asians." In *A History of British Columbia: Selected Readings,* ed. Patricia Roy, 285–99. Toronto: Copp Clark Pitman, 1989.

Rymhs, Deena. "Appropriating Guilt: Reconciliation in an Aboriginal Canadian Context." *English Studies in Canada* 32, 1 (2006): 105–23. http://dx.doi.org/10.1353/esc.2007.0068.

Scott, Joan W. "Storytelling." *History and Theory* 50, 2 (2011): 203–9. http://dx.doi.org/10.1111/j.1468-2303.2011.00577.x.

Shewell, Hugh. *'Enough to Keep Them Alive': Indian Welfare in Canada, 1873–1965.* Toronto: University of Toronto Press, 2004.

Simpson, Leanne. *Dancing on Our Turtle's Back: Stories of Nishnaabeg Re-creation, Resurgence and a New Emergence.* Winnipeg: Arbeiter Ring, 2011.

Smith, Keith D. *Liberalism, Surveillance, and Resistance: Indigenous Communities in Western Canada, 1877–1927.* Edmonton: Athabasca University Press, 2009.

Smith, Trefor. "John Freemont Smith and Indian Administration in the Kamloops Agency, 1912–1923." *Native Studies Review* 10, 2 (1995): 1–34.

Special Joint Committee of the Senate and the House of Commons Appointed to Examine and Consider the Indian Act. *Minutes of the Proceedings and Evidence, No. 5.* Ottawa: Edmond Cloutier, 1946.

St. Denis, Verna. "Rethinking Culture Theory in Aboriginal Education." In *Canadian Perspectives on the Sociology of Education,* ed. Cynthia Levine-Rasky, 163–82. Don Mills, ON: Oxford University Press, 2009.

Stern, H.H. *Fundamental Concepts of Language Teaching.* Oxford: Oxford University Press, 1986.

Stortz, Paul J., and J. Donald Wilson. "Education on the Frontier: Schools, Teachers and Community Influence in North-Central British Columbia." *Histoire Sociale/Social History* 26 (1993): 265–90.

Styres, Sandra, Dawn Zinga, Sheila Bennett, and Michelle Bomberry. "Walking in Two Worlds: Engaging the Space between Indigenous Community and Academia." *Canadian Journal of Education* 33, 3 (2010): 617–48.

Sutherland, Eileen. "My Skeena Childhood." *BC Historical News* 36, 2 (2003): 6–13.

Sutherland, Neil. *Children in English Canadian Society: Framing the Twentieth Century Consensus.* Toronto: University of Toronto Press, 1976.

Taylor, John. "Non-Native Teachers Teaching in Native Communities." In *Firsth Nations Education in Canada: The Circle Unfolds,* ed. Marie Battiste and Jean Barman, 224–42. Vancouver: UBC Press, 1995.

Tennant, Paul. *Aboriginal Peoples and Politics: The Indian Land Question in British Columbia, 1849–1989.* Vancouver: UBC Press, 1990.

Titley, E. Brian. "Duncan Campbell Scott and Indian Educational Policy." In *An Imperfect Past: Education and Society in Canadian History,* ed. J. Donald Wilson, 141–53. Vancouver: Canadian History in Education Association, 1984.

–. *The Indian Commissioners: Agents of the State and Indian Policy in Canada's Prairie West, 1873–1932.* Edmonton: University of Alberta Press, 2009.

–. "Indian Industrial Schools in Western Canada." In *Schools in the West: Essays in Canadian Educational History,* ed. Nancy M. Sheehan, J. Donald Wilson, and David C. Jones, 133–54. Calgary: Detselig, 1986.

–. *A Narrow Vision: Duncan Campbell Scott and the Administration of Indian Affairs in Canada.* Vancouver: UBC Press, 1986.

–. "Red Deer Indian Industrial School: A Case Study in the History of Native Education." In *Exploring Our Educational Past,* ed. Nick Kach and Kas Mazurek, 55–72. Calgary: Detselig, 1992.

–. "Unsteady Debut: J.A.N. Provencher and the Beginnings of Indian Administration in Manitoba." *Prairie Forum* 22, 1 (1997): 21–46.

Tomkins, George. *A Common Countenance: Stability and Change in the Canadian Curriculum.* Scarborough, ON: Prentice-Hall, 1986.

Tosh, John. *The Pursuit of History: Aims, Methods and New Directions in the Study of Modern History.* 3rd ed. London: Longman, 1999.

Toutant, Tara S. "Equality by Mail: Correspondence Education in British Columbia, 1919–1969." MA thesis, University of Victoria, 2003.

Wallace Adams, David. "Beyond Bleakness: The Brighter Side of Indian Boarding Schools, 1870–1940." In *Boarding School Blues: Revisiting American Indian Educational Experiences,* ed. Clifford E. Trafzer, Jean A. Keller, and Lorene Sisquoc, 35–64. Lincoln NB: University of Nebraska Press, 2006.

Walls, Martha E. "'The Teacher That Cannot Understand Their Language Should Not Be Allowed': Colonialism, Resistance, and Famale Mi'kmaw Teachers of New Brunswick Day Schools, 1900–1923." *Journal of the Canadian Historical Association* 22, 1 (2011): 35–67. http://dx.doi.org/10.7202/1008957ar.

Walsh, Andrea N. *Nk'Mip Chronicles: Art from the Inkameep Day School.* Osoyoos, BC: Osoyoos Indian Band, 2005.

Ward, Peter. "British Columbia and the Japanese Evacuation." *Canadian Historical Review* 57, 3 (1976): 289–308. http://dx.doi.org/10.3138/CHR-057-03-02.

Watt-Cloutier, Sheila. "Honouring Our Past, Creating Our Future: Education in Northern and Remote Communities." In *Aboriginal Education: Fulfilling the Promise,* ed. Marlene Brant Castellano, Lynne Davis, and Louise Lahache, 114–28. Vancouver: UBC Press, 2000.

Weber-Pillwax, Cora. "Indigenous Researchers and Indigenous Research Methods: Cultural Influences or Cultural Determinants of Research Methods." *Pimatisiwin: A Journal of Aboriginal and Indigenous Community Health* 2, 1 (2004): 77–90.

–. "What Is Indigenous Research?" *Canadian Journal of Native Education* 25, 2 (2001): 166–74.

Weiss, Gillian, ed., with Pearl McKenzie, Pauline Coulthard, Charlene Tree, Bernie Sound, Valerie Bourne, and Brandi McLeod. *Trying to Get It Back: Indigenous Women, Education and Culture.* Waterloo, ON: Wilfrid Laurier University Press, 2000.

Wexler, Lisa. "The Importance of Identity, History, and Culture in the Wellbeing of Indigenous Youth." *Journal of the History of Childhood and Youth* 2, 2 (2009): 267–76. http://dx.doi.org/10.1353/hcy.0.0055.

White, Ellen, and Jo-ann Archibald. "Kwulasulwut S yuth (Ellen White's Teachings)." *Canadian Journal of Native Education* 19, 2 (1992): 150–64.

White, Jerry P., and Julie Peters. "A Short History of Aboriginal Education in Canada." In *Aboriginal Education: Current Crisis and Future Alternatives,* ed. Jerry P. White, Julie Peters, Dan Beavon, and Nicholas Spence, 13–20. Toronto: Thompson Educational, 2009.

Wicks, Walter. *Memories of the Skeena.* Seattle: Hancock House, 1976.

Williams, Lorna. "Urban Aboriginal Education: The Vancouver Experience." In *Aboriginal Education: Fulfilling the Promise,* ed. Marlene Brant Castellano, Lynne Davis, and Louise Lahache, 129–46. Vancouver: UBC Press, 2000.

Wilson, J. Donald, and Paul J. Stortz. "May the Lord Have Mercy on You: The Rural School Problem in British Columbia in the 1920s." *BC Studies,* 79 (1988): 24–57.

Wilson, Peggy. "Trauma of Sioux Indian High School Students." *Anthropology and Education Quarterly* 22, 4 (1991): 367–83. http://dx.doi.org/10.1525/aeq.1991.22.4.05x1194x.

Wilson, Shawn. "Progressing towards an Indigenous Research Paradigm in Canada and Australia." *Canadian Journal of Native Education* 27, 2 (2003): 161–78.

–. *Research Is Ceremony: Indigenous Research Methods.* Blackpoint, NS: Fernwood, 2008.

–. "What Is an Indigenist Research Paradigm?" *Canadian Journal of Native Education* 30, 2 (2007): 193–95.

Woodworth-Ney, Laura. "The Diaries of a Day-School Teacher: Daily Realities on the Pine Ridge Indian Reservation, 1932–1942." *South Dakota History* 24, 3–4 (1994): 194–211.

Zusman, Angela. *Story Bridges: A Guide for Conducting Intergenerational Oral History Projects.* Walnut Creek, CA: Left Coast, 2010.

Index

Note: "(i)" after a page number indicates an illustration. In subentries, the Port Essington Indian Day School is referred to as the "Day School" (capitalized), and the Port Essington Elementary School is referred to as the "Elementary School" (capitalized).

Alaska, 7, 39; fishing off coast of, 71–73
All Hallows Residential School (Yale), 152
Anderson, Margaret Seguin, and Tammy Anderson Blumhagen: "Memories and Moments: Conversations and Recollections," 16
Anfield, F. Earl, 51–52
Anglican Church, 28, 40, 78. *See also* St. George's Residential School (Lytton)
Anglo-British Columbia Cannery (Port Essington), 61–62
animals, 39, 59–60; bears, 37, 57, 66, 74, 75; beaver, 104, 111; deer, 37, 66, 74, 75, 104, 109; mountain goat, 37, 60, 66, 74, 75; seals, 57, 66, 75, 83
attendance, student: at day schools, 29, 31, 42, 43, 51, 130, 141; at Elementary School, 52; Family Allowance cheques as tied to, 78, 173*n*47; during hunting/fishing seasons, 29, 43, 51, 69, 74, 139–40, 141; and railway construction, 42; during Vannatter's tenure, 50

Barbeau, Marius, 16
Barman, Jean, 31, 152
Barry, Gerald H., 48–49, 51, 139
Battiste, Marie, 27–28, 101, 103, 107, 108, 128, 135–36, 140, 144, 145, 146, 148
BC Hydro, 107
Bear Nicholas, Andrea, 136, 137
Bennett, Norma, 12
Bennett family, 65
berry picking and preserving, 3, 37, 58, 60, 66, 79, 97, 118
Bland, Hilda M. (Day School teacher), 42–43
Blue Quills Residential School (St. Paul, AB), 34
boarding homes: Crosbys' (Port Simpson), 40, 83, 171*n*10, 174*n*55; in Vancouver, 98
boarding schools, Canadian. *See* residential schools
boarding schools, US, 29, 138, 179*n*38
Boas, Franz, 14, 16, 24
Bob, Dempsey, 88

Boldt decision (*United States v. Washing-ton*), 34
Bolton, Alec, 86, 97
Bolton, Bobby, 97
Bolton, Charlotte (*née* Harrison), 96
Bolton, Clifford, 56, 82–91, 90(i), 133; as chief of Kitsumkalum, 89, 90(i), 91; childhood/Tsimshian education of, 82–84, 89; at Day School, 84–85, 174*n*58; at Elementary School, 85(i), 85–86; on his grandmother, 83–84, 135, 136; on importance of helping/sharing with others, 82–83; jewellery making by, 88, 90(i), 137; Kitselas canoe carved by, 88, 90(i); marksmanship ability of, 87(i), 87–88, 137; at residential school, 86–89, 89(i), 97, 135, 137–38, 145, 151; significant student-adult relationship of, 87–88, 89, 137, 138; on spirituality/ religion, 83–84, 102, 134, 135, 143; and Tsimshian cultural revival, 89, 90(i), 91, 123
Bolton, Edna, 53, 109
Bolton, Edward, 47, 67, 96, 131, 167*n*69, 175*n*73
Bolton, Elizabeth, 77
Bolton, Irene, 60–61
Bolton, James (father of Mildred Roberts), 57, 60, 64, 67, 171*n*10
Bolton, Laura, 86, 97
Bolton, Mark, 20, 172*n*39
Bolton, Rebecca (*née* Anderson), 117, 171*n*10
Bolton, Shirley, 86, 97
Bolton, William (Billy), 62, 64
Bolton family, 12
Booth Memorial Junior Secondary School (Prince Rupert), 92, 140
British-American Cannery, 9, 10(i), 120, 173*n*42
British Columbia Indian Commission, 97
British North America Act (1867; now Constitution Act, 1982), 28, 40, 148
Brooks, Norman, 73
Brooks family, 12
Brown, Ben, 78
Brown, Dan, 67

Brown, George, 88
Brown, James A., 173*n*41
Brown family, 12
Brown's Mill, 75, 77, 173*n*41, 177*n*22
Brown's Store, 108
Bryce, Peter, 31, 151

Campbell, Kenneth: *Persistence and Change: A History of the Tsimsyen Nation*, 16
camping, traditional, 35, 37–39; as largely lost to post-1950s generation, 113, 142–43; pre-1950s generation's memories of, 3–4, 60–61, 67, 74–75, 77–78, 83, 134; revival of, 26
Canadian Pacific Railway, 107
canneries, 9, 39, 61–62, 74–76, 91, 95, 109, 173*n*42; closure of, 11–12, 75, 96, 108, 171*n*13; of Cunningham, 8, 10(i), 157*n*17, 173*n*42; location of, 10(i); medical clinics at, 173*n*51; of Nelson family, 75, 95, 175*n*70. *See also specific canneries by name*; fishing industry
canoes: as carved by Clifford Bolton, 88, 90(i); community builders of, 38, 58; early use of, 8–9
Cardinal, Harold, 146
Cassiar Cannery (Prince Rupert), 62, 74, 75–76
Catholic Church, 28, 39, 179*n*43; sectarian tensions with, 49
Centennial Christian School (Terrace), 99–100
Champlain, Father, 49
chief (*sm'oogyet*), 39; House of Sm'oogyet (arts and crafts store), 89, 91
chiefs of Kitsumkalum, 20; interventions by, on behalf of students, 66, 70. *See also* Bolton, Clifford; Roberts, Don, Junior; Starr, Louis
childbirth: midwives and, 80, 117; on Skeena River, 82, 104, 113
Chilton, Francis W. (Day School teacher), 49–50, 63
chores: family, 37–38, 60–61, 62, 63, 101; fishing, 68–69, 98–99, 104, 111, 134; at residential school, 30, 86

Christmas activities: carolling door-to-door, 62, 172*n*32; Day School concerts/plays, 3, 44, 47, 62, 64, 79; Elementary School concerts/plays, 53, 97, 105(i), 109

Church Missionary Society (England), 39, 157*n*14

clans (*pteex*), Tsimshian, 35–37; and adoption of outsiders, 73; house groups within, 35, 36; and marriage, 35–36; as matrilineal, 35, 36; and names, 20, 36–37. *See also entry below*

clans (*pteex*), Tsimshian (specific): Eagle (Laxsgiik), 35; Killer Whale (Gispudwada), 35, 57, 117; Raven (Ganhada), 35, 77; Wolf (Laxgibuu), 35

Coast Mountain School District, 99, 100

Coast Salish, 25, 34, 136

Coates, Ken, 154

Collins, Gus, 73

Collins, Irene, 73

Collison, W.E., 49

Constitution Act, 1982, 28, 40

Cook, Constance Jane (Ga'axsta'las), 14–15

corporal punishment: abolition of, 123; as contrary to Native childrearing methods, 64–65, 171*n*21; at Day School, 64, 84, 104–5; at Elementary School, 52, 70, 74, 91; at Kalum School, 113–14; at residential schools, 30, 138

correspondence program, provincial, 70, 110, 172*n*35

Crosby, Thomas and Emma, 40

Crosby Home for Girls (Port Simpson), 40, 83, 171*n*10, 174*n*55

Cunningham, Robert, 7–8, 157*n*14; cannery of, 8, 10(i), 157*n*17, 173*n*42; reserve established by, 8, 9, 9(i), 10(i); and subdivision/"offers" of land, 8, 157*n*15

Darwin, Charles, 93

Davey, R.F., 52

Davin, Nicholas Flood, 29

day schools, 28–29; church management/mismanagement of, 28, 40–43, 45, 50, 131–32, 139, 147; compared to rural schools, 28, 40, 44, 63, 109, 110, 130, 138,

172*n*35; and erosion of Native culture, 152–53; government's arm's-length approach to, 28, 40–41, 131–32, 147; government's eagerness to close, 29; government's jurisdiction over/financing of, 28, 29, 31, 33, 40–42; local graduates as teachers in, 43, 152; as neglected by historians, 4, 16–17, 154–55; and postwar shift to integrated schooling, 17, 33–34; student attendance at, 29, 31, 42, 43, 51, 130, 139–40, 141; teacher qualifications/certification at, 28, 42, 132; teacher turnover at, 28, 40, 42, 130, 138. *See also* Port Essington Indian Day School

Deane, Dorothy (Day School teacher), 45, 132, 139

Delaney, Mrs. (Riverside School teacher), 106

Dewdney, Edgar, 29

Dick and Jane readers, 91, 104, 133

Dominie, Mr. (Elementary School teacher), 52

Donaldson, Jimmy, 12, 75, 173*n*41

Donaldson, Mrs. (teacher), 69, 70, 172*n*31

Dudoward, Alfred and Kate, 40

Duff, Wilson, 116

Duncan, Mikaiya, 82(i)

Duncan, Millie, 82(i)

Duncan, William, 39, 157*n*14

Easton, Miss A.M. (public school teacher), 32

Ecstall Mill, 12

Ecstall (Ocstall) River, 7, 9, 60, 75, 78, 120, 177*n*22

Elizabeth II, 88

Elkhorn Residential School (Elkhorn, MB), 152

Enfranchisement Act, 65, 172*n*23

ethnicity: Port Essington's diversity of, 9, 12, 69, 105. *See also* "Finntown," residents of; Indian status, loss of; Japanese Canadians; mixed marriages, children of; racism/discrimination

E.T. Kenney Elementary School (Terrace), 106, 111. *See also* Riverside Elementary School

Fakeley, Louise (Day School teacher), 45, 139

Family Allowance, 78, 147, 173*n*47

feasts (*luulgyit*), 20, 37, 39, 91, 107, 122, 123

Ferrier, Rev. Thompson, 42–43

Feuerstein, Reuven, 54, 144, 180*n*61

"Finntown," residents of, 9, 65, 69, 105, 108, 109, 118

fires in Port Essington: and destruction of town, 12, 53, 75, 103, 120, 175*n*73; early signalling system for, 84, 174*n*56; and government's decision not to rebuild, 65–66, 106–7

First Citizens Fund, 89, 174*n*62

First World War, 49, 167*n*68

fish and seafood: abalone, 37, 57–58, 74, 83, 97; clams and cockles, 57, 74, 77, 83, 97, 104; crab, 74, 118; halibut, 37, 67, 74, 77, 83, 104; oolichan, 37, 83, 97; salmon, 34, 37, 39, 83, 97, 104, 125

fishing, 26, 67; as casualty of wage labour economy, 127, 142–43; children's early start in, 68–69, 98–99, 104, 111, 134; and later need to buy licences, 66; as masculine activity, 37, 68–69, 78, 104, 127, 176*n*9; as not passed down to post-1950s generation, 113, 122, 123, 127; and poor seasonal student attendance, 29, 43, 51, 69, 74, 139–40; and respect for animals, 39; and seasons for specific fish, 37, 60; shaman's guidance in, 38; sites for, 34, 36; as skill used in real life/ subsistence of family, 71–72, 74, 75–76, 98–99, 104, 127, 130, 139–40; as stereotypical Native activity, 124, 145, 153. *See also* fish and seafood

fishing boats, 66, 67, 68–69, 71–72, 89, 95, 119; babies born on, 82, 104, 113; dangers of crossing the Skeena in, 65, 82–83, 122–23

fishing industry, 10, 11–12, 17, 51, 67, 68–69, 70–71, 73, 74, 75–76, 94(i), 95, 98–99, 104, 107, 113; and closure of canneries, 11–12, 75, 96, 108, 171*n*13; decline of, 77, 82, 113; gillnet/seine fishing, 68–69, 95, 113, 172*n*27. *See also* canneries

Fixico, Donald, 14

Fleras, Augie, 15, 16

food (fish and game). *See* animals; fish and seafood

food gathering, 26, 35, 37, 61, 77–78, 83, 113, 134; abalone, 37, 74, 83, 97; berries, 3, 37, 60, 66, 79, 97, 118; seaweed, 74, 83, 104

food preparation and preservation, 3, 26, 35, 37, 74, 77–78, 83, 113, 127, 130, 134, 140, 142, 143; canning, 57–58; drying/ salting fish, 37, 57, 59(i), 60; drying seaweed, 3, 37, 78; fileting fish, 60–61; preserving abalone, 57–58; preserving oolichan, 37

Ga'axsta'las (Constance Jane Cook), 14–15

games: community, 38, 73, 104, 118, 172*n*38; with non-Native children, 49; at school, 53, 63

Garfield, Viola, 16

Gillett, James, 50

gillnet fishing, 68, 95, 113, 172*n*27

Ging (Chinese-Canadian resident paid to carry water), 173*n*42

Gordon, Robert (Elementary School teacher), 52

Gosnell, Selina (mother of Mildred Roberts), 57, 61(i), 61–62, 65, 67, 171*n*n10–11

Gosnell, Jemima, 61(i)

Gower, Miss (Elementary School teacher), 52

Grand Trunk Pacific Railway, 11, 42, 158*n*26

Guno, Charlotte (*née* Bolton), 56, 96–100, 133; childhood of, 96–97; at Elementary School, 97, 175*n*75; high school/ vocational education of, 97–98; on importance of education, 97, 98–100; as Kitsumkalum education administrator, 99–100; on loneliness of Port Essington, 96–97, 102; as principal of Kitsumkalum learning centre, 99, 100(i); racism/discrimination against, 98, 140; at residential school, 97–98, 135, 137–38, 151; significant student-adult relationship of, 97–98, 138, 140

Haida Gwaii, 126, 146

Hankin, Thomas, 7

Happy Gang (children's performing group), 62, 69, 71(i), 73, 171*n*14, 172*n*32

Hare, Helena (Day School teacher), 45

Hargreaves, Margaret (Day School teacher), 40

Harris, Ernest A.: *Spokeshute: Skeena River Memory*, 7, 52, 163*n*35, 171*n*15

Harris, Harry, 163*n*31

Harris, Kenneth, with Frances M.P. Robinson: *Visitors Who Never Left: The Origin of the People of Damelahamid*, 16, 59

Harrison, Mr. and Mrs. (Elementary School teachers), 98

Hartley, W.C., 48

Hautenen, Mary, 118

Hedley Public School (Okanagan region), 32

Henderson, James (Sákéj) Youngblood, 17, 108, 135–36, 144

Hinchcliffe, Joshua, 32

Hoey, R.A., 51

hospitals: Port Essington, 10, 45, 57, 80, 170*n*3, 173*n*51; Prince Rupert, 82, 96, 104, 113; Vancouver (St. Paul's), 86

house groups (*waaps*), Tsimshian, 35, 36; and adoption of outsiders, 73; stories specific to, 38

Hudson's Bay Company, 39, 157*n*14

hunting, 26, 38, 75, 109; as casualty of wage labour economy, 127, 142–43; and later need to buy licences, 66; as masculine activity, 37, 78, 104, 127; as not passed down to post-1950s generation, 113, 122, 123, 124, 127, 142–43; and poor seasonal student attendance, 29, 43, 51, 74, 139–40, 141; and respect for animals, 39, 59–60; as skill used in real life/ subsistence of family, 130, 139–40; as stereotypical Native activity, 124, 145, 153; territories for, 35, 36, 37. *See also* animals

Hyndman, E.E., 52

Indian Act (1876), 41–42, 148; and compulsory education, 163*n*32; and integrated education, 33, 56, 103, 154; and status of women married to non-Natives, 19, 65, 69, 80, 153, 173*n*49

Indian Affairs, Department of: archives of, 6–7; assimilationist policy of, 27–28, 29, 31, 34, 132, 137–38; and Day School, 40–52, 131–32, 139, 141, 147; and Elementary School, 53; and integrated schooling, 31–33, 148; and residential schools, 29–31, 151; Tsimshian community members' work for, 88–89, 98

Indian Agents: and Charlotte Guno's request to attend residential school, 97; and Day School teachers, 43, 50, 51–52, 64; Wally Miller's interactions with, 69, 71, 134

Indian status, loss of: for wartime service, 65, 172*n*23; for women's marriages to non-Natives, 19, 65, 69, 80, 153, 173*n*49

Indigenous education, 27–34; assimilation through, 27–28, 34, 44, 101, 132, 137; funding of, 28, 30, 31, 32, 33–34, 41, 53, 146, 148, 155, 169*n*110; and postwar shift to integrated schooling, 6, 33–34. *See also entry below*

Indigenous education, forms of: boarding homes, 40, 83, 98, 171*n*10, 174*n*55; correspondence program, 70, 110, 172*n*35; day schools, 4, 28–29, 154–55; industrial schools, 29, 32; integrated schooling, 31–34; residential schools, 4, 29–31, 151–55. *See also entries for each topic*

industrial schools, 29, 32

Inkster, Verna (*née* Spalding), 56, 77–82, 79(i), 133; childhood/Tsimshian education of, 3–4, 26, 77–78, 134; at Day School, 78–79; at Elementary School/ residential school, 3–4, 79–80; four-generation family photograph of, 82(i); and help for blind community member, 78, 134; marriage of, 80, 81(i); on spirituality/religion, 78, 102, 134–35, 139, 143; Tsimshian Catering business of, 81

integrated schooling, 31–34; committee
  recommendation of, 33, 56, 164*n*38;
  earlier examples of (BC elementary
  schools), 31–33; and erosion of Native
  culture, 137, 147–48, 152–53; financial
  context of, 148; improved environment
  of, 127–28; as neglected by historians,
  17, 33–34; postwar policy shift toward,
  6, 33–34; at residential school, 34; at
  Washington State high school, 34. *See
  also* Port Essington Elementary School;
  Tsimshian students of post-1950s
  generation
Isaac, Miss (Elementary School teacher),
  79

Japanese Canadians, 9, 12, 51, 65, 69
Jenness, Diamond, 16
Jennings, Dennis (Day School teacher),
  40, 44(i)
Johnson, Miss (Elementary School
  teacher), 52
Johnston, Basil: *Indian School Days*, 152

Kalum School (Terrace), 53, 105–6, 111,
  113–14, 117, 120
Kameda, Mr. (store owner), 65
King Edward High School (Prince
  Rupert), 47, 131, 175*n*73
Kitimat, 7, 37, 45
Kitselas (Tsimshian winter village), 7, 35,
  37, 157*n*17; canoe carved by Clifford
  Brown for, 88, 90(i)
Kitsumkalum (Tsimshian winter village),
  7, 12, 37, 60, 73, 149; author's visit to,
  18–24; chiefs of, 18, 20, 66, 70, 89, 91,
  104, 108; community members' work
  at, 67, 99–100, 112; families' move to,
  4–5, 66, 103–28, 142, 143–44; fisheries
  at, 107, 125; later educational opportunities at, 67, 80, 123; as physically separated from Terrace schools, 5, 66,
  126–27, 143–46; Tsimshian cultural
  revival at, 26, 68, 89, 90(i), 91, 107–8,
  123, 126, 128
Kitsumkalum Band Council, 20, 22, 23,
  160*n*76

Kitsumkalum Fishery Program, 125
Kitsumkalum Salmonid Enhancement
  Development Project, 125
Kitsumkalum Treaty Office, 22
Klemtu, 35, 50
Kovach, Margaret, 13, 16, 18, 22, 23, 25, 134
Kwagu'l Gixsam Clan, 14–15

Large, Richard Geddes, 45, 173*n*51
Larkin School (Okanagan region), 32
LaRocque, Emma, 4, 24, 134
Lau, Ruby (Day School teacher), 50, 63,
  137
Lawrence, Miss K. (public school
  teacher), 32
Little, George, 74
Lockerby, Cecelia (*née* Nelson), 73, 74
Lockerby, Sam, 56, 73–77, 77(i), 133;
  childhood/Tsimshian education of,
  73–75, 135; at Day and Elementary
  Schools, 74; fishing industry experi-
  ences of, 75–77; as Happy Gang mem-
  ber, 73; and importance of sharing
  bounty, 74–75, 76
Lockerby, Sam, Senior, 73, 74–75
Lockerby family, 12
logging industry, 8, 17, 51, 66, 67, 75, 107;
  decline of, 82, 113, 116; in Terrace area,
  12, 53, 66, 80, 112, 115, 125
Lomawaima, K. Tsianina, and Teresa
  McCarty, 5–6, 54
Lummi high school students, in
  Washington State, 34
Lutz, John, 76, 140, 141
Lytton High School, 86

Macdonald, John A., 29
MacKenzie, A.F., 45, 46–48
Māori, 15
Marion, Lori, 82(i)
Marker, Michael, 34, 108, 136, 155
Marshall, Anne, 18, 19
Mayovski, Miss (Elementary School
  teacher), 52
McDonald, James (Jim), 17, 18–19, 20;
  *People of the Robin: The Tsimshian of
  Kitsumkalum*, 16

McDougall, Mrs. (Elementary School teacher), 52–53; class of (1950s), 110(i); class hikes led by, 109, 144

McLean, J.D., 42

McLeod, Neal, 135

Methodist Church missionaries, 28, 166n40; and Tsimshian communities, 39–40. See also entry below; Crosby Home for Girls

Methodist Church missionaries, as administrators of Port Essington Indian Day School, 3, 7, 40–52; and government officials, 40–43, 45–46, 48–51, 56, 130–32, 139; and preference for missionary teachers, 42–43, 50; and sectarian tensions, 49; and teacher appointments, 42, 43, 45, 50, 147; and teacher salaries/ expenses, 42–43, 44–45, 49–50; and teacher turnover, 40, 42–51; and teacher vetting, 50, 131, 132; and wartime loss of funds/personnel, 50

midwives, 80, 117

Mi'kmaq, of Nova Scotia, 27–28

Miller, James R.: Shingwauk's Vision, 34–35, 64–65, 131, 148, 152 , 153

Miller, Jay: Tsimshian Culture: A Light through the Ages, 16, 174n57

Miller, Wally, 56, 68–73, 72(i), 133; childhood fishing work by, 68–69, 134; and connection to Port Essington, 73, 135; at Elementary School, 69–70, 85(i); fishing industry experiences of, 71–73; as Happy Gang member, 69, 71(i); and mother's loss of Indian status, 69, 153; refusal of welfare by, 71, 134; and resistance to leaving reserve, 69, 101, 139, 153; Tsimshian education of, 69, 135, 139–40

Milloy, John, 34

mixed marriages, children of, 32, 48, 52, 69; as "nonstatus," 19, 65, 69, 80, 153, 173n49; racism/discrimination against, 53, 91, 92–93

Mussell, William Julius (Stó:lō educator), 153

'Na Aksa Gila Kyew Learning Centre (Kitsumkalum): Charlotte Guno as principal of, 99, 100(i)

names, Tsimshian, 36–37, 165n18; of Verna Inkster, 77

National Indian Brotherhood: Indian Control of Indian Education (policy paper), 21

National Rifle Association competitions (Bisley, England): Clifford Brown's participation/awards in, 87(i), 88

Nelson, Ethel, 43

Nelson Brothers Fisheries (Port Edward), 75, 95, 175n70

Neylan, Susan, 58, 134–35

Noble, Fanny (Day School teacher), 43–45, 44(i), 131, 167n52

North Pacific Cannery (Port Edward), 62, 113

Northwest Community College (Terrace), 18, 68, 99, 123

Ocstall (Ecstall) River, 7, 9, 60, 75, 78, 120, 177n22

Oka Crisis, 19

"Old Tom" ("one-base baseball" game), 63, 73, 104, 172n38, 176n3

Olynyk, Miss (Elementary School teacher), 52, 74, 79–80, 85(i), 85, 91

Parkside Alternative School (Terrace), 115, 128, 145

Parkside Elementary School (Terrace), 123

Pattison, Jim, 98

Pearl Harbor, bombing of, 12

Perry, C.C., 43

Pierce, Ernest H. (Day School teacher), 42, 43

Pierce, William Henry (missionary/ teacher), 40, 43

Plato, 36

Pogson, Elizabeth (Day School teacher), 45–48, 50–52, 74, 84–85, 167n65, 174n58; broken tenure of, 45; Christmas plays run by, 62, 64; and closure of Day School, 52, 85, 91; corporal punishment administered by, 64, 79, 84, 140; as "old," 48, 64; as residing on reserve, 46–48, 167n68; and school inspectors, 48, 50, 139; and Sm'algyax language, 84

Port Alberni Residential School, 80
Port Edward, 12, 119; canneries at, 62, 74, 75, 113; Wing family move to, 91–92
Port Essington, 7–12; on BC map, 8(i); boardwalks of, 10, 97, 118, 154(i); diversity of, 9, 12, 69, 105; early history/development of, 7–9; fires in, 12, 53, 65–66, 75, 84, 103, 106–7, 120, 174n56, 175n73; fish canning at, 8, 9, 11(i), 11–12; as frontier town, 10–11, 45; later decline of, 11–12, 96–97; shoreline of, today, 154(i); streets and buildings of, 10(i); summer hospital of, 10, 45, 57, 80, 170n3, 173n51; Tsimshian connection to, 57, 60, 73, 95, 102, 104, 117–20, 135–36, 143; water flume of, 75, 76(i), 93, 173n42, 176n8; wartime service in, 172n23. See also fires in Port Essington; water in Port Essington
Port Essington, Tsimshian children of. See Tsimshian student experience, as research topic, and entries following; Port Essington Elementary School; Port Essington Indian Day School; individual persons and schools by name
Port Essington Concert Band, 73, 172n39
Port Essington Elementary School, 4, 12, 52–53; Christmas play at (1950s), 105(i); class of (1947–48), 85(i); correspondence alternative to, 110, 172n35; corporal punishment at, 52, 70, 74, 91; curricula of, 52–53; events/activities at, 53; expansion of, 53; integration of Day School students into, 4, 6, 51–53; and loss of Japanese-Canadian students, 51; Mrs. McDougall's class at, 110(i); origins of, 158n21; remnants of, 107(i). See also teachers, at Port Essington Elementary School; Tsimshian students of post-1950s generation; Tsimshian students of pre-1950s generation
Port Essington Indian Day School, 3–5, 40–52; closure of, 6, 13, 51–52; corporal punishment at, 64, 84, 104–5; curricula/pedagogical issues at, 44, 48–49, 50–51, 84–85; early photos of teachers and students at, 41(i), 44(i); events/activities at, 43, 44; high teacher turnover at, 40, 42–51; last class list of, 6, 18, 149–50; missionary vs lay teachers at, 42–43, 50; sexual abuse at, 50, 64, 139, 147; and Sm'algyax language, 42, 63–64, 68, 70, 79, 84, 104–5, 111, 118–19, 136–37, 142; student achievements at, 45, 47; student attendance at, 43, 50, 51; and student poetry/artwork contest submissions, 45, 46(i), 47(i); and students' mixing with non-Native children, 49. See also Methodist Church missionaries, as administrators of Port Essington Indian Day School; teachers, at Port Essington Indian Day School; Tsimshian students of pre-1950s generation
Port Essington Indian Reserve, 8, 9, 9(i); location of, 10(i); Pogson's residence on, 46–48
Port Essington Water Company, 173n42
Port Simpson, 12, 35, 37, 73, 173n51; Crosby Girls' Home in, 40, 83, 171n10, 174n55; missions at, 39, 40
potlatch (xalait), 36, 76; government ban on, 14, 76, 83, 136
Presbyterian Church, 28
Prince Rupert, 7, 12, 45, 66, 75, 76, 80, 84, 98, 109; on BC map, 8(i); cannery in, 62, 74, 75–76; Donaldsons' hotel in, 172n31; hospital in, 82, 96, 104, 113, 117; as railway terminus, 11, 158n26; relocation of Port Essington residents to, 12, 18, 75, 106; school board of, 7, 51–52, 53; schools in, 44, 47, 71, 86, 91, 92, 131, 140, 175n73; wartime service in, 172n23
Prince Rupert Exhibition, work of Day School students entered in, 45, 167n65; artwork by 13-year-old girl, 47(i); poem by 10-year-old girl, 46(i)
Puget Sound, Native fishing rights in, 34
Purvis, Ron, 87–88, 89, 137, 138

racism/discrimination: against children of mixed marriages, 53, 91, 92–93; and choice not to acknowledge, 98, 140; and exclusion of Native students from integrated schooling, 32; among Native children, 80; of teachers, 34, 89, 92–93, 106, 113–16, 123–24, 145, 153

Raley, Rev. George H., 43, 131

residential schools, 4, 28, 29–31, 43, 107, 151–55; as available next step for Day School graduates, 44, 80, 86, 129; chores at, 30, 86, 101; government apology/compensation to survivors of, 151, 153; limitations of literature/discourse on, 4, 17, 29, 56, 101, 102, 137–39, 151–55; physical/sexual abuse at, 30–31, 50, 138, 151; positive experiences of Tsimshian students at, 86–89, 97–98, 137–38, 151; and postwar shift to integrated schooling, 33–34; as preferred to day schools, 29; resilience of students at, 152; as sometimes chosen by parents, 152; teachers/administrators at, 131–32; tuberculosis in, 31

respect: for all living things, 38, 39, 134; for animals, 39, 59–60; for community, 30, 59, 89, 99, 134; for elders, 83–84; in research with First Nations communities, 13–24, 150; and spirituality, 174n57

Richmond High School, 98

Riverside Elementary School (later E.T. Kenney Elementary School, Terrace), 54, 106, 111, 120–21

Roberts, Don, Junior, 103, 104–8, 107(i); author's contact/meeting with, 18–22; birth of, 104; as chief councillor of Kitsumkalum, 18, 104, 108; childhood/Tsimshian education of, 104, 108, 126, 127, 142–43, 144; on cultural/linguistic losses, 104–5; on demise of town, 106–7; at Elementary School, 104–5, 105(i); and family's move to Kitsumkalum, 66, 105; in fishing industry, 107, 144; at schools in Terrace, 105–6; on Tsimshian cultural revival, 107–8

Roberts, Don, Senior, 106, 109, 113, 114(i), 117

Roberts, Jim, 122(i), 122–26; childhood of, 122–23, 125–26; cultural/linguistic losses of, 122–24, 127, 143, 144; on education of his children, 126, 146; at elementary and high schools, 123–24; life skills

course taken by, 123; in logging and fisheries industries, 125, 144; racism/discrimination against, 123–24, 145, 153; on Tsimshian cultural revival, 123, 126, 146

Roberts, Mildred (née Bolton), 56, 57–68, 68(i), 133; cannery work by, 62, 109; childhood/Tsimshian education of, 57–61, 67, 102, 134; and connection to Port Essington, 60, 119; at Day School, 62–65, 67; as Happy Gang member, 62, 71(i); as punished for speaking in Sm'algyax, 63–64, 118–19, 137; and resistance to strap, 64, 140; on spirituality/religion, 58–59, 102, 134–35, 139, 143; as substance abuse counsellor, 67, 101; and Tsimshian revival/teaching of Sm'algyax, 68; and Xbishuunt legend, 60, 134; as young mother, 66, 67, 104, 106, 109, 113, 114(i), 117–18, 121, 143

Roberts, Richard, 103, 113–17, 114(i), 117(i); birth/childhood of, 113; cultural/linguistic losses of, 113, 127, 143, 144; on education of his children, 114–15, 116–17, 128, 145, 146; at Kalum School, 113–14, 117, 128, 145; in logging industry, 115, 116, 144; on racism/discrimination, 113–15; on today's teacher-pupil relationships, 114–16; and upgrading of education/fisheries enforcement work, 116

Roberts, Stella, 119(i)

Roberts, Steve, 103, 108–13, 112(i); author's contact with, 18–20; as chief/band manager at Kitsumkalum, 18, 112; childhood/Tsimshian education of, 108–9, 111, 126; class hikes remembered by, 109, 144; cultural/linguistic losses of, 111, 127, 142, 143, 144; and elementary school/correspondence program, 109–10, 110(i), 111, 144; and family's move to Kitsumkalum, 110, 111; logging work by, 112, 144; at schools in Terrace, 111; on today's economy/education needs, 112–13

Roberts, Victoria (Vicky), 66; as student spokesperson, 85

Roberts family, 113, 114(i)

Robertson, Leslie, 14–15

Roman Catholic Church. *See* Catholic Church

Roode, Annie (Day School teacher), 45

Roth, Christopher: *Becoming Tsimshian: The Social Life of Names*, 16, 36

rural schools, 28, 130; correspondence alternative to, 110, 172*n*35; older children helping younger ones at, 63, 109; teacher salaries at, 44; teacher turnover at, 28, 40, 130, 138

Russian Orthodox Church, 39

Rutherford, Andrew (Day School teacher), 49

Rymhs, Deena, 152

Saanich School Board (Vancouver Island), 32

Sainte-Marie, Buffy, 122

salmon berries, 37, 63, 97

Salvation Army, 40, 78, 173*n*48

Sam, Carol (*née* Roberts), 103, 117–22, 122(i); and childhood connection to/ summers at Port Essington, 117–20, 119(i); cultural/linguistic losses of, 118–19, 127, 143, 144; and family's move to Kitsumkalum, 117, 120; at Kalum and Riverside Schools, 120–21, 127, 145; marriage/family of, 121–22

School Act (BC), 53

school bus trips, 5, 86, 143; problems on, 66, 106

Scott, Duncan Campbell, 43

seaweed, 74, 83, 104; drying of, 3, 37, 78

Second World War, 5, 17, 152, 156*n*5; Day/ Elementary School issues during, 50–51, 53; Indian Act amendments after, 103; and Japanese Canadians, 12, 51, 65, 69; Native service during, 33, 172*n*23; and rise of social welfare state, 147; teacher service in, 88

seine fishing, 69, 95, 172*n*27

Severson, Benjamin (Day School teacher), 48–49, 63

shamans (*gwildmniits*), 38, 39, 54

Skeena Café, 91, 174*n*64

Skeena River, 7–9, 11, 35, 40, 42, 83, 95; on BC map, 8(i); children born on, 82, 104, 113; drownings on, 65, 82–83, 122–23; early surveying/land allotment along, 157*n*15; fishery program on, 125; gold rush near, 7–8; and meaning of "Tsimshian," 165*n*3; reserve on, 8, 9, 9(i); salmon in, 104, 125; shoreline of, today 154(i). *See also* canneries; fishing industry

Skeena River Commercial Cannery, 9, 10(i), 11(i), 173*n*42

Sm'algyax (Tsimshian language): Duncan's preaching in, 39; as forbidden at Day School, 63–64, 68, 70, 79, 84, 104–5, 111, 118–19, 136–37, 142; as not passed down to next generation, 111, 118–19, 123, 126–27, 136–37, 142; revival/ teaching of, 68, 91, 107; stories/songs in, 38, 68, 70, 118; Tranter's use of at Day School, 42

smallpox, 7, 39

Smith, Minnie (public school teacher), 32

social welfare programs, 147, 156*n*5; pre-1950s generation's refusal of, 71, 134; and tying of Family Allowance to student attendance, 78, 173*n*47

Spaksuut (Tsimshian camping site on which Port Essington was built), 3, 37, 104–7

Spalding, Bill (Willy), 62, 172*n*32

Spalding, David, 172*n*39

Spalding, Herbert, 77

Spalding, Peter, 65

Spalding family, 65

Special Joint Committee on the Indian Act (1946–48), 33, 56, 164*n*38

Spencer, John, 43

spirituality/worldview, Tsimshian, 36–39, 54–55, 148; and Christianity, 58–59, 134–35; and concept of eternal cosmos, 21–22; and continuum of Tsimshian education, 6, 21–22, 56–57, 100–2, 127, 133, 143; and government assimilation strategy, 27–28; importance of land/ ecosystem to, 38, 108, 134–36, 143–44, 176*n*5; importance of names in, 36–37,

165*n*18; loss of, 84, 142–44, 153–54, 174*n*57; pre-1950s generation on, 84, 102, 134–35, 143; revival/resilience and, 155; role of shaman and chief in, 39; in visions, 84, 135

sports, 3, 44, 79, 86–87, 91–92, 121, 172*n*39

Starr, Louis, 20, 68–69, 70, 172*n*39

Starr family, 12

St. George's Residential School (Lytton), 86–89, 97, 137, 151, 175*n*74; Charlotte Guno's experiences at, 4, 97–98, 137–38, 151; Clifford Bolton's experiences at, 4, 86–89, 89(i), 97, 137–38, 151

Stillwell, G.B., 48

strap. *See* corporal punishment

Tahltan, 18, 32

Tasaka, Jack, 95

teachers: physical/sexual abuse by, 30–31, 50, 64, 138, 139, 147, 151; racism/ discrimination shown by, 34, 89, 92–93, 106, 113–16, 123–24, 145, 153; as remembered with fondness, 63, 79–80, 87–88, 89, 98, 106, 109, 121, 124, 137, 138, 144, 145

teachers, at Port Essington Indian Day School, 40, 42–51; accommodation problems of, 45, 47–48; corporal punishment administered by, 64, 84, 104–5; curricula/pedagogical issues of, 44, 48–49, 50–51, 84–85; missionary vs lay, 42–43; qualifications/certification of, 28, 44–45, 46, 49–50, 131, 132; salaries of, 42–43, 44–45, 46, 49, 50; and Sm'algyax language, 42, 63–64, 68, 84, 104–5, 111, 118–19, 136–37, 142; vetting of, 50, 131, 132. *See also individual teachers by name*

teachers, at Port Essington Elementary School: corporal punishment administered by, 52, 70, 74, 91; curricula of, 52–53; qualifications/certification of, 52; and Sm'algyax language, 70, 79, 104; as well-liked, 79, 98, 109, 144. *See also individual teachers by name*

Telegraph Creek Elementary School, 32

Temple, Miriam (*née* Nelson), 61(i)

Terrace, 4–5, 7, 18, 20, 26, 37, 73, 81, 91; on BC map, 8(i); Centennial Christian School in, 99–100; founding of, 74; generation educated at, 13, 17, 22, 25, 65, 66, 103–28; Kalum School in, 53, 105–6, 111, 113–14, 117, 120; lifestyle changes/expenses in, 66; logging industry in, 12, 53, 66, 80, 112, 115, 125; Northwest Community College in, 18, 68, 99, 123; Parkside Alternative School in, 115, 128, 145; Parkside Elementary School in, 123; as physically separated from Tsimshian community, 5, 66, 126–27, 143–46; early public school education in, 171*nn*10–11; racism/ discrimination in, 88, 105–6, 113–15, 123–24, 145, 153; Riverside (later E.T. Kenney) Elementary School in, 54, 106, 111, 120–21; school bus trips to, 5, 66, 106, 143; as unfamiliar environment, 65, 66, 111, 142. *See also* Tsimshian students of post-1950s generation

Thomas, Robina, 25

Thompson, Judith (Edosdi), 18, 19

Thorsteinsson, Bergie, 51

Titley, E. Brian, 42, 131, 132

totem poles, 39; as carved out of jade by Clifford Bolton, 88; as raised at Kitsumkalum ceremony, 90(i), 91

Trafzer, Clifford, Jean Keller, and Lorene Sisquoc (eds.): *Boarding School Blues*, 138

Tranter, Catherine (Day School teacher), 42, 43, 166*n*47

Tsimshian: clans/family relationships of, 35–37, 38, 73; and connection to Port Essington, 57, 60, 73, 95, 102, 104, 117–20, 135–36, 143; and cycle of food gathering/preservation, 37; feasts of, 20, 37, 39, 91, 107, 122, 123; funerary practices of, 58, 59; and importance of helping/sharing with others, 30, 74–75, 76, 78, 82–83, 89, 93, 95, 134; leaders of, 39; matrilineal society of, 35, 36, 37–38, 42, 69; medicine of, 36, 39, 104; names of, 20, 36–37, 165*n*18; oral history tradition of, 38; and recognition of specialized knowledge, 38–39; religious conversion of, 39–40; and resistance to land appropriation, 157*n*15, 158*n*26; and respect for all people/living things, 38, 39, 59–60, 134, 174*n*57; and settler incursion/disease, 7, 39; social classes of, 36; spirituality/worldview of, 36–39, 54–55, 148; territory of, 7, 8(i), 35. *See also* Tsimshian education/learning

"Tsimshian," meaning of, 165*n*3

Tsimshian education/learning, 3–4, 5, 35, 37–39, 54–55; continuum of, 6, 21–22, 56–57, 100–2, 127, 133, 143; as gender-specific, 37–38, 57–58, 68–69, 78, 104, 127, 129, 176n9; and importance of mastering skills, 39; as lost to post-1950s generation, 5, 113, 122–24, 126–27, 142–46; and opposition to corporal punishment, 64–65, 171*n*21; as recognizing children's unique capabilities, 38–39, 54; of skills used in real life/subsistence of family, 54, 71–72, 74, 75–76, 98–99, 104, 127, 130, 139–40; as taught by example, 39, 57; vs Western education, 54–55, 129–33, 148–49. *See also* camping, traditional; fishing; food gathering; food preparation and preservation; hunting; Sm'algyax

Tsimshian student experience, as research topic, 3–26, 149–50; archival materials used in, 6–7; and author's "situating of herself," 18–19; and history of Port Essington, 7–12; and limitations of document analysis, 12–13; and need for respectful research with First Nations communities, 13–24, 150; and oral history approach, 13; and participant interviews/feedback, 23, 24–26; and representation of participants' stories, 25; and university ethics protocol, 22–24; and withdrawal of elder from project, 22–24

Tsimshian students of post-1950s generation, 4–5, 13, 17, 22, 25, 65, 66, 147–48, 149; author's interviews with, 103–28; cultural losses experienced by, 5, 113, 122–24, 126–27, 142–46; integrated education of, 4–5; and postwar economy, 5, 115, 116, 125, 144; racism/discrimination against, 105–6, 113–15, 123–24, 145, 153; and Sm'algyax language, 111, 118–19, 123, 126–27, 136–37, 142; themes in narratives of, 141–46. *See also individual persons*; Terrace

Tsimshian students of pre-1950s generation, 4, 6, 13, 17, 18, 147, 149; author's interviews with, 56–102; integrated education of, 4, 6, 51–53; as participants in both subsistence and wage labour economies, 76, 140–41, 142; and Sm'algyax language, 42, 63–64, 68, 70, 79, 84, 91, 104–5, 107, 111, 118–19, 136–37, 142; themes in narratives of, 133–41; traditional education/learning of, 3–4, 5, 37–39. *See also individual persons*

Tyson, A.M., 42

United Church of Canada: archives of, 7; formation of, 168*n*7; in Port Essington, 78, 173*n*48

Vancouver Vocational Institute, 98, 175*n*77

Vannatter, Roy B. (Day School teacher): criminal record of, 131, 132; sexual abuse by, 50, 64, 139, 147

Walker, Nettie (public school teacher), 32

Washington State: integration of Native high school students in, 34

water in Port Essington: and absence of indoor plumbing, 82, 108, 120; as carried "Chinese fashion" by resident, 173*n*42; as carted on sleigh, 93–94; and firefighting, 84, 120; as flowing through flume, 75, 76(i), 93, 173*n*42, 176*n*8; as packed in buckets, 108

Weber-Pillwax, Cora, 13, 15

Wesley, John, 20, 172*n*39

Wesley family, 12, 65

"Where go the boats?" (poem by 10-year-old girl), 46(i)

Wickwire, Wendy, 24

Wilson, Peggy, 115–16
Wilson, Shawn, 13, 15, 18
Wilson, T.A. and Belle (Elementary School teachers), 52
Wing, Charlotte, 91
Wing, Eileen (*née* Wesley), 65, 91
Wing, Faith, 95–96, 96(i)
Wing, Harvey, 56, 91–96, 96(i), 133; and connection to Port Essington, 93, 95, 126; at elementary/high schools, 91–93, 140; family of, 95–96; in fishing industry, 92, 95; on importance of helping others, 93, 94–95, 101; and racism/discrimination, 91, 92–93, 140; strong work ethic of, 93–95, 113, 135
Wing, Lee, 91, 93
Wing family, 65
Wood Lake School (Okanagan region), 32

Xbishuunt, legend of, 60, 134

Printed and bound in Canada by Friesens
Set in Garamond by Artegraphica Design Co. Ltd.
Copy editor: Robert Lewis
Indexer: Cheryl Lemmens